GETTING IT RIGHT

GEOFFREY GALT HARPHAM

GETTING IT RIGHT

Language, Literature, and Ethics

THE UNIVERSITY OF CHICAGO PRESS

Chicago and London

BJ1012

.H3174

1992

GEOFFREY GALT HARPHAM is professor of English and director
of the Program in Literary Theory at Tulane University

The University of Chicago Press, Chicago 60637
The University of Chicago Press, Ltd., London
© 1992 by The University of Chicago
All rights reserved. Published 1992
Printed in the United States of America

01 00 99 98 97 96 95 94 93 92   54321

ISBN (cloth): 0-226-31693-9
ISBN (paper): 0-226-31694-7

Library of Congress Cataloging-in-Publication Data

Harpham, Geoffrey Galt, 1946–
    Getting it right : language, literature, and ethics / Geoffrey
Galt Harpham.
        p. cm.
    Includes bibliographical references (p.   ) and index.
    1. Ethics. 2. Language and ethics.   I. Title
BJ1012.H3174 1992
170'.42—dc20   91-35267

CONTENTS

ACKNOWLEDGMENTS

This book was conceived and largely written in 1989 in conditions of ideal freedom, in a small room rented for the purpose in Cambridge, England. My first thanks are to Elizabeth Leedham-Green of Darwin College, who kindly rented me the room, and to whom this book constitutes my final payment. I was able to be in Cambridge because of a fellowship from the J. S. Guggenheim Foundation, generously supplemented by a leave from Tulane University. I would like to thank colleagues and friends at various institutions who read, listened to, or generally encouraged the project, including J. Hillis Miller, Tobin Siebers, Joseph Valente, Dan Latimer, Martin Jay, Christopher Norris, Simon Critchley, Robert Weimann, Hayden White, Molly Rothenberg, Tom Mitchell, Howard Eiland, and especially Robert Storey. For the second time, I am indebted to Clare Hall, Cambridge University, for its hospitality. Versions of some parts of this book have appeared in *Textual Practice* and *Representations*. I would like to thank the editors for permission to reprint. Thanks, finally to Mrs. Sandra Haro for her tolerant professionalism and good cheer in helping to prepare the final manuscript.

The project was powerfully affected by the events of 1989, a year that, from a certain point of view, was dominated by the power of ethics. It was, in the view of many analysts, a specifically ethical power that was triumphantly on display in the huge collapse of state-administered socialism in Eastern Europe, and in the rapid erosion of some of the institutions of apartheid in South Africa; and ethical power that suffered a disastrous, and hopefully temporary, defeat in China; and ethical power that was, and is, claimed by both sides in the hostilities between Israel and the Palestinians. Throughout the year, ethics was represented as a force capable of standing against massed military and economic might, a way of advancing the claims of rightness as such over and against pragmatism, complacency, or manifest injustice. "We must learn," Vaclav Havel said after assuming the presidency of

Czechoslovakia, "how to put morality ahead of politics, science and economics." The world was schooled, for a few months, in what I call in this book the ethical "mode of presentation" by the spectacle of men and women opposing tanks and machine guns protected by nothing more substantial than a passionate and ideal desire to live free from coercive or oppressive power. Equally instructive concerning that mode of presentation were the much more dubious and altogether strategic ethical claims made by the Bush administration in defense of interventions in Panama and, more recently, the Persian Gulf, claims in which morality was made to front for politics and economics without being placed precisely "ahead of" them.

The most intimate setting for ethical issues is the family, with its complex interplay of rights, interests, ideals, idealizations, ideologies, obligations, and brute facts. Accordingly, this book is lovingly dedicated to Joan Barasovska, Adrian Harpham, Clare Harpham, and John Harpham.

INTRODUCTION

I use the term *ethics* in this book in the spirit of what Jacques Derrida calls "paleonymy": an "old name" strategically retrieved in order to launch a new inquiry (*Positions* 71). The term invokes an ancient tradition of meditation, speculation, and debate which, however diverse, has maintained at least the continuity of its perennially paleonymic name, as if to signal a yearning for convergence, rationality, closure, transcendence. For many people today, these terms evoke the bathos of obsolescence; and ethics itself has become, especially for non-philosophers, an embattled concept. It is depicted by some as an atavism, a bourgeois pretension, a delusion, the enemy of historical or critical thinking. For others, however, ethics is nothing less than the privileged form of commitment to justice. Contemporary enthusiasm for ethics takes roughly two forms. Those on the right claim that the "restoration" of ethics to its "rightful place" in contemporary discourse would produce a return to central or essential "values," helping to revitalize a degenerate humanism and reaffirm a battered tradition; while for many on the left, ethics names the obligation to empower the hitherto deprivileged, silenced, or colonized other.

The anti-ethical argument might best be characterized as using an old name to underscore the contemporary irrelevance of the inquiry, while pro-ethical arguments often employ an old name to cover for the lack of an inquiry. Typically, both employ ethics as an uncontroversial or unproblematic concept. In both instances, polemics have supplanted paleonymics, bringing with them a general refusal of the task of rethinking. My wish for this book is that it may serve to advance the "new inquiry" that ought to accompany the rejuvenation of an old name.

The shape and force of this inquiry can be anticipated by contrasting it with another recent paleonymic strategy. In 1972, Roland Barthes argued that the modern human sciences were bringing into being not interdisciplinary cooperation in the study of a traditionally

1

defined object (such cooperation often being no more than a collection of parochialisms anyway), but rather the invention of a new object ("Jeunes chercheurs"). This object was the linguistic-semiotic "text," and his suggestion collaborated with powerful energies elsewhere in making the text the fetish of the following decade. But that was, it seems, long ago and in another land—or, rather, in no land at all; and recent reactions to what Richard Rorty called "textualism" from Marxism, feminism, historicism, pragmatism, cultural studies, and various minority perspectives have stressed the idea of historical and cultural locality as a way of correcting a certain indifference to material life that had been fostered by the textual orientation. Together, all these resistances to the text have implied another object, the act. The making and reading of texts are, of course, acts, but the emphasis on action encourages an attention to embedded, assessable practices that the emphasis on textuality does not. Even in philosophy, which never had much truck with the text, the most interesting recent work—by thinkers as diverse as Rorty, Stanley Cavell, Robert Nozick, Thomas Nagel, Emmanuel Levinas, Jeffrey Stout, Agnes Heller, Michel Foucault, Bernard Williams, Martha Nussbaum—focuses on the worldliness, rather than on the language or logic, of ethics. And in the disciplines such as deconstruction and literary theory that found the text most seductive, a "turn to ethics" can be traced in the late work of Paul de Man and in recent work by Wayne Booth, Charles Altieri, Tobin Siebers, J. Hillis Miller, Derrida, and many others.

My primary aims can all be briefly stated. First, I want to try to understand what constitutes "ethics itself," to understand the *ought*, the "resisted imperative," that centers all ethical discourses. *Getting It Right* is not a "meta-ethical" reflection on the timeless constants of the moral law, justice, rationality, maximal social utility, or the Good Life; it is rather a "sub-ethical" account of the conditions and characteristics of the discourse of what I call the "underdetermined ought," regardless of content. It is evident, to begin with, that all forms of the ethical imperative gather around the structurally obscure but commanding figure that contemporary thought has called "the other." What might be less evident is that "otherness" touches all aspects of ethics, beginning with the most important ethical terms, such as "freedom," "obligation," "subject," and "ought" itself. All of these, when used in a specifically ethical context, are inhabited and inhibited by othernesses, energies that contradict their manifest meanings. The phenomenon of "otherness" applies equally, I argue, to the obligations of the individual, the structure of ethical terms, the subject as constructed by ethics, and even to the position of ethical discourse with respect to other discourses. Like any institutionalized and professionalized discourse, ethics seeks clarity and precision; it posits rules, laws, conditions, implications, entailments, values, hierarchies. In the case of ethics, however, all this positing is both necessitated and frustrated by a radical and ineradicable unclarity built into the discourse itself. If this unclarity could be respected as constitutive, if the quest for a certain kind of lucidity could be suspended, then ethics might discover some path between, or other than, the depressing reduction to strictly logical rules and a more or less covert utopianism, paths that largely define the possibilities for ethics today.

While an ethical imperative is often described as standing alone unsupported by reasons, this underdetermination applies only to the ethical "mode of presentation." As a condition of their "unclarity," ethical imperatives are also, and necessarily, overdetermined. The first chapter concludes with an account of one of the primary forms of overdetermination in the relation between the global and the local. My candidate for a truly universal imperative, a law that would work the way Kant, for example, saw such a law as working, is "Act on principle." This apparently vacuous but truly noncontingent imperative does not specify or warrant any particular act, choice, or decision. Ethical legitimacy for particular acts can only be claimed through a synergistic convergence of "Act on principle" and some more definite or specific code—an other within ethics that, out of respect for a traditional distinction, I call morality. Morality is what Foucault seems to me to be talking about when he describes a "prescriptive ensemble," a "set of values and rules of action that are recommended to individuals through the intermediary of various prescriptive agencies such as the family (in one of its roles), educational institutions, churches, and so forth" (*Use of Pleasure* 25). These values and rules become not just "good for" but also simply "good" when they are convincingly situated within a larger imperative to act on principle. What interests me is the lamination of two kinds of prescription, with the moral representing a class of contingently desirable acts—"Honor thy father and thy mother"; "Don't steal that book"; "Help your brother tie his shoes"— whose contingency is transcended but not fully cancelled by the appeal to the universal. Saturated with particularity and circumstance, morality fuses interest with principle, both fulfilling and negating the global imperative on which it depends for its effectiveness.

Second, I want to try to account for the transcultural, panhistorical grip of ethics by exploring language as a primary site of the phenomenon of a "global" imperative operating in tension with local choices and acts. The argument of chapter 2 may have more relevance to what Benjamin Lee Whorf called "SAE" or Standard Average European languages than it might to others; but I am not arguing, as Whorf and

3

other linguists and philosophers have, for a value (and even a perceptual) system embedded in a particular language. The mass of local and contingent factors that make any natural language slanted, inflected, non-neutral, belongs, in the terms of my initial distinction, to the moral. The ethics of language are situated in very general features—the capacity for the same utterance to be referential or nonreferential, for example; or the capacity of all pronouns to refer to all persons; or the grammar of the sentence. The case I make, accordingly, is not the case that Whorf or his successors might make, that our language inclines us to certain evaluations or perceptions. Such arguments, no matter how persuasive in some respects, are generally based on the meanings of certain words, and seem founded on a misconception of what language does, or rather what language is; for they presume that language is an agent with, if not intentions, at least positive and identifiable effects on the subjects who use it. My premise is rather that language cannot be sharply distinguished from its users and so cannot truly be regarded as an agent at all. Accordingly, I argue that the ethics of language do not reside in the way *it* orients *us* towards or against certain values, but rather in the fact that language use itself requires certain recognitions and kinds of choices essential to ethics. It is the presence of these recognitions and choices in language that makes language itself seem to have an ethical dimension.

The third chapter concentrates on another site of universality, conversion. The role in ethical prescriptions of conversion—whether of impulse to reflection, the mutable to the permanent, immoderation to moderation, the apparent to the true, self-ends to the common good, etc.—has been widely noted but, I think, little understood. What has escaped detection is that all such prescriptions urge either a conversion from a condition of pain to one of pleasure, or the reverse. This fact suggests that conversion itself is the common and essential factor, and that ethics is in some sense indifferent to the particulars, satisfied by any conversion. I argue this point through an analysis of Freud's *Beyond the Pleasure Principle*, which, despite its author's repudiation of ethics, enacts an exemplary ethical process, converting, with a deeply ambivalent success, what it describes as the unconquerable quest for pleasure into the pain of its own "scientific" methods and discoveries. I then try to generalize the discussion of conversion in Freud to a consideration of the role of conversion in analysis in general.

The first part of the fourth chapter carries over the analysis of conversion to an inquiry into narrative, whose form, as classically defined, pivots on a conversion, the reversal-recognition said to occur at the climactic moment of plot development. The ethics of narrative are not strictly formal, however, for the determination of plot requires the

4

agency of a reader who, while binding the narrative into form, is also bound by the narrative through a passivity imprinted in the act of reading.

My last project is to investigate, through a study of the genesis of Joseph Conrad's *The Secret Agent,* the role of ethics in creation, another word used in a paleonymic sense. I am not, except incidentally, concerned with the relation of the aesthetic object to ethical "disinterestedness," but focus instead on the act of creation. First-hand accounts of creation exhibit sufficient regularities to enable us to speak of a "creative process"; and these regularities gather around some of the most familiar concepts of ethical discourse—the interplay of freedom and obligation, the imperative to honor the other, the necessity of "getting it right." That such accounts are not generally considered as fit material for theoretical contemplation, and are relegated to reductive psychologizers; and that the process of creation has been considered to be beneath the attention of a critical community concerned more with the creativity of understanding than with the understanding of creativity—this circumstance remains one of the most disturbing and curious features of contemporary critical thought.

My presumption throughout is that ethics is not properly understood as an ultimately coherent set of concepts, rules, or principles—that it ought not even be considered a truly distinct discourse—but rather that it is best conceived as a factor of "imperativity" immanent in, but not confined to, the practices of language, analysis, narrative, and creation. Whatever else these may or may not have in common, they share an investment in ethics. Popularly identified with exclusion, ethics can, I believe, also be construed as a principle of commonality between practices and discourses often considered to be independent both from each other and from the world of action.

5

1

ETHICS AND ITS OTHERS

It is easy enough to say: All this has to do with the nature of morality itself. What we don't know is: what is this nature with which all this has to do?

Stanley Cavell, *The Claim of Reason*

1. The Discourse of the Other and Other Discourses

No single term currently enjoys a greater prestige within the world of academic discourse than "the other." Derived from Hegel, this term figures prominently in the work of Freud, Mikhail Bakhtin, Jean-Paul Sartre, T. W. Adorno, Jürgen Habermas, Jacques Lacan, Iris Murdoch, Maurice Merleau-Ponty, Georges Bataille, Maurice Blanchot, Claude Lévi-Strauss, Tzvetan Todorov, Simone de Beauvoir, Vincent Descombes, Julia Kristeva, Jacques Derrida, Stanley Cavell, H. R. Jauss, Michel Foucault, Luce Irigaray, Edward Said, Hélène Cixous, Stephen Greenblatt, and Michel de Certeau, and in the controversies that swirl about them. Although the other may have an Hegelian origin, it has played an especially prominent and powerful role in the critique of Hegel, often conducted in the name of Kant, that has been played out chiefly in French thought since the 1960s (see Dews). Whereas (it is often maintained) Hegel posited an ultimately triumphant and harmonious reconciliation of matter and spirit as the end of history, Kant insisted on the incongruity between the ethical law and all our inclinations. Contemporary thinking seems inspired by the idea of an otherness that remains other, that resists assimilation, accommodation, and reconciliation. The notion of an otherness with integrity is applied to discussions of, for example, the constitution of the subject, the status of the object of knowledge, representations of imperial or colonial power, ideas of "presence" and "absence," social or cultural "alterity," the relation of signs to consciousness, the nature of justice in a conflictual and heterogeneous society, gender and canon formations, the theory of interartistic relations, the condition of our understanding of history, and, in the late work of Roland Barthes, love.

If the dominance of "the other" over "the same" signals a massive and general shift towards figures of fragmentation, difference, "heterology," "paralogism," and locality—towards what has been called, collectively, "enclave theory"—it has also helped to promote a renewed attention to ethics. For what all these discourses have in common is a powerful, and very often explicit, ethical component. The other does not simply exist; it imposes responsibilities, obligations, constraints, regulations: it claims its rights. Taking the forms of Reason, God, the injunction to care, objectivity, the unconscious, communal norms, or the Good, the other impinges on the subject from the outside, or from some interiority so profound as to escape the control of the *cogito*. The appearance of the other marks an "ethical moment" even in discourses not obviously concerned with ethics. Have we attended to the voice, the face, the law, of the other? Have we been faithful to its dictates? Have we permitted the other to be itself, to retain its autonomy? Have we taken proper care, proper responsibility? The answers to such questions form the content of ethical self-awareness.

Perhaps the most pertinent recent invention of the other in this respect can be found in the work of Emmanuel Levinas, the Lithuanian philosopher whose work (particularly *Totality and Infinity* and *Time and the Other*) has proven to be influential for a number of French thinkers, including Jean-Paul Sartre, Jacques Derrida, and Jean-François Lyotard. Levinas's complex and highly abstract work resists summary paraphrase, partly because it is still evolving—and, as Lyotard comments, it "sets a trap for commentary, attracting it and deceiving it" ("Levinas' Logic" 275; hereafter LL). But it can be responsibly stated that it focuses on an elaborate, radical, and uncompromising account of the absolute and primordial obligation placed on the subject by the "face of the other." For Levinas, ethics—unlike his formulations of it—is not abstract, not a function of reason, not a matter for reflection, not even something to be understood. Rather, the ethical obligation issues directly from the encounter with the luminous and alien other in its human density, and it both precedes and exceeds any cognitive grasp of duty.

While ethics is often considered a branch of philosophy, its basic project, the postulation of the *ought,* is uneasy in the company of philosophy's metaphysical, ontological, phenomenological, or epistemological explorations of what *is.* In his "Letter on Humanism," Heidegger expressed a "philosophical" hesitation concerning ethics, commenting that ethics "begins to flourish only when original thinking

7

comes to an end" (195). The whole question of the *ought* is, Heidegger continues, belated and derivative, participating in the displacement of the question of Being, the issue of "fundamental ontology." Levinas repeats and amplifies Heidegger's reservations from a point of view outside philosophy, whose fundamental task from the Greeks onward has been, he charges, the reduction of Other to Same. Philosophy, Levinas says, has devoted itself to containing disturbing alterities (e.g., materialism, madness, history) within conceptual categories that philosophy lays down in advance in such a way that, as Christopher Norris says, "as soon as they enter the discourse of philosophy—whether Kantian, Hegelian or Marxist—these categories are subject to a kind of conceptual sea-change which renders them henceforth intra-philosophical" (*Derrida* 231). The agent and beneficiary of this violent suppression of the other is not just philosophy but the philosopher, the masterful knowing subject who stands apart in sublime detachment from all forms of interest, desire, circumstance, or noncognitive obligation. Hence, for Levinas, "philosophy is egology," the systematic marginalization of the ethical *ought* as a means of protecting the privileges of the autonomous subject.

According to one of his recent critics, Wittgenstein imagined an "ethics without philosophy" (see Edwards). In a similar spirit, Levinas has devoted himself to articulating, or to rediscovering, an ethical discourse not simply adjacent to philosophy but beneath it, a discourse that has been victimized and dissimulated, a vanished and radically other "first philosophy" based on the experience of decentering imposed by an infinite otherness. As Lyotard puts the "essential statements" of Levinas, "*The self (soi) does not proceed from the other; the other befalls the self*" (LL 278). The aberrance of such formulations within the discourse of philosophy can hardly be overstated. Unlike Kant, Levinas proposes no universally binding principles or rules of reason; nor does he claim that the self draws its dictates from within its own deepest nature; nor does he describe obligations in terms of norms (see LL 298–303). Unlike Hegel, he does not insist on the inexorable advance or ultimate triumph of Absolute Idea. Unlike thinkers in the Christian tradition, he does not advocate a logocentric metaphysics: the face of the other is "other" above all to the logos. Unlike Husserl, he does not focus on the phenomenological experience of a transcendental ego. Unlike Sartre, he rejects the notion of a primordial experience of selfhood, and rejects, too, the Sartrean paranoia concerning the gaze of the other. Levinas bases his entire discourse on the asymmetrical encounter between self and other, an encounter that places the self under an infinite obligation, dominating it "from a height" (*Totality and Infinity* 214). An unphilosophical concept—not even a "concept" at all—the encounter with the other marks the difference between ethics and philosophy: ethics may be the "more things in heaven and earth" of which Hamlet warns Horatio. Himself reluctant to engage in ethical discourse, Derrida, whose "Violence and Metaphysics," appearing in *Writing and Difference*, was one of the crucial texts in bringing Levinas to the attention of a wider public, points out that Levinas's ethical break depends on conceptual resources borrowed from Husserl, Hegel, and Heidegger. But he also appreciates the singularity of Levinas's position. "I believe," Derrida tells an interviewer, "that when Levinas speaks of ethics—I wouldn't say that this has nothing in common with what has been covered over in this word from Greece to the German philosophy of the 19th century, ethics is wholly other (*tout autre*); and yet it is the same word" (*Altérités* 71).

Derrida's comments indicate that Levinas stands in much the same relation to "ethics" as Levinas says "ethics" stands to "philosophy"— "wholly other" and yet "the same." An anomalous instance of an anomalous practice, Levinas's work could even be considered paradoxically typical of ethical discourse in general. For, especially in its troubled but intimate relationship with philosophy, it exemplifies the relationship that ethics has with a number of discourses, with respect to which it is consistently "other."

Ethics often provokes from other discourses the same resentment and belligerence provoked in the subject by ethical laws or by the conscience. Nowhere is this more evident than in the domain of materialist or Marxist thought. If, as Alasdair MacIntyre has remarked, every ethics "characteristically presupposes a sociology," the sociological dimension of ethics is characteristically suppressed (*After Virtue* 22; hereafter *AV*). As if in revenge, those who study actual socio-historical practices have always reserved their most astringent skepticism for ethics, with its ahistorical principles, rules, and prescriptions. In *The German Ideology* of 1845 and the 1848 "Communist Manifesto," Marx repudiated ethics in favor of scientific materialism. Henceforth, as Louis Althusser has argued, Marx increasingly devoted himself to a study of power, an inquiry without idealist or essentialist illusions about human nature or the *ought* (*German Ideology* 154–55; Althusser, *For Marx* 222–34, and *Lenin and Philosophy* 159–65). The argument that ethics constitutes a kind of lie or obliviousness to material reality is stated in the most uncompromising terms by Nietzsche, who holds that ethics is the pretentious, idealizing form of "the herd instinct in the individual," a strategic "forgetting" of tradition, custom, and authority, a bad-faith apologia for the status quo, a laundering of the contingent and advantageous so that it appears necessary and worthy (*Gay Science* 116). Trotsky continues this argument, stating that ethics properly interpreted reveals an ideological basis: "morality more than any other form of ideology has a class character" (*Their Morals and Ours* 13).

The famous opening trumpet blast of *The Political Unconscious*—"'Always historicize!'"—announces that Fredric Jameson has inherited the anti-ethical prejudice. This ringing imperative is followed, in the first chapter of that book, by the claim that "ethics itself" has been responsible for arranging the loaded binary oppositions (such as self and other or, to use his own recurrent example, the "primitive" dualism of Good and Evil) by which the Western mind has been seduced and by which it exercises its hegemonic power. Ethics, for Jameson, is "the ideological vehicle and the legitimation of concrete structures of power and domination," and actually works against society's "others" (*Political Unconscious* 114; hereafter *PU*). Ethics in this account is not truly disinterested or transcendent; rather, it serves the powers that be by deflecting an ideological critique of their practices and values. If the "single fundamental theme" of history is "the collective struggle to wrest a realm of Freedom from a realm of Necessity," then the polemical form of historicizing critique would be the demonstration that every law or obligation posited by ethics is in fact a mystified form of the interests of power (*PU* 19).

According to the Marxist argument, post-Kantian ethics individualizes what is properly collective. Some recent thinkers have sought to neutralize this feature of ethics by recycling the theories of Aristotle, for whom ethics is a branch of politics that constantly refers to the values and practices of the polis, with which the desires of the individual must be harmonized. But Aristotle's ethics, perhaps for this reason, perhaps because it applies only to a portion of the population, or perhaps because it is baldly represented as ending in pleasure, seems to many contemporary readers to be unrepresentative of the long tradition of ethical discourse, indeed hardly an ethics at all. More typical of this tradition is Levinas, who epitomizes the egological orientation that he repudiates by representing the unsocialized individual as the site of the ethical event. The marble smoothness of the Levinasian "face," its otherness unscored by the differences of social existence, confirms an "ethical" suppression of the polis. Marxism itself has found the ethics/politics distinction worth preserving, pointing out, for example, that the terms generally preferred by ethical discourse—Reason, Virtue, Duty, the Good—are ideological growths that flourish especially in the climate of capitalism. Thinking "ethically," Jameson has said, people acquire a warrant for a self-interested disinterest in collective attitudes and communal practices (*PU* 116; see also Jameson, *Fables of Aggression* 56). The fundamental problem becomes, in the climate of this disinterest, what Iris Murdoch has scathingly called "sincerity" ("Against Dryness" 44–45). And with the reduction of the polis to the individual, everything else shrinks. The deeply sedimented and traditional practices of everyday life, the longer durations of the events of communal history, the phenomenon of group or mob behavior, the circumstances of a class, social group, race, or religion—all become crushed into the "ethical moment" when an individual confronts a choice and makes a decision.

Marxism undertakes the recovery of what has become, in an ethical age, a "political unconscious," an impoverished collective narrative that has been sacrificed to the powerful advance of the individual. The extreme form of historicist skepticism about ethics is attained, once again, by Nietzsche, who attacks the "error of accountability." No one, Nietzsche says, is accountable for his or her nature "in as much as it is altogether a necessary consequence and assembled from the elements and influences of things past and present: that is to say, that man can be made accountable for nothing" (*Human, All Too Human* 39). In place of the subject of liberal humanism, Nietzsche would put the historicized subject embedded in and constituted by the "chain" of the past. "The single one, the 'individual',," Nietzsche says, "is an error . . . he is the whole single line of humanity up to himself" (*Twilight of the Idols* 9 : 33). Correcting this error is, Jameson argues, the fundamental task of Marxist criticism today, as it seeks to "[transcend] the 'ethical' in the direction of the political and the collective" (*PU* 60).

Marxism also seeks to reverse the direction of judgment. In ethical discourse, judgment tends to issue from the future: the energies of the *ought* concentrate in promises, responsibilities, and commitments. Indeed, in a recent essay on Levinas, Derrida invents a cryptic sentence that condenses the essence of Levinas's message: "Il aura obligé" (He will have obligated) ("At this very moment"). The specifically ethical other obligates the subject from a future anterior which can never be made present. Marxist judgment, by contrast, falls on the present from the otherness of the past, which will, Jameson promises, "begin to come before us as a radically different life form which rises up to call our own form of life into question and to pass judgment on us . . . imposing the painful knowledge of what we are not, what we are no longer, what we are not yet" ("Marxism and Historicism" 175).

Perhaps a sentence from Georges Bataille's *Visions of Excess* most succinctly expresses the Marxist antipathy to ethics: "Materialism," Bataille says, "is a crude liberation from the imprisonment and masked pathology of ethics" (32). Bataille's sense of the irreconcilability of the two discourses is matched by Levinas, who expends enormous effort *not* to "presuppose a sociology," or indeed to presuppose

11

anything but "ethics itself." Ethics, Levinas says in *Totality and Infinity*, goes "beyond History"; in the ethical encounter, the subject is "uprooted from history" (52).

But the strain on Levinas's discourse of repressing history is considerable, and produces a sense of sterility, abstraction, reduction, and even self-absorption. To be sure, the history of the ethical repression of history is marked by failure; and the entire tradition of ethics that leads from Aristotle through Hume to the Utilitarians, shunting over to Hegel, and on to such contemporary pragmatists and communitarians as Bernard Williams, Jeffrey Stout, Richard Rorty, Martha Nussbaum, and Alasdair MacIntyre, refuses to make the Kantian or Levinasian distinction between the laws of ethical theory and the ways of life in which these laws might be realized. One of the defining moments of this tradition was Hegel's attack on the "empty formalism" of the Kantian categorical imperative (Act only according to that maxim by which you can at the same time will that it should become a universal law), and his insistence that the content of ethical life was to be found in the cultural and institutional ethos, the *Sittlichkeit,* of the community. For Hegel and his descendants, the categorical imperative not only evaded this truth but enabled the bourgeois subject to dignify his values and prejudices, to dress them up in the guise of Reason itself. Anti-Kantians of all kinds relish moments in the second *Critique* in which Kant confesses to the difficulty of grounding ethics in abstract principles, moments such as the one in which Kant admits that "one cannot hope to have everything as easy as it was with the principles of pure theoretical understanding" (V.46).

Kant's difficulty, his opponents claim, derives from the real impossibility of straining out a purified Reason from the rest of life, an impossibility that dooms any effort to uproot ethics from history. But, to turn the tables, how likely would be the success of an effort to uproot history from ethics? According to Philip J. Kain, Marx actually began his intellectual career as an Aristotelian ethical thinker, renounced ethics for a brief moment in the mid-1840s, and then—*contra* Althusser—returned to a more critical and nuanced ethics in his late writings. Recent studies of Sartre's late notebooks have confirmed that Sartre was trying in his last years to develop an ethical theory that would moderate the existentialist absolutism of his earlier writings. And Jameson presents his "Always historicize!" as a "transhistorical" and "absolute" imperative that is closely modeled on the ethical commands he rejects—it is, he notes, "the moral of *The Political Unconscious*" (9). In fact, in his critical practice, Jameson treats the ethical not simply as the unhistorical, but almost as the *form* of the historical.

Middlemarch, for example, may appear to foreground "ethical concerns"; but if these concerns are recoded they reveal "the surest clue to the concrete historical reality in question" ("Criticism in History" 125–26). So despite the tensions on both sides of the ethico-historical divide, there is reason to think that there are not two sides at all, but rather two emphases or dimensions of an essentially convergent inquiry. Even Bataille, according to Maurice Blanchot, was engaged in an "ethical quest," haunted by "the demand for a morality" (Blanchot, *The Unavowable Community* 18).

The situation is comparably ambivalent when we turn to psychoanalytic theory. As will become clearer—or perhaps more complicated—in chapter 3, psychoanalytic discourse typically portrays itself as the antagonist of and alternative to ethics, but just as typically finds a way to return to and promote an ethics of its own. Despite Freud's corrosive skepticism about any form of idealism or any postulation of an ethical "instinct," and despite the refusal of psychoanalysis to offer a new ethical system to replace the ones that it discredits, the therapeutic situation is inescapably predicated, as Philip Rieff has argued, on an "ethics of honesty" (see *Freud: The Mind of the Moralist*). Jacques Lacan is, if anything, even more merciless than Freud on ethical idealism, but while criticizing Kant's "bachelor's ethic," as well as the altruism and reciprocity of all humanistic ethics, he has characterized his own analytic practice as an "ethic of the Well-Spoken," and has even stated that "the status of the unconscious . . . is ethical" (*Television* 42, 41; *Four Fundamental Concepts* 33). In an article entitled "Lacan and the Ethics of Modernity," John Rajchman has argued that Lacan should be seen as an advocate of an "ethopoetics" based on the "resistance to the tyranny of the very idea of an objectively good human arrangement" (55). So psychoanalysis, too, begins with a repudiation of ethics only to end with an embrace.

Freud also points to another trouble spot for ethics. Counting women's indifference to "the great exigencies of life," that is, their characteristic subordination of justice to "feelings of affection or hostility," among the "psychical consequences of the anatomical distinction between the sexes," Freud confessed that he could not "evade the notion . . . that for women the level of what is ethically normal is different from what it is in men. Their super-ego is never so inexorable, so impersonal, so independent of its emotional origins as we require it to be in men" ("Some Psychical Consequences" 257). In such comments, Freud joins a tradition that extends back to the Greek ethic of virility, the code of free men in an undemocratic society, a code articulated decisively in the *Nichomachean Ethics.*

Traditionally, ethics has pointed to humanity and said, "Ecce homo." Those interested in ethics today must reckon with a stubborn and resilient streak of patriarchalism within ethical discourse, and with the possibility that a contemporary revival of ethics as an area of academic interest signals not just a resistance to various forms of anti-humanism or irrationalism but also a specific resistance to feminism as a discipline and a cultural force. The masculine bias seems especially sinister in ethical discourse, which typically seeks to define the universally binding or necessary constraints on human conduct, and to interrogate the norms and general conditions of value in human life. Manifested without apology in Classical ethics, patriarchalism still dominates traditional Christian ethics, and silently informs, according to Luce Irigaray and others, the Kantian idea of the neutral but implicitly male "universal subject." In our century, patriarchalism has become if anything less neutral and altogether less silent. Sartre, for example, spoke of his efforts late in life to develop an ethics based on a "fundamental bond" obtaining between human beings simply on the basis of their common humanity. How to express this fundament? "When I see a man," Sartre said in an interview (whose title in translation, "The Last Words of Jean-Paul Sartre," may not have been of his own choosing), "I think, his origin is the same as mine; he comes as do I from, let's say, mother-humanity, from mother earth. . . . We call the relationship of a man to his neighbor fraternal because they feel they are of the same origin" (413). The insistent gendering of this primal scene of recognition resists the universalization Sartre seems to want to promote, and resists as well the benign interpretation that he is simply and uncritically adopting a conventional use of the "generic" masculine. Similarly, MacIntyre actively generalizes a use of "man" that is originally *not* generic when he says that moral arguments "within the classical, Aristotelian tradition" involve "one central functional concept, the concept of *man* understood as having an essential nature and an essential purpose or function." Aristotle's "starting-point for ethical inquiry" is, MacIntyre says, the premise "that the relationship of 'man' to 'living well' is analogous to that of 'harpist' to 'playing the harp well' " (*AV* 56). Taking what appears to be the opposite position, a nonessentialist or "particularist" conception of ethics, Isaiah Berlin gives the same answer to the unasked question of gender when he argues that "there are many different ends that men may seek and still be fully rational, fully men, capable of understanding each other and sympathizing and deriving light from each other, as we derive it from reading Plato or the novels of medieval Japan" ("Pursuit of the Ideal" 14). The tradition is generous, it makes room for all kinds of men.

It is often difficult to know exactly what to attribute to carelessness or insensitivity, to the actual prejudice of an individual writer, to a cultural predisposition, to a linguistic convention, or to some inherent tendency of "ethics itself." Take for example Stuart Hampshire's description of the manner in which a "way of life" gently guides one's thoughts towards one's own kind, causing "a man to think of selected aspects and features of his future, which become focuses of his desire or aversion, and to be wholly uninterested in features that are strongly marked in the moral vocabulary attached to another way of life" (*Morality and Conflict* 24; hereafter *MC*). Is it possible not to suspect that these desires and aversions run toward and away from woman, and that this boring "other way of life" is the life of woman? And when Hampshire refers to "that sense of freedom which men take to be peculiar to themselves," is it possible not to wonder whether the implied contrast is not with other sentient beings but with enslaved woman (78)? And when Hampshire, once again, describes "the intrinsic character of thought" as "self-correcting, when thinking reaches a first stage of complexity," and then gratuitously adds, "as it does in adult men"—well, enough (54). Such usages in Hampshire, MacIntyre, Sartre, and many others have provoked the suspicion that ethics as a discourse is predisposed to honor a masculine "way of life" as especially free, and masculine "impersonality" as especially worthy. Routinely casting men as the heroes of Duty and women as the magnets of Inclination, ethical discourse has historically dramatized an ideology of gender on the stage of philosophy. In a culture in which this ideology is challenged, the use in ethical discourse of the generic masculine will inevitably come to seem ironic, if not invidious.

Levinas's position in feminist discussions of ethics has been pivotal. His texts are heavy with a highly theorized feminine, a concept that ripens within such freighted terms as "fecundity," "voluptuousness," "tenderness," and "virginity," coming to rest in the idea of "Dwelling." This attention to feminine alterity is intended to disrupt a dominantly masculine or "absolute" metaphysics, and Levinas has been praised by Alison Ainley and, in a subtle and important essay, "The Fecundity of the Caress," by Luce Irigaray. On the other hand, both the Levinasian subject who confronts the face of the other, as well as that face itself, are decisively masculine; and this has not escaped the attention of feminists since Simone de Beauvoir's criticism in *The Second Sex* of passages from *Time and the Other* on the "mystery of the feminine" (see *Time and the Other* 85–94). In a more recent essay, even Irigaray charges that Levinas "cling[s] on to the rock of patriarchy" precisely in the area of "carnal love" by submitting the female to the *telos* of

15

paternity ("Questions to Emmanuel Levinas: On the Divinity of Love").

Derrida's most recent meditation on Levinas suggests the intricacy of the issue of gender. The essay originally appeared in a volume called *Textes pour Emmanuel Levinas*, and so took as a starting point the question of what it would mean to write a text on Levinas *pour* Levinas. For Levinas himself had stipulated that "the Work . . . demands a radical generosity of the Same who, in the Work, goes towards the other. In consequence the Work demands an *ingratitude* of the other. Gratitude would be precisely the return of the movement to its origin" (see Levinas, *En découvrant l'existence avec Husserl et Heidegger* 191). The task of writing a text *for* Levinas then, must not only gratefully or generously show how Levinas's text works by repeating its resistance to the Same, its generous movement towards the other; it must also ungratefully show how it does *not* work. Accordingly, Derrida engages, serially, in two related but opposite activities, the first of which might be called faithful commentary, and the second a more independent practice of interpretation that ungratefully honors the other by revealing its fault. The fault, according to Derrida, is nothing other than the subordination of sexual difference in the name of a spuriously gender-neutral ethical difference, a subordination that repeats the unethical mastery of masculine over feminine. This movement from gratitude to ingratitude, required after all by Levinas, is signalled in Derrida's text by a gradual slippage from the faithful summation—the "*Il aura obligé*" mentioned earlier—to a more precise but still grateful naming of "*Il*" as Levinas, or "E. L." for short, and for Elohim, concluding with the violent but inevitable conversion of "E. L." into "*Elle*": "*Elle aura obligé.*" Other to the other, Derrida asks, "does 'She' not demand greater ethical respect and priority than 'He'?" ("At this very moment"; see also Critchley, "Bois").

The point to be stressed is that although both Irigaray and Derrida question Levinas's practices, neither rejects "ethics itself." Derrida discovers a more ethical and more just ethics through the deconstruction of Levinas; and Irigaray, while calling for a "destruction of metalanguages," does not call for a destruction of ethics. True, she does call for women to repudiate a certain kind of ethics. "Women, stop trying," she writes; "Do what comes to mind, do what you like: without 'reasons,' without 'valid motives,' without 'justification.' You don't have to raise your impulses to the lofty status of categorical imperatives" (*This Sex Which Is Not One* 203; see also Chanter and Chalier). But "doing what you like" is a principled position, the basis of an ethic of difference, a different ethic, or as Irigaray puts it in a recent book, an Ét-

hique de la différence sexuelle. Visible as theory in much "essentialist" feminism, this putative difference is presented as empirical fact by the sociologist Carol Gilligan, who claims to have discovered a specifically feminine model of "moral development" based not on transcendental imperatives or ideals of justice but on "responsibility" and "the injunction to care" (*In a Different Voice* 100; see also *Mapping the Moral Domain* 3–20, 73–86). Feminism today might reject the ethics of Levinas, or Kant, or Aristotle, but as several recent books attest, feminism is keenly interested in and increasingly committed to ethics both as an area of inquiry and as a polemical instrument (see Griffiths, *Feminist Perspectives in Philosophy*; Ellison, *Delicate Subjects*; Daly, *Gyn/Ecology*; and Andolsen et al., *Women's Consciousness, Women's Conscience*).

The tar-baby character of ethics which permits it to absorb its enemies actually illuminates what might be referred to by the phrase "ethics itself." As a discourse of the other, we have seen, ethics also assumes the marginal position of otherness with respect to other discourses. Philosophical ethics collaborates in its own marginalization by being persistently abstract, graceless, pretentious, essentialist, antihistorical, and arguably antifeminist. But ethics itself seems to possess its own best antidotes, providing the most pertinent solutions to the problems it has itself generated, solutions that confess their origins by repeatedly designating themselves as yet more "ethics." Ethics always has a response to arguments raised against it. In fact, at least one writer has argued that Heidegger, whose "philosophical" hesitation about ethics was cited earlier, was actually engaged in a protracted "retrieval" of Kantian ethics, providing a more concrete phenomenological grounding for "conscience" than had Kant himself (see Schalow). The attempt to go beyond, beneath, or outside ethics by proposing an alternative ethical theory happens with sufficient regularity to prompt the reflection that these pseudo-disputes recur not *between* ethics and some other perspective or discourse, but *within* ethics: complaints or hesitations about ethics constitute a recurrent side-effect of the central project of ethical discourse, which is not just to describe a state of affairs but to prescribe an "other" state of affairs, to imagine an ideal or an alternative, to articulate a difference between what is and what ought to be.

How to think of ethics? *Can* one think of ethics? As the locus of otherness, ethics lacks integrity in "itself," and ought rather to be considered a matrix, a hub from which the various discourses and disciplines fan out and at which they meet, crossing out of themselves to encounter the other. Ethics is perhaps best conceived as a "conceptual base"—neither as organic drive nor as properly conceptual superstructure, but rather as a necessary, and necessarily impure and un-systematic, mediation between unconscious or instinctual life and its cognitive and cultural transformation.

2. Incoherence and the Ethical Mode of Presentation

At the dead center of ethics lies the *ought*, which defines what Stanley Cavell calls the ethical "mode of presentation." A word hovering be-tween the "constative" and the "performative," a word that dictates through an appeal to freedom, a word, as G. E. M. Anscombe has commented, of "mere mesmeric force," *ought* is the defining term and most powerful resource of ethical discourse (Anscombe, "Modern Moral Philosophy" 219).

What makes *ought* so distinctive in the company of words is its en-croachment on the realm of power. Hugh Kenner has commented that language consists entirely of names; but unlike *sprinting, ocean, strike three, quark, constraint, is,* or *ouch, ought* not only names nothing, but seems to embody a wish that things become different, and there-fore unfit to bear the names they have (Kenner, "Modernism" 98). The *OED* defines it as "the general verb to express duty or obligation," used "strictly" only in "a moral sense"; but as a verb it is strangely empty. In the "strict" moral sense it is, in fact, necessarily empty. For what distinguishes the moral sense from other senses is the absence of support for its imperativity. It is often argued that in "ethical" discus-sion reasons are given for preferring one course over another, while in non-ethical discussion, if two people disagree, there's no more to be said. But the reasons ethics gives are in a sense no reasons at all, for they begin and end with the bare, stark, noncontingent, self-validating *ought.* As Stuart Hampshire says, ethical choice is always "underdeter-mined by the arguments," predicated on norms and ideal conceptions that stand beyond reasons and must simply be accepted or rejected by a person whose choice reflects not the set of circumstances that con-fronts him but rather his commitments, values, character. To be ethi-cal, an *ought* must not refer itself to threats or desires, coercion or self-ends. Only a choice based on such a liberated *ought* is truly free, or, as Hampshire says in his characteristic way, "his and his alone" (*MC* 42). Accordingly, ethical arguments invariably round on them-selves: You ought to because you ought to. Speculation on what pre-cedes this terminus can take any tack. You ought to because: it is consistent with a vision of the good life for man, it produces the great-est good for the greatest number, it is dictated by sovereign Reason, *x* always overrides *y*, it furthers the revolution, God hath decreed it, it feels good, it feels bad. But these justifications are themselves self-justifying, simply deferring the "ethical moment," the moment of "strictness," which is achieved when reasoning becomes tautological.

We are now perhaps a bit closer to understanding the "mesmeric force" of the *ought*; but what might remain puzzling is why Anscombe, or anyone, would regard this force as "mere." Anscombe's argument is historical. The modern *ought* is alien to Aristotle, and makes sense only in the context of a "*law* conception of ethics" (216). Naturalized after centuries of Christianity, this conception has survived Christianity's decline still powerful but hollow. Deprived of context, the special "moral" use of *ought* is also deprived of content, except, as Anscombe says, for "a certain compelling force, which I should call purely psychological" (232). Anscombe repeats Hegel's attack on Kant's formalism in the name of logic rather than communal norms and practices, and extends it beyond Kant to take in virtually everything since Aristotle. What she finds especially "detestable" is that philosophers and others should wish to retain the "atmosphere" of the *ought* when clear and definable terms such as "unjust" are available. But even in the course of an argument that recommends "*banishing ethics totally* from our minds," Anscombe recognizes that the *ought* "is such an extremely frequent term of human language that it is difficult to imagine getting on without it" (228, 232). Anscombe, like MacIntyre, Basil Mitchell, and others who complain of the "confusion" of modern moral discourse, its clinging to the rocks not only of patriarchy, but of Christianity, Kant, Utilitarianism, Nietzsche, and various other pernicious doctrines of the past, situates the problem in the use of what MacIntyre calls the "emphatic *ought*," the impoverished idea of an autonomous "good" with no connection to a "good for" or grounding in human nature (see MacIntyre, "Hume on 'is' and 'ought'" 49). But once identified, the problem remains, for the "moral" sense of the *ought* cannot be siphoned off, especially as it is the simplest and most primitive sense—the unsupported, underdetermined, unargued, autonomous *ought* itself—and since the *ought* cannot be extirpated from human language no matter what confusion it sows.

Anscombe's vehemence, which is far from hers alone, bespeaks something more and other than mere disagreement, something closer to the panic and nausea associated with the "return of the repressed." But why would the philosophical mind repress the discourse of the *ought* when so much of philosophy is concerned with ethics? How can a philosopher urge, virtually in the name of philosophy itself, that we banish ethics *totally* not just from the pages of philosophical texts, but "from our minds?" One possibility is that the ethical *ought* enacts, in its mode of presentation, an autonomy, or rather a semi-autonomy from the kind of logic on which philosophy rests by giving reasons

19

that are no reasons. Another possibility is that the *ought* is irreducible to the clarity and transparency that philosophy seeks, in one of its moods, to exact and promote. If this last were so, the reason must be that the *ought* is itself a figure of repression, a repressed figure; that its mode of presentation, so naked, so brazen, so categorical, drives down to invisibility other—perhaps "hypothetical"—factors that it cannot admit on principle. And if all this were so, then we could make a beginning, if only a beginning, by saying that the ethical *ought* is *apparently* underdetermined but *actually* overdetermined.

Anscombe and MacIntyre try to ground the *ought* in the *is*, so that one could never say, "One ought to because one ought to," but only, "One ought to because [say] it is required by one's socially-determined responsibilities." Others repress the *ought* by advocating its rigorous segregation from *is*. For Levinas, the priority of the *ought* is absolute and must not be confused with knowledge in the form of descriptive statements about what is. Only prescriptive absoluteness will secure the radical "passivity" of the subject. And for Lyotard, the conflation of *is* and *ought* represents not just confusion but "terror." The rhetoric of literal description, Lyotard insists, terroristically silences resistance by grounding itself, and no others, in the real (see *Just Gaming*; hereafter *JG*). Cutting the prescriptive loose from its other guarantees, Lyotard argues, not the radical passivity but the radical freedom of the subject. What both the integrationists like Anscombe and MacIntyre and the segregationists like Levinas and Lyotard have in common is the Cartesian commitment to clear and distinct ideas. To the (very great) extent that philosophy itself is committed to such ideas, the *ought* constitutes a perpetual crisis, even a scandal. Among philosophers, few can be found who would share Wittgenstein's enthusiasm for concepts "with blurred edges": "isn't the indistinct [concept]," Wittgenstein asks, "often exactly what we need?"—especially "in aesthetics or ethics?" (*Philosophical Investigations* 77).

The shock registered by thinkers of widely divergent persuasions at the prospect of miscegenation between *is's* and *oughts* of equal status suggests that philosophy sees not just a few ideas but its own discursive identity at stake. To see why this should be so we must turn for a moment to the "original" and still the most enigmatic and unsettling discussion of the question, the passage in Hume's *A Treatise of Human Nature* where he notes that in "every system of morality, which I have hitherto met with, I have always remark'd, that the author proceeds for some time in the ordinary way of reasoning, and establishes the being of a God, or makes observations concerning human affairs; when of a sudden I am surpris'd to find that instead of the usual copulations of propositions, *is*, and *is not*, I meet with no proposition that is not connected with an *ought,* or *ought not*" (196). Hume's surprise at this often "imperceptible" passage has led many to feel that Hume is saying that *ought* cannot be logically or legitimately derived from *is* at all. In what the editor of a collection of essays on *The Is-Ought Question* calls the "standard interpretation," no description has legitimate prescriptive force, no fact grounds a value, no ethical choice can be compelled by a value-neutral representation (see Hudson). The subsequent history of philosophical ethics returns again and again to "Hume's Law": No Ought from an Is. Hampshire's "underdetermination," R. M. Hare's "decisionism," Sartre's "commitment," and Lyotard's "judgment without criteria" all represent modern elaborations of this construction of Hume.

But other constructions abound. MacIntyre, to take one example from a large literature on the subject, claims Hume's support for his position that the two ought not to be distinguished. In a detailed argument that often hinges on the historical meanings of words and on the probable opinions of Hume, MacIntyre argues that Hume was condemning "specific religious moral views" that effected the passage from *is* to *ought* in illegitimate ways, and that he encouraged the proper kind of connection through reference to the facts of human wants and needs ("Hume on 'is' and 'ought'" 46–48). "Hume's support" bolsters many arguments, including the suggestion that *is* and *ought* represent the terms of a developmental sequence, from the immature immersion in the comforts of the *is* to a more austere commitment to the *ought.* In terms of cultural "development," similar arguments have been made, to the effect that the effort to distinguish between the two terms marks a perennial modernity, a mark of cultural maturity as well as philosophical rigor, while the effacement of this distinction constitutes a perennial form of nostalgia.

For thinkers as different from each other as MacIntyre, Georg Lukács, and Martha Nussbaum, the passing of the Greek consensus on the good life has virtually created the distinction. In the speculative "Greece" that might be constructed from their works, the passage from *is* to *ought* was negotiated by a social consensus based on traditional roles or "characters" that defined the ends of action. A more "modern" view of Greek culture would point not to the consensus dreamed of in philosophy but to the very different world of blindness and ignorance in *Oedipus Rex* or of conflicting imperatives in *Antigone.* But the strain between "traditional" and "modern" is reborn continually. An example of the "traditional" attitude towards *is* and *ought,* or, more precisely, description and prescription, abruptly occupied the stage of international diplomacy when it occurred in a speech delivered by the then-Speaker of the Iranian Parliament, Hashemi Rafsanjani, in early May 1989. Here, Rafsanjani apparently recommended to the Palestinians that they kill five Westerners for every Palestinian killed by the Israelis: "It is not hard to kill Americans or Frenchmen," he pointed out; "it is a bit difficult to kill Israelis, but there are so many [Americans and Frenchmen] in the world . . ." (Hawkes 21). Those in his audience, their interpretation perhaps guided by the sight of Rafsanjani leaning on an AK-47 attack rifle as he spoke, were widely reported to understand the speech as an authoritative *ought*, a call to kill Americans and Frenchmen. In the face of a storm of international denunciation the following day, Rafsanjani, reinforcing his "moderate" or "pragmatist," i.e., modern, image, redrew the distinction that had been effaced, insisting that the *ought* had been illegitimately derived. As the report in *The Observer* put it, "What he had meant to say was that Israeli oppression of the Palestinians would naturally lead to violent reactions" ("Rafsanjani backs down on his 'kill Westerners' call"). In a "modern" world, prescriptions are not entailed by descriptions (e.g., that it is easy to kill Americans and Frenchmen); the agent is "free."

The belief in political, ethical, artistic, and epistemological freedom—a belief articulated, we should recall, for the first time within scientific discourse during the period in which Hume wrote—virtually defines modernity. But regardless of how attractive and useful the *is/ought* distinction has proven to be, the first to violate Hume's Law was Hume himself, who conceded that *ought* was deduced from *is* in every system he had met with. Nor did Hume say he was opposed in principle to the deduction; rather, he was simply amazed by it, and demanded an explanation. "'Tis necessary," he said, "that it shou'd be observ'd and explain'd; and at the same time that a reason should be given, for what seems altogether inconceivable, how this new relation can be a deduction from others, which are entirely different from it" (*Treatise* 196). The deduction *seems* inconceivable, Hume admits; but he does not assert that it cannot be done; moreover, he may be being ironic, and he explicitly urges that *when* it occurs it should be explained.

The discussion of *is* and *ought* follows a passage on fact and value, a relation Robert Nozick, reflecting the customary interpretation of Hume as the inventor of clear philosophical distinctions, describes as a "chasm" that "despite determined efforts no one has been able to leap across or bridge" (*Philosophical Explanations* 535). But on this point, too, Hume has already performed the feat his readers think he has demonstrated to be impossible, arguing that morality did not consist merely in facts or in reason, but rather in "our own sentiments" of approbation or revulsion. "Take any action allowed to be vicious,"

Hume writes. "Willful murder, for instance. Examine it in all lights, and see if you can find that matter of fact, or real existence, which you call *vice*. In which-ever way you take it, you find only certain passions, motives, volitions and thoughts. . . . The vice entirely escapes you, as long as you consider the object" (195). The viciousness of the vice declares itself not in the action but in one's sentiments, which are still so solid as to be factual. "Here is a matter of fact," Hume says of morality; "but 'tis the object of feeling, not of reason. It lies in yourself, not in the object" (196, 195). Far from distinguishing absolutely between facts and values, Hume asserts that, in the realm of morality, evaluative feelings *are* facts. In the case of *is* and *ought*, then, Hume makes the distinction, but fails to make it rigorous; while in the related if not identical case of fact and value, he insists that there is no distinction at all. The true Humean law, in other words, might be less epigrammatic, less "emphatic," less like a law and more like a riddle.

When is a fact like a value? When it is ethical. In ethics, *is* and *ought*, descriptions and prescriptions, facts and values can be turned inside out, and can easily, if not exactly logically, convert into each other. A prominent feature of ethics is its structural hospitality to such fusions and conversions. In ethics, *is* and *ought* achieve a kind of dynamic lamination in which alterities are joined without losing their identities. Both are essential: without the bracing *is* to stipulate an "objective" condition, a "cognitive" necessity, a reality, the *ought* appears vacuous and unmotivated, and risks seeming a mere arbitrary, subjectively determined pronouncement; and without the animating *ought* to indicate a subjective sense of commitment to a goal, ideal, or value, the *is* becomes dull, inert, worthless. Hence the weakness of both strict segregationist and strict integrationist cases, which tend to caricature and even sometimes to reverse themselves. Levinas, for example, writes a descriptive discourse about the priority and autonomy of the prescriptive, while MacIntyre first describes as a historical fact and then prescribes as a cultural goal the fusion of description and prescription. MacIntyre, we may recall, claims that contemporary moral discourse is the product of a historical "confusion" in which the terms of obligation have survived any general sense of the nature of man, in the context of which obligation could make sense. From this perspective, we can perhaps come to a more positive appreciation of ethical "confusion" based on the recognition that such confusion is inherent and irreducible. Ethics entails a necessary and principled confusion: the ethical *is* is an *is* that *ought* to be; the ethical *ought* is an *ought* that *is*.

Other equally principled confusions follow in the wake of the *ought*. Many of these gather around the issue of freedom. Kant's aphorism, "*Ought* implies *can*," summons up the luminous figure, central to ethics, of the self-determining, integrated subject, the subject for whom action is, in the title of Stuart Hampshire's well-known book, a matter of *The Freedom of the Individual* (hereafter *FI*). Ethical imperatives address the subject *qua* subject, the hero of its own narrative, enjoying both the power to do what is required and the freedom not to do it. This last point is essential, for it underscores the freedom of the subject even from the law. The defining act of the ethical subject is choice. As opposed to the coercive *must*, the *ought* speaks to the circumstance of choice, and even recognizes a certain equality between options. As Stanley Cavell says, "'Ought', unlike 'must', implies that there is an alternative course you *may* take, may take responsibility for; but reasons are brought to urge you not to" (*Claim of Reason* 309). *Ought* urges you, therefore, to regard a certain action *as a* choice rather than as a brute necessity; and urges you, therefore, to declare your identity by making your choice. Indifferent to identity and hostile to choice, the *must* represents a necessity rather than an imperative. Foucault signals his turn from an attention to coercive mechanisms of normalization and discipline to an interest in freedom by taking up the discourse of ethics. "I am a moralist," he says in a late interview, "insofar as I believe that one of the tasks, one of the meanings of human existence—the source of human freedom—is never to accept anything as definitive, untouchable, obvious, or immobile" ("Power, Moral Values, and the Intellectual" 1).

Many commentators have read Foucault as endorsing an "ethical" freedom that is virtually unrestricted when he makes statements such as "Liberty is the ontological condition of ethics" ("Ethic of Care for the Self" 115; see Rajchman, *Michel Foucault: The Freedom of Philosophy*). But it is precisely in ethics that one finds the most rigorous insistence that freedom is necessarily complicated or qualified by its other. In the interview just quoted, Foucault comments that "ethics is the deliberate form assumed by liberty" (115), and the emphasis on "deliberate form," as on "self-fashioning" in his later works, suggests a nearly Kantian notion of freedom attained through the act of giving oneself the law. Foucauldian freedom is not, then, anarchically unregulated; nor could it be, as long as it is "ethical." To represent the *ought*, as Cavell often does, as singlemindedly generous and nonrestrictive, is to repress a necessary dimension of the imperative, the dimension of necessity itself—the *must*.

Necessity cannot be evaded. When we decide to do something because we ought to, the decision itself implies a *must:* we must have chosen between certain, fixed alternatives. In fact, once a choice is posited, we have no alternative but to choose. We need not choose between the things originally presented to us—to marry or not, to return the wallet I found or not, to lie or to tell the truth—but we must choose because any act represents a choice. If we go to sleep, translate the original issue into some other issue, or forget about it, we have simply posited a different choice, between choosing between two alternatives and not choosing between them. Hence from the moment of its first possibility, the imperative to choose will necessarily be obeyed. But if the *must* is a "terroristic" form in one respect, especially in contrast to an *ought* that liberally acknowledges the resistance to its imperative in the free will of the subject, the opposite can also be maintained: the *ought* specifies, defines, and limits, urging a particular choice, while the *must* scatters possibilities, dictating only that one choose. The containment of the *must* within the *ought* means that ethics contains its distinctive terrors, albeit in repressed form.

These terrors converge in the figure—the trope, the image, the idea, the pathology—of the ethical law. In Kant's formulation, we must follow duty rather than inclination; moreover, we must follow duty out of respect for the law rather than from any selfish motive, any "allurement." If, for example, I return the wallet because I wish to be thought honest, my act reflects a "hypothetical" rather than a properly categorical imperative, a narrow or material conception of interest, a means to some end rather than the expression of an enlightened self-interest based solely on a universalizable principle of reason with which I rejoice to concur. We cannot, according to Kant's merciless argument, be considered praiseworthy if we maintain our lives merely *as* duty requires; we must do so *because* duty requires (see *Metaphysical Foundations of Morals* 145). Corresponding to no possible arrangement of "phenomenal" interests, the law imposes, as one of Kant's recent readers complains, "a tyranny of reason on the weak and human too great to be endured for long"; and grounds, as Richard Rorty argues, an "ethics of purity" based on an inhuman fantasy of a "true self" living in a "true world" that was "nothing but point: nothing but a moral imperative, nothing but a call to moral purity" (MacRae 83; Rorty, "Freud and Moral Reflection" 13). So perversely uncompromising has Kant appeared on this point that, in a dazzling essay, Jacques Lacan was able to argue that the law itself was perverse by drawing a structural analogy between Kantian rationality and the rigors of sado-masochism. In Kant, Lacan argues, the subject is stripped of its pleasures and sequestered with the law in a confinement that duplicates in many respects the fascination with the pleasure of the other at the expense of one's own that is so endlessly represented in the work of de Sade (see "Kant avec Sade").

The point in the present context is that the terroristic purity of the law does not produce or even presume purity in the subject whose law in a sense it is. The very idea of an "ethical" law is strictly inconsistent with the integrated, self-consistent agent who alone, supposedly, can follow it. This inconsistency may account for a neo-Kantian strain in contemporary postmodern thinkers whose route to ethics runs through the decentered, pluralized, or shattered self. One of these thinkers, Kristeva, is drawn to ethics because it enforces and reinforces the effect of "poetic language," "the negativizing of narcissism" (*Revolution in Poetic Language* 233). Another, Lyotard, urges, in a complex meditation on "Obligation" in *The Differend*, a return to the position that "the law is transcendent to all intellection." This transcendence may be experienced as a "scandal" for the subject "abandoned by one's narcissistic image, opposed in this, inhibited in that. . . ." But can't we, Lyotard asks hopefully, "begin with the dispersion, without any nostalgia for the self?" (109–10). Levinas's concept of ethical "passivity" might be one non-nostalgic way of imagining the "ethical" disconfirmation of the subject, the seizing of its liberties, the denial or appropriation of its powers. Another way is opaquely indicated by Paul de Man and articulated more fully by J. Hillis Miller, who gives the Kantian antinomies their sharpest possible formulations. In Miller's "ethics of reading," the reader is wholly responsible for her acts, while the text is imagined as compelling from the reader, in a moment "neither cognitive, nor political, nor social, nor interpersonal, but properly and independently ethical," an abject "I must" (*Ethics of Reading* 1). Even within the less extreme and more humanistic forms of contemporary ethical discourse, the limits to agency are registered, often in the form of a meditation on what philosophers like Thomas Nagel, Bernard Williams, and Martha Nussbaum have called "moral luck," or, in Nussbaum's resonant phrase, "the fragility of goodness." "Moral luck" suggests the idea that although one can be held responsible only for what one can control, the area of "genuine agency," as Nagel puts it, seems to shrink under inspection to an "extensionless point." "Everything," Nagel writes, "seems to result from the combined influence of factors, antecedent and posterior to action, that are not within the agent's control" (*Mortal Questions* 35; see also Williams, *Moral Luck*, and Nussbaum, *The Fragility of Goodness* 1–21, 378–94). Even philosophers remote in spirit from Nietzsche are drawn to a critique of the "error of accountability."

But if they were as convinced of this error as Nietzsche was—if, for example, they believed, as he did, that "Everything is necessity," and therefore that "Everything is innocence"—then they might regain philosophical clarity and self-consistency, but they would also enter, as he did, a truly post-ethical world (*Human, All Too Human* 39). And if, on the other hand, they believed that nothing at all resulted from factors beyond the agent's control, that the agent enjoyed a perfect and unresisted agency, then ethics would be circumvented in the opposite way, for the subject would encounter nothing but itself. Whatever freedoms it enjoys to stipulate the exact ratios as well as the ultimate rationale, the discourse of ethics is constrained to represent some coincidence or coimplication of freedom and the law, free agency and obligation.

Some representations, such as Aristotle's, can minimize the strain of accommodation between these factors; and others, such as Kant's, can emphasize that strain. But strain there will always be in ethics; and the sign of strain is the compulsive drawing of unpersuasive or unconvincing distinctions. Take for example Cavell's discrimination between "persuading" and "convincing," where persuading involves getting another person to do something and convincing involves getting that person to see something in a certain way. "You can (grammatically) persuade someone to take a course of action," Cavell says, "but must convince them of the truth or soundness of a judgment." Persuasion may proceed by appeals "to his fears, your prestige, or another's money"; but convincing can only be effected by *"using reasons which convince you,"* that is, by reasons whose rightness compels assent (*CR* 278). The point of the distinction is to specify a practice of freedom as opposed to one of coercion. But the imbrication of the two, to which "ethics" bears perpetual witness, makes rigorous distinctions of this sort, however desirable, hard to maintain. Cavell's game is actually given away by Rorty, who, in defending freedom from encroachments by coercion, describes "persuasion" as the form of liberty: "Whatever else rationality may be," Rorty writes, "it is something that obtains when persuasion is substituted for force" ("Truth and Freedom" 634). Rorty's "persuasion" is Cavell's "convincing," while Rorty's "force" is Cavell's "persuasion." This is no mere verbal confusion that could be cleared up by greater precision, for the issue is ultimately what lies "inside" and what "outside" the human will, a question that becomes not just difficult but undecidable when the will in question is responding to an *ought.*

Where, exactly, does an "ethical" obligation come from—from the face of the other, human nature, the consensual view of the good life, the natural *telos* of the species, our nature as rational beings, the subject's deepest self-interest, prevailing community standards, our duty as God's creatures? Does it come from the inside or the outside? The history of ethical discourse consists of oscillations, vacillations, negotiations, and compromises between the given and the created, the nonnegotiable and the negotiable. One recent collection of essays is entitled *Universalism vs. Communitarianism: Contemporary Debates in Ethics* (Rasmussen); and other titles could be readily be imagined: *Reason vs. History, Idealism vs. Pragmatism, Objectivity vs. Will.* MacIntyre argues that the "incoherent" application of a lexicon of timelessness and impersonality—*right, good, worthy, just,* and so on—to the mere judgments of subjective will testifies to an aspiration to morality even in our degraded times. But, especially considering the history of ethical discourse, a subject on which MacIntyre is a leading expert, it makes more sense to say that what MacIntyre calls incoherence is simply the characteristic feature of ethical discourse in any age.

As a consequence of this incoherence, a kind of auto-deconstruction typifies ethical arguments. Cavell provides once again an excellent example in his insistence on a "point of crucial importance," that a "moral" reason must be "conceived in terms of what will morally benefit the person the speaker adduces his reasons to" (*CR* 281). What is a "moral" benefit? On the strength of Cavell's distinction between coercive persuading and the ideal freedom associated with convincing, we might expect that such a benefit does not answer to political, utilitarian, or psychological needs. Our expectation might be buttressed by Cavell's invocation of the necessity of an unworldly perspective: "However finally unsatisfactory a moral theory may be which invokes the idea of an Ideal Spectator as the optimal moral judge," he comments, "it contains that ineluctable truth" that "not every opinion has the same weight nor every disagreement the same significance" (*CR* 270). But such an inference would conflict with other elements in Cavell's account of ethics. For as Cavell develops this account, worldly and especially social needs dominate. Ethics, it turns out, is "a way of encompassing conflict which allows the continuance of personal relationships against the hard and apparently inevitable fact of misunderstanding, mutually incompatible wishes, commitments, loyalties, interests and needs, a way of mending relationships and maintaining the self in opposition to itself or others" (*CR* 269). So, while Cavell can argue that ethics is not a branch of "propaganda," in which any reason at all might count as legitimate (a position he associates with Charles Stevenson's *Ethics and Language*), but rather a force of principle, he can still claim that the point and value of ethics is to be found in the social realm of "relationships." For Cavell, at least sometimes, the proper center of ethical thought is not the undeviating and absolute prescriptions of the sovereign Law, not the rationality of the rules of mutual obligation, not the greatest good for the greatest number, not the logical implications of certain sentences. The center of ethics is rather the intelligible human community knit together by commitments, cares, responsibilities, and obligations. "We do not have to agree with one another in order to live in the same moral world," Cavell says, striking the social tone; "but we do have to know and respect one another's differences" (*CR* 269).

How does Cavell reach this ultimately utilitarian point of social humanism through the ethical when he had begun by insisting precisely on the difference between the utilitarian and the ethical as the difference between persuading and convincing? How does he arrive at the primacy of "personal relationships" *through* the ethical when his entire painstaking argument is built on the distinction between the contingencies of such relationships and noncontingent purity of the ethical? One explanation is that, in summing up, Cavell has gone sentimental, wiping out the tough distinctions on which his argument had been based, to conclude with a vision of the "family of man." But a more accurate and sympathetic explanation would recognize the peculiar nature of the distinctions Cavell is working with, the distinctions of ethics itself. What might be called sentimentalism or confusion or inattention could also be regarded as a rigorous working out of certain structural implications or inevitabilities within ethics itself. For distinctions between what might broadly be called the "political" (utilitarian, hypothetical, pragmatic, social, historical, etc.) and what Miller calls the "properly and independently ethical" must be made but cannot be made rigorous or "clean"; nor—in "ethics"—can they simply be collapsed so that there is no distinction at all. Ethical rigor is achieved precisely insofar as a strictly conceptual or logical rigor is suspended. For this reason, the introduction of "ethics" into a discussion often produces a sense of logical ineptitude or lexical unclarity, as the following example illustrates.

While they both saw integration as a solution to what journalist Nicholas Lemann calls "racial problems," Lyndon Johnson and Robert Kennedy approached these problems from altogether different premises. "Johnson's views on how to solve racial problems," Lemann writes, "were those of a man whose whole world was politics" ("The Unfinished War" 54). On the premise that politicians were prisoners of their constituencies, Johnson's solution to injustice was "vote power": "'If they give the blacks the vote, ol' Strom Thurmond will be kissing every black ass in South Carolina,' he told a friend once" (55). According to Johnson, interest binds the representational relationship: if blacks could express their interests through the vote, then politicians, protecting their own interests, would try to represent black interests effectively. Seeking many of the same ultimate ends, Kennedy disdained the deal-making pragmatism of Johnsonian politics;

he "saw life as a morality play" (55). For Kennedy, one ought to because one ought to. Kennedy's principled indifference to, even contempt for, the imperfect human community struck Johnson as
incomprehensible. Kennedy himself he regarded, in the words of one
of Johnson's aides, as "'a man of narrow sensibilities and totalitarian
instincts'" (54).

Does the distinction between the political and the ethical survive
the Kennedy-Johnson confrontation? Cavell seems to sum up the
Johnsonian criticism of Kennedy when he describes how one can
"make oneself a stranger to the human race, perhaps with the help of
philosophy"; and seems to support Johnsonian pragmatism when he
urges as ethically desirable "your being willing, from whatever cause,
to take his or her position into account" (*CR* 326). But terms appear
to have gotten reversed somehow, for it is the moralist, Kennedy, who
is criticized as unethical; and the politician, Johnson, (who occasionally, Lemann reports, "used the word 'nigger' in private" [54]), who
exemplifies the ethical respect for the other.

Such a confusion of terms suggests that the terms themselves may
be simply imprecise. In fact, however, they are too precise: the distinction between ethics and politics is too crisp to describe a complex
real-world situation. What the Kennedy-Johnson split dramatizes is a
division *within* the ethical between two kinds of "autonomy," with Kennedy standing for respect for the autonomy of the law, and Johnson,
respect for the autonomy of the other. Ethics, we must conclude, contains both a "political" humanism and a counter- or antihumanism of
the law. Neither Kennedy nor Johnson, in this account, would stand
for the ethical; nor would either stand for the political. Each would,
however, represent a particular mix of "politics" and "ethics," without
which neither politics nor ethics would be coherent in principle or
effective in practice.

We are compelled, further, to conclude that an entirely self-consistent law cannot be fully ethical. Uncrossed or unmediated by its other,
the principle of the autonomy of the law is compatible with narrow
sensibilities and totalitarian instincts. But, too, the uncompromised
principle of respect for the other risks a culpable failure to guide the
other towards the right judgment or decision out of mere consideration for his or her autonomy. One can over-respect the other if one
does not also respect the law. Moreover, the child-beater, the wife-
rapist, the police torturer, could, under accusation, appeal to the principle of the autonomy of the other—themselves—to claim that their
actions were "internal" to a domestic or institutional dynamic to which
others remained strangers and whose otherness demanded respect.
The only protection for the child, the wife, the prisoner, against such

an indifferent and often cowardly respect is provided by the principle of the autonomy of a law that is strictly out of control, a law apparently drawn from no interest and no context, a law effectively represented as being compelled by Reason rather than reasons, the Good rather than the Good for Me. Neither form of "respect" or "autonomy" can serve as the basis of an ethical practice unless accompanied, qualified, crossed by the other.

Ethics necessarily entails, then, two types of respect, a respect for the law and a respect for the other. Joseph Valente analyzes this situation with great succinctness and theoretical clarity. Considering "the law as social agency," Valente points out an "asymmetrical relation" between the "criteria of assessment" and "the various claims, viewpoints, and circumstances they affect." The law, he notes, is "by nature universalizing to some degree and so tends to adequate similar and dissimilar elements, to decide like and unlike cases by a univocal standard." The very equity of the law, however, its "systematic failure to account or adjust for the full play" of social or individual circumstances, calls forth, by violating through the *in*equity of its effects on variously situated people, another principle of justice, the respect for difference. Thus, Valente concludes, "the notion of justice not only legitimates and delegitimates existing law in a single blow but performs each function by way of the other; i.e. a law can only be held just on principles which, operating on another plane of analysis serve to dispute certain of its implicit assumptions"; but also "a law can only be held unjust on principles which, operating on another plane, form a part of its rationale." The enabling condition of this rough justice is most aptly described in terms of repression. Underdetermined on the representational surface but overdetermined in its actual force or content, the ethical *ought* is constituted by a mutual repression of its double imperative, with each form of respect provisionally negating or dominating the other within a system that, to be ethical, must include both.

The repression and internal division within ethics replicates itself in the relations established by the discourse of ethics with its others. The distinction between ethics and politics, for example, is both easily drawn and easily erased, precisely because each is defined as the repression of the other, as a certain emphasis occurring in a larger field—call it "justice"—that contains both. Jameson's "transhistorical imperative," "'Always historicize!',", suggests, in its pretermission of differences, in its suppression of justifications or reasons, and in its unconditioned absolutism, an operative but covert "ethical" respect for the ahistorical autonomy of the law. Arguing that ethics ought not to be, and that ethical criticism ought to be transcended in the direc-

31

tion of the collective and political, Jameson has only ethics, only the transhistorical imperative addressed to the individual, to appeal to. His politics betrays an "ethical unconscious" that mirrors and counterbalances the "political unconscious" his analysis reveals in the ethically-coded works of literature he discusses.

Indeed, even his critics on the left who attack him for his political shortcomings revert to the ethical in order to do so. "Jameson's works," one writes, are "too theoretical": "his welcome call for a political hermeneutics is too far removed from the heat of political battles . . . Jameson [should] write less Frenchified, expand his fascinating Marxist discourse to include talented American friends and foes, and situate himself more clearly within the American Marxist tradition. . . . Jameson's own historical predicament . . . should become more an object of his dialectical deliberations" (West, "Ethics and Action" 140–41). The case is not just theoretical (claiming to possess theoretical knowledge about what another person should think and write, about the proper "distance" between a discourse and political "heat," even about the right "amount" of theory), but ethical, insofar as the reasons for the recommendations and the consequences for failing to follow them are repressed and out of sight. Jameson is addressed in his freedom, insofar as he is free, and urged freely to choose based on principle. Thus ethics is reaffirmed through its very repudiation.

Cavell makes a routine if (by now) dubious distinction between a "properly ethical" *ought* that bears a message of consideration for the other that is independent of whatever reasons might accompany it, and a "utilitarian" *ought* whose content is "exhausted by reasons" (*CR* 317–18). Statements such as those by Jameson and his critic both illustrate this distinction and jeopardize it. For while, in their advocacy of politics, they do repress reasons and consequences, and thereby suggest a "properly ethical" consideration for the autonomy of the other, utilitarian factors are never far away. "You ought to write less Frenchified" virtually exhales "if you want to get along with me and my friends," "because you owe it to us," and "because you obviously don't know what you're doing." "Expand your fascinating discourse" trails its utilitarian consequences behind it in a cape of implication. Ethics and politics turn out to be not identical, but coimplicated, each dependent upon the repression, and support, of the other.

For reasons can always be adduced, and always suppressed, determining the mode of presentation as utilitarian or "properly ethical," universalistic or communitarian. Nor does anything prevent a synergistic convergence of both modes. In a statement made during the 1989 election campaign in Poland, Lech Walesa called on Poles to respect the autonomy of the other—the numerous linguistic, ethnic, ra-

32

cial, and religious minorities living in Poland. Walesa urged his fellow citizens to "find responsible positions for them in this campaign, so that they may participate with the dignity to which they are entitled. This is our human and moral duty." But lest this categorical duty prove too abstract to be persuasive to some, he adds a hypothetical complement in the next sentence: "It is also our political, and specifically Polish duty. After all, we have millions of Poles living beyond our present frontiers, and we naturally demand that their identity and civil rights be respected" ("Letter" 72). The "human and moral" duty is urged to those who position themselves in relation to history-transcending laws or obligations, while the "political and specifically Polish" duty speaks to those who see themselves situated in a world of nontranscendent force.

Ethics, or the "ethics-effect," depends, then, on the effectiveness of a certain representation, its ability to stand without visible means of support. Acts whose rationales are open to question—such as the American interventions in Grenada, Panama, Vietnam, and the Middle East, or insurrections in the Philippines, Lithuania, East Germany, Romania, Czechoslovakia, and Poland—are often represented as acts of fidelity to "human and moral duty" in an effort not just to dignify the agents but to place their motives out of play, to represent them as necessary consequences of the ensemble of fundamental beliefs that any rational (or "human," or "God-created," or "justice-seeking," or "socially responsible") being must hold, beliefs we are not at liberty to contest. But in fact an ethical representation is always contestable. Indeed, "pragmatists" such as Jeffrey Stout and Richard Rorty reject the fact-value distinction as well a number of other distinctions associated with it precisely for this reason, that to set up separate categories of "fact" and "value" is to paralyze discussion and critique by rendering "values" "noncognitive" and "not rationally discussable," while "truth" and "objectivity" are severed from will, desire, and belief (see Rorty, *Philosophy and the Mirror of Nature* 363; Stout, *Ethics after Babel* 255–65). Excessively rigorous distinctions imperil ethics, which lives by the permeability or deconstructability of the distinctions on which it is founded.

A reported incident involving Heidegger illustrates a few of the complexities arising from the recodability of ethical representations. In 1938, Heidegger blocked the appointment of a former student, Max Müller, to a teaching position at Freiburg by informing the university administration that Müller was "unfavorably disposed" toward the regime. Confronted by Müller, Heidegger explained that he had been asked about Müller's politics and "I gave the answer that simply corresponded to the truth," adding that, "As a Catholic you must know that everyone has to tell the truth." As Müller was leaving, Heidegger asked him not to take things badly. "It's not a question of taking things badly," Müller replied. "It's a question of my existence" (Sheehan 41). What is the question? How do we decide the ethical status of the act, which involved "telling the truth" *and* "imperilling Müller's existence?" According to an ethic of truth, Heidegger was right to respond honestly to questions about Müller's beliefs; but of course, Heidegger could have been lying or confused about his motives. According to an ethic of loyalty, Heidegger was wrong to give the answers he did; but of course, loyalty to the Führer might occupy a higher place in a patriot's values than loyalty to friends. How do we decide which principle ought to prevail when both principles can be so easily redescribed in terms of the other as a failure of principle? And how, for that matter, can we decide what principle or "maxim" is illustrated by the act? What *is* the act? What is the ultimate difference between a principle and a motive? Perhaps Heidegger's loyalty to the regime determined his truth-telling; perhaps a desire to seem loyal determined the apparent loyalty; perhaps a desire to protect his relatives, or to provide covert aid to the persecuted Jewish scholars working with him in the university, determined the desire to seem loyal; perhaps Müller *deserved* to be betrayed. *What*, finally, is at issue here—the act, the principle, the application of principle to act, the motive behind the principle, the motive for representing the motive as the principle? In its disinterestedness, ethics, the discourse of bridged gaps, the discourse of resistance, does not solve such questions; ethics is their articulation. The fact that the application of sound ethical principle to action cannot prohibit such acts as the betrayal of friends to Nazis is the nausea of ethics, that which it can neither reject nor swallow.

Another example, again connected to the ultimate issue of human life and death, suggests even more disturbing implications about recodability and about the ethical indifference to, or "disinterest" in, rightness as such in favor of a certain style of representation. In a recent article, Bruce Jennings discusses the options confronting doctors in the treatment of mortally ill newborns whose existence can be prolonged by the technology of Neonatal Intensive Care Units. The question is especially resonant since advanced cultures often affirm their advancement by contrasting their own treatment of sickly infants to the brutal pragmatism of primitive cultures which, we are told, simply pitch the babies off the cliff. The question is, Should doctors—our enlightened, modern doctors—pull the plug? Jennings never asks the question in this crude form, but argues that decisions of this type be decided not by an "ethic of rights," which he says is misplaced, but by an "ethic of the good" "in the context of [the infant's] future family life and in terms of its potential for development and self-realization." Jennings concludes that doctors should pull the plug, and should do so in full confidence that their choice, phrased in the elaborate deferrals of the discourse of first principles, is ethical. We can, in a word, kill sick babies and maintain our ethical self-respect simply by reclassifying the act.

Jennings's point, again delicately stated, is that pulling the plug according to the ethic of the good makes a hopeless situation easier on the family. Jennings himself makes the choice of this principle easier on the family through an elaborate metaphoricity whenever he approaches a description of the terrible act itself. "The flame we kindle in the process of rescue," he writes (assuming the community of "we") "need not be exceptionally or even normally bright. The human community is lit by the small candles among us as well as by our shining stars. But some flame must be kindled; if there is no viable spark there to begin with . . . then the benevolent act of rescue turns into a maleficent display of technological virtuosity in which Faust triumphs over Prometheus." Hence, in the service of the good, we should discourage "aggressive rescue" and encourage "conservative and palliative care, even if that means a foreshortened life" (92). If (we are to understand) the child had a "viable spark," then we would surely "kindle" it, regardless of our opinion of its luminosity; we respect the other and do not presume to judge his worth. But the dying child, Jennings implies, while unmistakably a "human being," does not qualify as such a spark, and therefore cannot claim our unreserved benevolence in the way that, presumably, all truly viable sparks can. Arguing for obedience, submission, passivity before an imperative, Jennings's "ethical" argument—aided by rhetorical indirection—sanctions a decision that exhausted and anguished parents might find appalling but welcome—to spare themselves the agony and let the baby die—and permits that decision to remain mercifully and powerfully unarticulated by characterizing it as no decision at all.

It is easy to imagine—indeed, possible to infer from Jennings's own argument—a counterargument on behalf of medical researchers that advances, say, an "ethic of ultimate social good" as the justification for prolonging the lives of such infants as long as possible so as to learn as much as possible from their response to treatment. Both this ethic and Jennings's "ethic of the good" could be cast in terms of a desire to avoid pain and pursue pleasure. But neither would proceed along those lines, for arguments based on mere personal pain or personal pleasure are not convincing to people who wish to be seen as, and indeed to be, ethical. Such people are convinced, as we recall from

Cavell, by arguments that could apply equally to anybody, that is, arguments not rooted in *my* pain, *my* pleasure. Promoting a pain-reducing choice, Jennings can—indeed, must, to be ethical—still assail the "excessively hedonistic conception of interest" indulged in by partisans of an ethic of rights (91). Ethical interest is interested to appear disinterested. It is the task of ethical discourse convincingly to represent as "principle" some interests designated as "deeper" or "truer" than others, which it stigmatizes as "egoistic," "material," or "narrow." Only "earned" interest becomes principle. Discriminating between earned and unearned, ethical discourse accommodates the fact of the universal pursuit of interest to the value of law, duty, principle. It is "ethical" in this sense to say things like "'The good' dictates that the plug be pulled." Not every action can be convincingly represented as obedient to every principle, and not every principle can be convincingly advanced as worthy. But the effort to relate act and principle in a convincing way binds one to a world of discourse, of conventions, material conditions, habits, values, ideals, commitments, norms, others. Only in terms of this world can one even attempt to convince oneself or anyone else that a certain principle truly is a principle, a world-transcending *ought*.

Jennings's argument suggests that no act is so unreservedly vile, contemptible, or unworthy as to be altogether uncatchable by the net of ethical redemption. Virtually anything can be justified, anything condemned, on ethical grounds. The "virtues" themselves—those tokens of the desire for formalism—are just words, no less arbitrary than any other signs, and can, with determination and wit, be applied to any act. Terrorism, torture, chemical warfare, slavery, the denunciation of one's family demanded by both the French and Russian Revolutions and more recently by the authorities in China, the deliberate starvation of civilian populations by their own governments, the destruction of rainforests and ozone by commercial interests, the "slaughter of innocent babies," the "state takeover of a woman's body"—all these acts have been defended as acts of principle, obedience to the law, instances of courage, loyalty, progress, liberation, respect. The destruction of Jews, Gypsies, Communists, and others during the Second World War was not unjustifiable, but eminently justifiable: before, during, and after, it was the object of a fantastic elaboration of justification.

Ethics is a spacious discipline, a mansion with many rooms, as a final example should demonstrate. "Terrorism is for us a part of the political battle being conducted under the present circumstances, and it has a great part to play. . . . It proclaims our war against the occupier. . . . Neither Jewish ethics nor Jewish tradition can disqualify terrorism as a means of combat" (quoted in Shammas 47). The author is the current (1991) prime minister of Israel, Yitzhak Shamir, writing in 1943. Even Jewish writers in the darkest hours of the Holocaust can claim ethical credentials—*Jewish* ethical credentials—for terrorism.

At the bottom of this deep and troubled well lies the enabling, and disabling, circumstance of ethics, the ambivalence that determines the ethical imperative as simultaneously interested and principled, an ambivalence or undecidability that installs arbitrariness and therefore choice at the heart of obligation. One can—one must—choose which principle to be governed by. In one sense, the fact of choice corrupts the law; but in the absence of choice the law could not be followed or obeyed in any properly ethical sense at all, for the agent would have no responsibility for the act. Rather, choice systematically *risks* corruption. Ethics in general is a species of risk that affords no rigorous way to tell ethical reasons from other reasons, choices from obligations.

In fact, the deep and troubled well in question is not just a discursive ambivalence, but the mind capable of repression. While one can say that everything about ethics is choice, one can also say that everything is determined. One does not, after all, choose one's parents, one's initial and formative circumstances, one's siblings, one's aptitudes or abilities, one's desires or hungers or tastes or revulsions, or countless other facts about oneself and the world one lives in: one does not choose who one is. Nor, one could say, does one choose one's actions, which are all the issue of previous acts, prior conditions, none of them altogether one's own. One *can* say these things; but if one wishes to be ethical, one will say, and believe—one will be convinced—that principle is underdetermined and binds all alike, while the decision to follow the principle is freely chosen.

Principles, as all the previous examples testify, do not just announce themselves and declare their intentions. However implicitly, they must be argued for, their claims established through, and enmeshed in, strategies, ploys, appeals, devices that persuade us we are convinced, that manipulate us into the conviction of freedom. A principle is what is taken for a principle, and the ethicity of a practice must be worked out in a climate of doubt. Kant, supposedly the inventor of a purely abstract, nonsubjective, and ahistorical notion of duty, grants without hesitation that the agent can never rid herself of doubt, for there is no reliable way of determining one's true motive. He begins the second section of the *Metaphysical Foundations of Morals*, for example, by noting that "the sharpest self-examination" cannot reveal whether we acted out of duty or out of "some secret impulse of self-love, under the false appearance of that idea." We like to flatter ourselves with a "pretended nobler motive," but in fact can never know "the secret springs of action, since when we ask about moral worth, we are not concerned with actions but with their inward principles which we do not see" (155). Following, perhaps, an irresistible temptation, we often think in terms of a binary view of agency—we deny ourselves or we gratify ourselves, we follow the law or we transgress against it. But an ethical action is one of which it might be said that the agent *either* followed Reason or reasons, "the good" or "hedonism," some "nobler motive" or some "secret impulse of self-love." Principles command; but the machinery of command is operated by the human hands of choice in a strictly undecidable but always contestable relation. In ethics, the crucial, evidentiary factor remains permanently inward and invisible, permanently under suspicion, and the subject permanently at risk.

3. Double Agent, Double Duty

What *is* the subject, according to ethics? *What* is an ethical person? As we have already seen, ethical discourse compulsively represents a heterogeneous subject. One of the canonical forms of this heterogeneity was given by Kant, who in "The Doctrine of Virtue" said that we obey our consciences as if they were not our own. In the court of conscience the accused is one with the judge, and becomes "a twofold personage, a doubled self who, on the one hand, has to stand in fear and trembling at the bar of the tribunal which is yet entrusted to him, but who, on the other hand, must himself administer the office of the judge which he holds by inborn authority" (104). At odds with Kant on most things, Nietzsche agrees with him on this. In morality, Nietzsche says, "man treats himself not as *individuum* but as *dividuum*"; morality is the stage for the ascetic spectacle of the "uncanny, dreadfully joyous labor of a soul voluntarily at odds with itself" (*Human, All Too Human* 57; *Genealogy of Morals* 87). Even in Levinas, who begins with the dreary and apparently absolute binary of Same and Other, the subject is compelled—by the sheer discursive requirements of ethics, one might argue—to complicate itself. "Paternity," Levinas writes, is "the relationship with a stranger who, entirely while being Other, is myself, the relationship of the ego with a myself who is nonetheless a stranger to me" (*Time and the Other* 91).

In Kant, Nietzsche, and Levinas, the adversarial "relationship" is between the impulse to follow the law and the impulse to pursue desire or inclination. But Cavell indicates a further dualism *within* the dutiful subject. According to Cavell, a person is, first, an integrated, conscious agent capable of accurate assessment and principled choice. A person, moreover, occupies a certain place and operates from a certain point of view that must be respected. But a person is not simply a centered, concentrated, autonomous node of consciousness. A person is also known if not by his enemies then by his others; he is partly defined by forces, agencies, and imperatives that come from "outside" or "beyond." A person is, for example, always in relation to others whom he addresses and is addressed by. And one has one's principles. Here, Cavell is explicit. The point of assessing a claim by someone to moral rightness is, he argues, "to determine *what* position you are taking, that is to say, *what position you are taking responsibility for*—and whether it is one I can respect." "Principles" or "positions" thus make community possible: to know one's position is to know oneself, and to know oneself is to be able to understand and situate others. "What is at stake," Cavell concludes, "is not the validity of morality as a whole, but the nature or quality of our relationship to one another" (*CR* 268). Cavell's ethical agent, then, commands respect both for its own autonomy and for its responsiveness to communal commitments and values, to "positions." An autonomous *cogito,* the ethical subject is yet permeable to alien forces and energies.

This division within the dutiful subject is urged in traditional ethical discourse by the posing of two questions. The first, corresponding roughly to the "autonomy of values," is Socrates' majestic "How should one live?" Corresponding to the "autonomy of the agent," the second is Lenin-Chernyshevsky's "What is to be done?" or, more pointedly, "What should I do?" To ask "How should one live" is to see the subject as generalized and abstracted, an ideally uncircumstanced being concerned with norms, principles, values, universals. To think of oneself as "one" is to "transcend" the particularities of one's life. Even those who reject the very possibility of transcendence recognize, as Bernard Williams puts it, that Socrates' question has a "peculiar emphasis" that distances the asker from any actual occasion of considering what to do. The question's form, Williams says, "invites me to think about my life from no particular point in it," and so leads away from the immediate and egoistic and towards the impersonal, the nonsubjective, the disinterested (*Ethics and the Limits of Philosophy* 19; hereafter *ELP*). "One's" values are represented not as one's own, nor as prevailing community prejudices. Other than an "I," "one" has, ideally, nothing of one's own, no specific content, no life at all outside the activity of reflection. "One" reflects on the life of "I," and, again ideally, is reflected in it.

Meanwhile, on the other side of the mirror of reflection stands "I," a creature of concreteness and specificity, a being with a particular point of view from which it is emphatically not distanced. It makes a difference to "I," if not to "one," that one is a nineteen-year-old mother of three, one retarded; or that it is monsoon season; or that the applicant is an old drinking buddy; or that the others did it and got away with it; or that today is one's fifth birthday; or that one distrusts all Hispanics, especially men.

On occasion, the split between "one" and "I" can manifest itself in radical and painful ways. It is one thing, for example, to believe in the general right to abortion, and almost quite another to contemplate aborting your own baby, especially if you have seen it through ultrasound imaging; it is one thing to believe in equal treatment under the law, and almost quite another to find oneself punished as a "common criminal." In two distinguished books, Thomas Nagel has explained such disjunctions in terms of the radical difference between "objectivity" and "subjectivity." The "coordination of the points of view of different individuals toward their own experiences," is, Nagel asserts, "totally different from the coordination of their points of view toward the external world," because while the subject knows itself through itself in an intimate and immediate way, the "pursuit of objectivity involves a transcendence of the self, in two ways: a transcendence of particularity and a transcendence of one's type" (*Mortal Questions* 207, 209; see also *The View from Nowhere*). According to Nagel, the self has the unconquerable capacity, and in some circumstances the duty, to shear off from itself, to transcend itself in the direction of "one."

Despite the subjective experience of "transcendence," or of internal division, however, the distinction is not rigorous or absolute. The "total difference" Nagel posits between subjective and objective "coordinations" does not fully apply to the distinction made here between the "one" and the "I"; nor do all of Nagel's formulations support such a rigid distinction. In *The View from Nowhere*, Nagel describes as "an aspect of what we are" the workings of an "objective self" with the power to detach from, refer to, and oppose the rest of the self. The apparent autonomy of the faculty of objectivity suggests that the human subject is at once inside and outside the world, with the project of reconciling these two aspects of the self constituting the primary task of philosophy, or indeed of intelligence. "It turns out," Nagel writes, "that the human mind is much larger than it needs to be merely to accommodate the perspective of an individual human perceiver and agent within the world" (66). Nagel does not argue here for a total autonomy of the objective self. "However often we may try to step outside of ourselves," he writes, "something will have to stay behind the lens, something in us will determine the resulting picture, and this will give grounds for doubt that we are getting any closer to reality" (68). A record of the complex simultaneous experience of transcendence and the skepticism that accompanies it—an experience that received its decisive philosophical formulation in Spinoza's *Ethics*—is provided by the meditations of Italo Calvino's Mr. Palomar:

> But how can you look at something and set your own ego aside? Whose eyes are doing the looking? As a rule, you think of the ego as one who is peering out of your own eyes as if leaning on a window sill, looking at the world stretching out before him in all its immensity. So, then: a window looks out on the world. The world is out there; and in here, what do we have? The world still—what else could there be? With a little effort of concentration, Mr. Palomar manages to shift the world from in front of him and set it on the sill, looking out. Now, beyond the window, what do we have? The world is also there, and for the occasion has been split into a looking world and a world looked at. And what about him, also known as "I," namely Mr. Palomar? Is he not a piece of the world that is looking at another piece of the world? (*Mr. Palomar* 114)

The enclosure of both "object" and "subject" within "the world" overcomes any possibility of a "total" difference between them. This does not mean, however, that there is no difference at all. Mr. Palomar and the objects of his vision are not just equivalent and interchangeable "pieces of the world," for one piece is looking at and reflecting on the other. A similar difference without distinction characterizes the self-reflective subject itself. A factor of "objectivity" and "transcendence," "one" is yet able to reflect only on the particular experiences of "I": "one" can only transcend oneself. And for its part, the "I," a factor of "subjectivity" and concrete particularity, is not confined to its "own" circumstances and aptitudes; for everyone, as Charles Altieri has commented, has "the same experience of what it is like to be an I or a me. Each of us experiences an 'I,' so that the very intimacy of the 'I' is at once elemental and abstract" ("Contemporary Philosophy and Modernist Writing" 7). Even the "I," then, maintains a critical distance from its own particularity. The totality is—as ethical discourse ceaselessly insists—both part of the observable, contingent order of things and necessarily capable of and duty-bound to reflection upon itself.

The transpersonal "I," as Altieri describes it, serves at once as the basis of subjective isolation and as the ground of all community. Once again, Mr. Palomar has the exact formulation. Pondering the "sword" of light extending over the sea from the swimmer's eye towards the setting sun, he reflects that "the sword is imposed equally on the eye of each swimmer; there is no avoiding it. 'Is what we have in common precisely what is given to each of us as something exclusively his?'" (14). Despite the theoretical break between "one" and "I," they share

41

a certain inclination towards or even obligation to the other: the faculty of the subject whose allegorical name is "one" reflects, generalizes, regulates, and idealizes the circumstances of the "I" to which it is bound and limited; while the faculty named "I" individualizes, instantiates, tests, and grounds the norms and principles of "one."

The two primary ethical questions suggest not only a doubled subject but a doubled duty as well. The chief duty demanded of "one" is reflection, whose differentness from practical life and any duties centered there is conceded even by the urbane Williams. Reflection inserts into the flow of action a principle of inhibition that a moment's reflection will tell us is theoretically infinite. "One must always reflect," Lyotard says, "in order to know if in repaying a loan or in refusing to give away a friend, etc., one is actually acting, *in every single instance,* in such a way as to maintain the Idea of a society of free beings" (*JG* 85). One must always reflect: this is the law that ethical discourse virtually presumes as well as teaches. But the law cannot be followed, for perpetual reflection, like the early Christians' ideal of perpetual prayer, would leave no room for anything else, devouring the "material" on which it is supposed to meditate. This was, in fact, part of the point of the injunction to perpetual prayer, to keep one out of trouble by occupying all one's time.

And all one's energy as well. As Lyotard suggests, specifically ethical reflection carried out by "one" demands in even the simplest cases a continual exploratory application of principle (or "maxim") to action, an elaborate sifting and searching for definitions, motives, and effects that sorely tests the Enlightenment claim that knowledge of right and wrong is immediate, universal, and intuitive. Say I want to spank my whining and cantankerous child right now, but I hesitate to do so, and while I hesitate I reflect. What should I do? Should I spank her? What sort of discipline should I provide? Should I prepare my child for the realities of a harsh world? (*Is* it harsh? *primarily* harsh? *characteristically* harsh? harsh in what ways?) Should I mimetically embody that harshness, or try to reinforce her self-esteem through unconditional love so that she can confront harshness confidently when she encounters it outside the home? Should I represent the world or myself? Should I think teleologically or deontologically? Should I represent my intentions directly or indirectly, physically or verbally? Would it be a good thing if every parent in similar circumstances spanked his child? If I spanked her, would I be maintaining the Idea of a society of free beings? Should I think about the future? Should I try to anticipate the consequences of all my acts? Should I think, or just act instinctively? (What *are* my instincts?) Should I? Should one? How should one live? My hand suspended in mid-air, I remain in the ethical moment of reflection, a moment of thought-crowded paralysis that may be marginal to "my," and to my child's, life but is central to the distanced life of "one." One's ethical duty—perhaps the only duty that "one" could recognize as one's own—is to reflect. The real question, as Heidegger said, is, How must we think?

Insofar as ethics commands reflection above all else, it defers action by rotting its basis in certainty. This is the startling conclusion reached by Williams, who, having argued that ethical reflection arises *within* our generalized worldly interests, states that *"reflection can destroy knowledge"* (*ELP* 148). Proliferating questions, generating perspectives ever more spacious and general, making us uncertain of what we know and doubtful whether we know anything at all, ethical reflection subverts the assurance, the "knowledge," on which action is based, resists action's finality, and undermines the will to ignorance implicit in action's foreclosure of alternatives. It was to resist this corrosive effect of reflection, in fact, that Sartre argued in *Un Théâtre de situations* that action should maintain its "freedom" by suppressing knowledge, especially psychological knowledge, and should contain its justification within itself: "chaque acte comprend ses propres fins et son système d'unification" (30).

Sartre's is an extreme statement of the proposition that an ethic of reflection cannot by itself be ethical. The ethical *ought* also dictates action, and does so in the most direct and least persuasive way possible, with no arguments, reasons, or appeals. In this respect, ethics is the perennial innocence of action. In Aristotle, for example, ethics is conceived as a branch of politics precisely because of the power of ethics to guide and legitimate certain actions; ethical knowledge, according to Aristotle, naturally "finds expression in actions" (*Nic. Eth.* 1.7:38). This element in Aristotle's ethics badly compromises Martha Nussbaum's claims for an Aristotelian basis for the ethic she derives from Henry James's novels, according to which "perception" is the highest act. The idea that "seeing a complex, concrete reality in a highly lucid and richly responsive way" constitutes the essence or end of ethics is profoundly anti-Aristotelian (*Love's Knowledge* 152). If knowledge does not find expression in action, if it remains on the level of perception or apprehension, or if the gap between reflective sophistication and the coarseness of action becomes unbridgeable, then ethics itself is brought into disrepute. The real question, some Aristotelian anti-Heidegger might have said, is, How must we—or I—act?

How to negotiate the double demands, the doubled demand, of reflection and action? Can we ever achieve such a perfected ripeness of understanding that knowledge might pass over directly into justified action; or must action always remain a blind wager? Can reflection be considered a kind of action, and action a species of reflection, so that the two converge on, and convert into, each other? Or do they remain apart, each the other's goal, or degradation? "Ethics" does not provide an answer to such fundamental questions, but simply raises them by positing, both in the subject and in the idea of duty, what might be called a relation of *resistance,* a constitutive reciprocity between shared or mutually implicated but not identical—indeed, apparently opposed—forces.

This resistance appears in primary form in what has been described as the real overdetermination, as opposed to the apparent underdetermination, of the ethical *ought.* When proposed norms or principles cannot demonstrate a vital connection or responsiveness to concrete particulars, the effectiveness of their *oughts* dwindles, and the entire discourse thins out into what Schopenhauer called "stilted maxims, from which it is no longer possible to look down and see life as it really is with all its turmoil" (*The Basis of Morality* 133). Any truly forceful and convincing principle will betray, at some remove, the urgencies of a particular point of view on a particular world. When Plato describes four things as absolutely forbidden—murder, bestiality, incest, and sacrilege; or when Aristotle describes a "natural" convergence between the highest ethical development of the individual and the objective needs of the polis, a modern reader can recognize the preferred terms of Greek aristocracy as well as that class's efforts to resist its peculiar temptations, temptations classically elaborated in Nietzsche's *The Birth of Tragedy* and E. R. Dodds's *The Greeks and the Irrational.* When Kant proposes a categorical imperative, it is obvious to a thinker like Hegel that he is merely inscribing the self-conception of his class as a universal subject; but when Hegel corrects Kant by insisting on the importance of *Sittlichkeit,* he reveals to later generations the distinctly German idealization of "community." When Lyotard launches a polemic against "terror, that is, the blackmail of death toward one's partners, the blackmail that a prescriptive system does not fail to make use of in order to become the majority in most of the games" (*JG* 100), this prohibition is shadowed and defined by Lyotard's version of principle, a "pagan" multiplicity of "games" and a model of "judgment without criteria." And when Irving Massey proposes as the ultimate violation of ethics any act "that, without sufficient reason, reduces . . . someone else's ability, or desire, to survive," the connection between global principle and the highly particular Jewish post-Holocaust experience which forms the stated background of his meditation is not remote (*Find You the Virtue* xviii). Such traces of worldly implication do not cripple or compromise the principle; they simply make it intelligible and effective as a worldly force even as they qualify its claims to autonomy or global applicability. The relative visibility of worldly circumstances and a circumstantial point of view makes an *ought* "persuasive"; their relative invisibility makes it "convincing." Ethical discourse thus operates through a calculation of "distance": too great a distance between principle and interest produces stilted maxims; too little produces apologias, bad faith, and false consciousness. As the distance "itself," ethics is equally removed from one-dimensional conceptions of ideality and of interest. The essence of ethics is its form, its structure of resistances; but, formally, ethics constitutes a resistance to formalism through the overdetermination of all its elements, which are not simply themselves, but rather entangled, compromised, formed and deformed by otherness.

This dialectical series of negotiations between resistant elements does not merely apply to ethics; it constitutes the ethical dimension of dialectic itself. Take as one contemporary instance the debate between Hans-Georg Gadamer and Jürgen Habermas on the relation of understanding to its objects. Gadamer insists that all understanding occurs within the "hermeneutic circle," with the present engaging in an essentially prereflective dialogue with the past, a dialogue that enables understanding even as it effectively prevents the possibility of an objective or absolute judgment. Habermas disagrees, defending the power and right of rational critique to unmask and criticize the often irrational interests that constitute discourses. Especially in this reductive précis of a complex and evolving discussion, it is apparent that the essential issue is the relation of the terms of a binary opposition—past and present, rationality and interest—with Gadamer arguing for no essential difference and Habermas standing up for radical difference. To the Gadamerians, Habermas proposes stilted maxims with no worldly force; to the Habermasians, Gadamer irresponsibly abandons the world to its own unprincipled devices. Each argues, accordingly, for an "ethical" corrective to the other, an adjustment of the distance between understanding and what is understood in light of certain desirable ends.

This debate is replayed continually, providing a kind of "ethical" subtext for debates that appear to be based on empirical or technical questions. Does a "moment of *unconditionedness*" inhere, as Habermas claims, in the condition of all action oriented towards reaching understanding; should ideology and theory, as Althusser argues, both be grouped into a larger class, the production of social relations; is the concept of a structuralist "center," as Derrida says, merely relational and "functional" rather than transcendental; can what Stout calls a "fittingly modest pragmatism" that abandons the hope for ultimate grounding of principles still hope to work on behalf of justice (see

Habermas, "Questions and Counterquestions" 195; Althusser, "Ideology and Ideological State Apparatuses"; Derrida, "Structure, Sign, and Play in the Discourse of the Human Sciences"; Stout 257–60)? Any discussion of the relation between the regulator and the regulated, the center and the margins, the grounded and the ungrounded, will be at least implicitly "ethical" in that it will involve issues of governance, and will turn on the question of how the relationship between distinct but manifestly co-implicated terms *ought* to be construed. The *ought* de-neutralizes even the driest conceptual settings.

The ethical dimension of the relation between theory and practice is nowhere more apparent than in recent debates about the role of literary theory, which has been criticized for being too categorical, too eager to regulate the practice of interpretation by appeals to a general theory of meaning, too quick to promote certain practices as though they were imperative. Stanley Fish points, for example, to Chomsky's attempt to construct a "competence model" of linguistic use, a model "which reflects the timeless and contextless workings of an abiding formalism," as an instance of the ambitions of "theory" to define the abstract, general, and invariant rules that would determine the course of research in linguistics (*Doing What Comes Naturally* 318). Theory is marked, Fish says, by a reformist impulse that seeks to substitute "for the parochial perspective of some local or partisan point of view the perspective of a general rationality to which the individual subordinates his contextually conditioned opinions and beliefs" (319). This Habermasian substitution, he argues at length, can never be achieved because the "rules" are themselves "interpretive products," and so theory as a whole "cannot help but borrow its terms and its contents from that which it claims to transcend" (320, 321). Thus theory cannot govern practice from above because it is itself originally and decisively "below."

Fish's method is startling. He takes the presumptions of theory to neutrality and transcendence and relentlessly redescribes them in terms of their others—politics, practice, interpretation, history. Fish vehemently denies that these latter terms are unconstrained, insisting rather that constraints are "built into practices" themselves (13). In the present context, we could say that Fish tries to deny the idea of "distance." But the denial of distance returns to haunt him, for the "distance" between his constraints "built into practices" and Habermas's "moment of *unconditionedness* built into the conditions of action" is perhaps not as large as either might like to believe. Moreover, Fish's characterization of the effects of theory as "political rather than theoretical" might protect his argument from one danger but exposes him to another, for it reinstitutes the very distinction between politics and

46

theory that he is trying to deny (331). The provocative upending of stilted maxims about truth, objectivity, and theory ends up, at least in Fish's less circumspect formulations, by replicating those maxims. What neither Fish nor anyone else can succeed in doing is convincingly to represent the relation between the activity and the object of reflection, between "politics" and "theory," without recourse to the idea, however compromised or complicated, of distance. And this distance institutes ethics.

In contemporary academic discourse, the term "theory" is under siege. Evidence of the radical loss of status by "theory," once the key term and proudest claim of the discourse of ethics, is everywhere. A recent collection of essays including work by some of the most eminent and influential people writing about ethics today, including Charles Taylor, Annette Baier, Richard Rorty, Stuart Hampshire, Bernard Williams, Martha Nussbaum, and Alasdair MacIntyre—and the editor claims Iris Murdoch, Jeffrey Stout, Cora Diamond, Michael Walzer, and unnamed others as colleagues in spirit—is entitled *Antitheory in Ethics*. The project of a systematic understanding of ethics on the theoretical level lies in ruins, the victim of a triumphant anti-Kantian localism. Speaking for the anti-theoreticians, Agnes Heller urges a reflection on "certain issues in their fixed and concrete situations without attempting to interrelate the results of such a detached reflection within the framework of a coherent and internally consistent moral theory" (*General Ethics* 5).

If theory were only the collection of stilted maxims its opponents picture it to be, it would deserve the oblivion to which they have consigned it. But theory need not and ought not to be outcast in the contemporary discourse of ethics. For a conception of theory and practice that contemporary thinkers might respect, one need look no farther than Kant's essay on the subject. Theory, Kant argues there, does not constitute a one-way critique or regulation of practice. Rather, theory and practice engage in a reciprocal self-definition in terms of the other. "An aggregation of rules, even of practical rules, is called a *theory*," Kant writes, "as long as these rules are thought of as principles possessing a certain generality and, consequently, as being abstracted from a multitude of conditions that nonetheless influence their application. Conversely, not every undertaking is a *practice*; rather, only such ends as are thought of as being brought about in consequence of certain generally conceived principles of procedure are designated practices" ("On the Proverb" 61). This brief formulation proves to be surprisingly supple in its evocation of resistance: in the first sentence, theory is said to be governed or "influenced" by practical "conditions" from which it is "abstracted" (a formulation that, in other contexts, might be consistent with the "autonomy of the agent"); while in the second sentence, practice is governed or "brought about" by theory (a recognition of the "autonomy of values"). The consequences of theory that Fish describes as "political" could, in light of this model, more appropriately be seen as the only kind of effects that theory could possibly have—effects in and on practice, effects that enter the world, there to be realized and deformed, there to be risked.

Such an elastic model could accommodate any ethical system that posited overlapping or conflicting imperatives, which is to say, any ethical system whatsoever. On the basis of Kant's theory/practice distinction, ethics could be conceived as *both* a systematization of the principles that might be inferred from practice *and* a criticism of practice that seeks to regulate it as if from the outside. A contradiction in strictly logical terms, such a doubled and self-resistant concept is strictly routine in ethical terms.

The foregoing discussion has sought to demonstrate that every one of those ethical terms is impinged upon by its other, cloven and divided against itself, neither one nor two. No matter how urgently ethical discourse describes a principled difference between right and wrong, good and evil, worthy and unworthy, reasonable and unreasonable, the unavoidable lesson of that discourse is that differences shatter each term itself. As a consequence, ethical decision-making takes the form of a sequence that refuses to take form, that refuses to become a narrative. The ethical subject is, as we have seen, divided between inclination and duty, between which one must choose. But since such acts as betraying friends to Nazis and letting sick babies die can be represented as acts of duty, this choice accomplishes no exclusionary work. Instead, it leads to the next question, which requires another principle, another choice. We decide, say, to follow duty; but duty takes two forms, respect for the moral law and respect for the human community. If, on principle, we choose one of these, we are brought to the next choice, between reflection and action. Making a principled decision for, say, action, we arrive at a solution, and, almost simultaneously, at another question: which action to take? This oscillation between choice and resolution continues all the way down the line, with each decision producing a new choice.

Thus ethical problems constitute a theoretically endless chain, a chain of command in which command is always countermanded by alternatives whose recurrence, like a trick candle that refuses to be blown out, resists the commands it calls forth. This resistance is inherited, as it were, from the basic terms of ethical discourse, whose paradigm is the compromised binary. From is/ought, through freedom/

obligation, I/one, subjective/objective, integration/permeability, universalism/communitarianism, and other relations yet to be explored, ethics is a garden of forking paths, a discourse of mitosis that urges all who will listen to become such gardens themselves, to assume the form of ethics.

4. Morality and the Chain of Command

Western ethical thought since Kant has witnessed a steady erosion in the status of the ethical law. It has become all but impossible even to imagine the law in its ideal purity as a pancultural, transhistorical force, an imperative operating everywhere in perfect undeflected consistency. Few arguments have caught the spirit of the times more decisively than a 1973 essay on "Is Morality a System of Hypothetical Imperatives?" in which Philippa Foot tried to demolish the Kantian claim that morality could not be referred to any other end than rationality itself. Rejecting the very concept of the categorical by comparing it with the "silly rules" of etiquette, Foot proposed instead that the marginalized category of the hypothetical, where action was referred to certain specific ends, illuminated ethical action far more powerfully by acknowledging the contextual nature of action, agency, and identity. Even many of the more sympathetic recent readings of Kant have stressed the political dimension of his ethical thought, especially his emphasis on the necessity of representative democracy. The fundamental idea behind the categorical imperative is, as Hilary Putnam says in this revisionist vein, consent, that is, the idea "that the maxim of one's action should be one to which others can be imagined as *consenting*" ("Rules" 194). Such comments promote what Kant, and then Hegel, called *Sitten* or *Sittlichkeit,* social convention or communal norms, at the expense of the term Kant wanted to siphon off from the merely cultural, *Ethik.* Bernard Williams, Cavell, and Rorty all argue that ethics, the discourse of the underdetermined *ought,* has no particular privilege or separate station within culture, but is simply one force jostling among others such as love and armed revolution (*ELP* 184; *CR* 269; Rorty, "Freud and Moral Reflection"). Insofar as "modernity" can be associated with the autonomy of different discourses, the new tendency constitutes a "de-modernization" of ethics.

The prevailing opinion seems to be that ethics, while highly useful on occasion, is nothing special; that while any evaluation of human action may be ethical in part, no such evaluation can be exclusively ethical; and that when we speak of ethical decisions, judgments, considerations, values, and so forth, we are actually speaking of mixtures, overdeterminations, compromises, in which something called the ethical participates alongside other nonethical factors from which it cannot, and ought not, be clearly distinguished. The epigraph for such a mood comes from William James: *"All Goods are disguised by the vulgarity of their concomitants, in this work-a-day world"* (*Habit* 62).

A number of the most influential ethical thinkers today are producing a "soft" or pragmatist ethics in which the place formerly held by such terms as the law, reason, or the Good is taken by history, gender, cultural norms, perspectives, or consensus. The accounts of ethics that seem to find the greatest acceptance are those that advance concepts that stand somewhere between the poles of duty and a transgressive inclination, terms that resist equally an outmoded absolutism and a postmodernist "universal abandon." One such term is "tradition," which MacIntyre uses in *After Virtue* to argue for a redefinition of virtue. According to MacIntyre, the "core conception of the virtues"—justice, courage, truthfulness—must be recast in terms of the idea of "goods internal to practices." Not, that is, the rewards to be gained from success in a particular practice but rather the rewards inherent in the performance of the practice itself. Stout's example is "in baseball, what Mattingly achieves, Red Smith appreciated, and Steinbrenner violates" (303). MacIntyre's own preferred set of "practices" include those such as chess, teaching, law, or home construction, that are sustained by institutions and history: "To enter into a practice," MacIntyre says, in terms that evoke both baseball and T. S. Eliot's definition of "tradition," "is to enter into a relationship not only with its contemporary practitioners, but also with those who have preceded us in the practice, particularly those whose achievements extended the reach of the practice to its present point" (*AV* 194). This historicist revision of the virtues culminates in the claim that the good for human beings can be elaborated and possessed only "within an ongoing social tradition," and that debates between rival ethical principles can only be settled where they arise, in history (273). In *Whose Justice? Which Rationality?* (1988), MacIntyre candidly declares himself an "Augustinian Christian," thereby settling many questions; but in *After Virtue* he formulates the challenge that resonates throughout much contemporary thinking on ethics: When was there ever *"morality as such?"*; and where can be found any set of "universally necessary principles" that bind behavior at all times and places (266)?

If "tradition" is the historicized version of the law, then "confidence" might be the socialized version of certainty. "Basically a social phenomenon," Bernard Williams writes, ethical confidence requires confirmation by others and depends in various ways on institutions and public discourse (*ELP* 170). Legitimation is in the hands of the local authorities, who are conspicuously unarmed, more like the British police than like their American counterparts. For Williams, every-thing floats; but the fact that it has always floated suggests that it will continue to do so, and that, despite certain leaks in the vessel, we need not worry about sinking; as he comments, we repair the ship while on the sea. So confident is Williams's ethical subject that he loses sight of the social origins of his confidence and becomes persuaded that he possesses an unmediated perception of the truth. The ethical subject does not feel as though he is merely imitating others or inhabiting tradition; his confidence seems, Williams reports, to "stretch beyond its boundaries," beyond the vulgarity of the work-a-day, towards a "world-guided" objectivity.

Despite the comforting expansiveness of this argument, however, its progress may in fact be the best possible demonstration of how reflection destroys knowledge; for the revelation that our invulnerable towers of objectivity or rationality have been constructed of mere brick or timber and are secured not by earthquake-proof stabilizers but only, like the stock market or one's fragile composure on the tennis court, by "confidence," gives us excellent reasons to withdraw our confidence from confidence altogether. Still, Williams claims that con-fidence gives us not only all we can ever have, but all that we might ever need.

Williams argues in the name of Aristotle against Kant; MacIntyre, for Aristotle against Nietzsche. Both urge a return to a lost sense of the wholeness and oneness of life in which the individual inhabits a community, evaluates properly, and behaves appropriately in a world without gaps, without theory. What offends both is the idea of the otherness, the distance, of ethics, the notion that ethical imperatives might be hostile or indifferent to one's general worldly interests and circumstances. That such terms as culture, politics, pragmatism, de-sire, economics, gender, and history itself might be seen as others to the ethical *ought* is, to an increasing number, an absurd and anti-quated notion. These forces should, as many now argue, be rede-scribed and incorporated within a new, historically aware, pragmatic study of the relative or contingent good—a "modest pragmatism," to recall Stout's term, an ethics without metaphysics, without otherness, without the law.

Self-evident though it may seem that people get their ideas of what is just, worthy, and right from the options that their circumstances offer, a powerful case can nonetheless be made for retaining the idea of the otherness of the law. Indeed, Williams himself acknowledges as much in his grudging concession that ethics contains its own internal other in "morality." Williams adapts here a distinction made by Kant in the *Metaphysical Foundations of Morals* (*Metaphysik der Sitten*), where the duties that can be enjoined by external laws are segregated from those that cannot. The meanings of these terms slide around within Kant's discourse, and Kant complains about the inadequacy of the German language to his purposes. But generally speaking, "morality" refers to right action itself, while "ethics" indicates a subclass defined both by propriety of action and of motive—doing the right thing for the right reason (see Murphy). Giving the terms a rather different inflection, Williams treats morality as a "peculiar system" within ethics, a cultural aberration that repels him as much as "ethics" repels Jameson, and for many of the same reasons. Williams's "morality system" stresses the idea of obligation; it is predicated on the reductive response of blame; it presumes a perfect, unimpaired individual agency, repressing "the dimension in which ethical life lies outside the individual" (*ELP* 191); it overrates rationality; it falsely represents obligations as "pure," ideally independent from circumstance and desire (Williams's "morality" includes Kant's "metaphysics"); it suggests that beyond such pure obligations lies only a less-worthy "inclination"; it refuses to distinguish social influence from force and constraint, and condemns both.

Williams's morality seems to represent a caricature of those passages in Kant where a free agent hears the voice of Reason calling from within and instantly purges his inclinations so that he may do what he does not want to do, blaming others who don't do the same. Williams's moral person is not just confident but overconfident, displaying a crudeness, a contempt for nuance, an overbearing and unsophisticated decisiveness that offends against society and its more bevelled edges and circumambient pressures. "We would be better off without it," Williams says of morality; and yet there it is, incongruously but—the imprecision of language once again—"irremovably, one name" for ethics in general (*ELP* 174, 6). Wishing to preserve Williams's use of the term, I would suggest that it designates, rather, one name for a particular moment of ethics, not the static passivity of the virtuous will but rather the punctual, purist moment of decision when all but one of the available alternatives, no matter what their claims to rationality or justice, are excluded. The imperative that presides over and legitimates such a moment of decision must be "transcendent," crushing all opposition in its drive to self-actualization and resolution. As the secret agent of the virtuous will, then, morality represents the ethics of ethics. The policeman's gun, morality refuses disarmament.

Could ethics be disarmed and still be ethical? The example of MacIntyre's and Williams's hero, Aristotle, suggests that the answer is no. Aristotle's silent and complacent acceptance of slavery and numerous other forms of privilege and exploitation, his conviction that humanity was divided into "natural types," betrays the secret of an ethics of social confidence—that it defines values primarily in terms of culturally sanctioned attitudes and opinions and promotes the undistanced local social order to the status of a universal order of the worthy. Unless it contains a "moral" image of the law as a resistant other to society, history, or to the uncritical beliefs and prejudices of the individual, ethics can only be an apology for interest even more ignoble than interest itself.

Society does not necessarily suffer from ethical armament. For just as ethics must be other to society in order to be ethical, so does society require an other in order to be truly social. MacIntyre's and Williams's images of a society whose othernesses are all internal are smoother, more homogeneous, and better intentioned than any society ever is in practice, and are best described as types of metaphysical nostalgia—despite Williams's ostensible disdain for any form of nostalgia. Indeed, from the Marxist point of view with which Williams flirts, the salient features of any culture are its ideological clefts, divisions, and conflicts, all of which make it impossible for the individual to be fully synchronized with the social because the social is not synchronized with itself. In a complex, stratified, and variously divided society, shared values, norms, and confidence are hard to come by, and the realities of social life can destroy knowledge just as surely as reflection on duty. With increasing numbers of economically disadvantaged minorities, constant threats from the IRA and other terrorist groups, and the urban violence associated with the drug trade, even the British police are arming themselves. Referring ethics to "practices," "institutions," "history," and "culture," Williams wants, it seems, not just the law without otherness, but Marxism without revolution, and civil order without force.

Strikingly, it is when culture is analyzed from a Marxist perspective as a self-transforming, self-discovering, self-defining body politic, that the purely social necessity of morality emerges most powerfully. For when cultural values are unworthy, uncertain, or disputed, only an appeal to some imperative that convincingly transcends culture and privatized conceptions of interest can legitimate action. In a society that holds slaves and disempowers women, exploitation and misogyny express shared values, and those who hold these values hold them with confidence. Any effort to question these practices, or indeed the autistic tendencies of any localism, must base itself on some value or standard that lies—again, convincingly—outside the cultural horizon (see Wolin).

Consider, as an example, the dilemma confronting Israel over the

Palestinian *intifada*. Unable to destroy the Palestinian nationalists, Israel could at least suppress them, according to Irving Howe, if it were "willing to resort to the kinds of slaughter that Hussein used against the PLO and Assad against Syrian dissidents." Clearly, many Israelis are willing, perhaps in the belief that Mr. Shamir expressed many years ago that "the Jewish ethic" would not be offended; and a wholesale massacre has been averted so far, Howe says, only because "moral constraints still work within Israeli society" (13). The effect of morality is not transcendental, but worldly; it achieves its worldly force, however, through its claim to universality and transcendence.

Morality thus deconstructs the opposition Rorty has articulated in an essay called "Solidarity or Objectivity?" in which he posits a choice between pretending to an impossible universal toleration or an "ethnocentrism" in which one chooses to regard as best the institutions and practices of one's own community. Rorty chooses the second of these depressing alternatives, speaking up in solidarity with the liberal democracies of North America. But from morality we could learn that we do not necessarily make such a choice, for, as the putatively transcendental legitimation of worldly action, morality presumes a unity between the relative and the absolute: moral constraints work, as Howe says, "within Israeli society," many of whose members surely feel that a rigorous obedience to the law characterizes that society. Providing one of the principal ways by which cultures regulate and transform themselves, morality is an engine of change and evolution just as often as it is a reactionary, regressive, or stabilizing force. In both respects, morality serves culture rather than simply opposing it or seeking to dominate it. Morality is, then, not only conceptually necessary—"the outlook, or, incoherently, part of the outlook, of almost all of us," as Williams notes with obvious dismay—but useful (*ELP* 174). It is in the cultural interest to cultivate the notion of morality; and so in acceding finally to morality, in accepting its "incoherence" as inevitable, however lamentable, Williams at once subverts his project of a social ethics, and strengthens it as well: he strengthens it at the cost of its subversion.

Williams discovers *malgré lui* that while an ethics based on unopposed or self-contained principles of pragmatism, rational self-interest, and social legitimation may be *coherent,* it cannot be *complete* or *effective.* What is missing is the "peculiar system" he calls morality, the claim to an "irrational," unargued, unjustifiable, unassimilable, and absolutist force, which alone can justify actions or choices that run against the social grain or the dictates of self-interest. In his effort to humble Kantian ethics by unifying the ethical agent, Williams has nearly made both ethics and the agent structurally irresolute. Morality is summoned to legitimate action that apparently conflicts with social propriety or convention. When society yields no confidence, or when one loses confidence in society, only morality, with its clarity and rapid discharge in action, can decide the issue. Thus, by a curious route, morality, described a moment ago as the ethics of ethics, emerges as the politics of politics, the very *principle* of politics itself; for only on a "moral" basis can political action ground itself, or represent itself not just as desirable or useful but as necessary and right from a standpoint that "transcends" mere politics. The moral other *in* ethics aligns itself finally, then, with the political others *of* ethics; a difference *between* is repeated and in a certain sense resolved through a difference *within*.

For Levinas, too, morality performs the worldly work of ethics. "By morality," he tells an interviewer,

> I mean a series of rules relating to social behavior and civic duty. But while morality thus operates in the socio-political order of organizing and improving our human survival, it is ultimately founded in an ethical responsibility towards the other. As *prima philosophia,* ethics cannot itself legislate for society or produce rules of conduct whereby society might be revolutionized or transformed. It does not operate at the level of the manifesto or *call to order*; it is not a *savoir vivre*.

Ethics is properly dis-interested, preceding and governing our "political 'inter-estedness' " ("Dialogue" 29). But, as the name for the principle of the "extreme exposure and sensitivity of one subjectivity to another," ethics requires a lieutenant; or rather, it must become its own lieutenant, "harden[ing] its skin as soon as we move into the political world" (29–30). In response to the interviewer's charge of "Utopianism," Levinas gives an example that shows how morality both realizes the ethical ideal and de-idealizes ethics itself—and, incidentally, disputes Foot's point about the triviality of etiquette. "This is the great objection to my thought," he says; " 'Where did you ever see the ethical relation practiced?' people say to me. I reply that . . . even the smallest and most commonplace gestures, such as saying 'after you' as we sit at the dinner table or walk through a door, bear witness to the ethical" ("Dialogue" 32; see Stent and Martin).

According to Levinas, ethics without morality, if there were such a thing, would be ill-equipped to prescribe "rules of conduct," for its province would extend only to the border between theory and practice (if there were such a thing). Ethics places imperatives, alternatives, and possibilities of redescription on a balanced scale; by itself, it sustains an august reticence, a principled irresolution to which, nevertheless, the limited and precise prescriptions of morality, which Foucault called the "code" or "prescriptive ensemble," must refer for their authority. Ethics, the strictly undecidable, suffers determination by morality, a further imperative nested within the ethical whose business is to activate the chain of command, to pull the trigger. Morality both realizes and negates ethics, as death both realizes and negates life.

Hillis Miller's "ethics of reading" provides an acute angle of vision on the relation between ethics and morality. "Language," Miller argues, compels us to read; thus reading "*has* to take place, by an implacable necessity, as the response to a categorical demand" (*Ethics of Reading* 59). Linked to the pragmatics of narrative, which, he says, continually defers its own fulfillment, reading (or "Reading") inhibits the tempting quest for meaning, commanding readers not to decide on a final interpretation. Miller has been accused by Martin Jay of a theoretical imperialism on behalf of literature for stuffing into the "ethical moment" of Reading not only reading as such but "sensation, perception, and therefore every human act whatsoever" (58; see Jay, "The Morals of Genealogy" 72). But his formulation of ethical unworldliness gives a countenance, and a specifically linguistic emphasis, to ethical reticence or irresolution. Miller's Reading corresponds precisely to what I have been calling ethics; morality is, one might infer, what happens when you stop Reading.

For Levinas, the ethical imperative issues from the human other, and exceeds all knowledge. But if it did take articulate form, if it spoke, it might command one to "Act on principle." "Principle" is today as stigmatized a term as "theory," because, like theory, it suggests what Cavell calls "universal simples," universal rules that bind human beings at all times, equally, and everywhere, eternal commandments resonating across and over history. Since history proves there are none of these, then ethical action, Cavell says, cannot be action on principle. Many thinkers today are skeptical of neo-Kantian distinctions between formal "principles" and the more haphazard "rules of thumb designed to promote one's aim" (see Baier 191). But "Act on principle" must be acquitted of the charges against it. What Cavell appears to mean is that no universal simples actually exist, and therefore that there are no real "principles." But principle can be defined differently.

"Principle" suggests freedom from coercion: one cannot act on principle because one is forced to. It also suggests obedience to an imperative that runs "against nature," "against inclination," or "against interest." Imbricating these two principles, "principle" expresses precisely the sense of free obedience to the law that underwrites all ethics.

More importantly, "principle" is altogether nonspecific. It does not, as the article by Baier cited above confidently states, presume to guarantee rightness or appropriateness, or any absolute or unconvertible quality. "Principle" directs attention not to essences but to representations. In July 1990, the newly-liberated Nelson Mandela came to the United States, where he was often asked about his apparent indifference to human rights violations in Libya, Cuba, and by the PLO. This indifference had disappointed many in the United States who had supported Mandela's African National Congress as part of a general repudiation of state and organizational terrorism. Mandela's reply, that he did not judge the internal affairs of other countries, that his approbation of Gadhafy, Castro, and Arafat derived exclusively from their support for the African National Congress, was an even more bitter disappointment for many Americans because it appeared to be based on a calculation of interests and strategies and, in a word, indifferent to principle. But at this point the limits of the undifferentiated term "principle" have been reached. For interests, as many examples have demonstrated, are always redescribable as principles, and vice versa. Supporters of Mandela could rescue the situation by arguing that support for the ANC is Mandela's highest principle, and one that could hardly, in light of his twenty-seven years of incarceration, be considered to serve his mere or narrow or material interest. The confusion and dismay of Mandela's American supporters reflected a preference for a different principle, such as "Condemn injustice," and not a difference over the commitment to principle itself. It is, indeed, the common commitment to principle that enabled this disappointment and may yet enable some more productive understanding. With those who do not or cannot represent their acts in terms of any principle at all, no conversation or even communication is possible.

Valente describes the difference "between restricted economies of justice which nonetheless open toward a theoretical maximum" and an unrestricted or "Kantian" idea of "justice that is still bound to its conditions of formulation"; and this exactly expresses the condition of resistance obtaining between ethics and morality. We behave morally when we act not just on principle but on the right principle, when we act properly in our circumstances, according to standards that "we," the relevant cultural entity, agree should prevail. This restricted economy opens toward, because it is structured and empowered by, a "theoretical maximum" whose purest formulation is the unrestricted ethical imperative. We are commanded by ethics to act on principle, and by morality to do the right thing. Ethics leads into conflicts only morality can settle. The hands of ethics are clean, because they have touched nothing; the hands of morality are bloody, but effective.

Ethics is independent of context and hence out of control; morality represents what is specifically worthy in a particular context, the ends that particular people ought to try to secure. Ethics is born free, but is everywhere in chains, bound by morality to particular values, communities, institutions, codes, and conventions. And, like "natural man," ethics has never existed in a pure state, for it is always in resistance with its other and in this resistance accomplishing its work. Any representation of an action as worthy, just, or right will, then, necessarily entail two claims: an ethical claim that the action is based on principle, and a moral claim that the action is based on the right principle.

As developed here, the relation between ethics and its other bears some resemblance to other conceptual schemes, including the classic Marxist distinction between base and superstructure; also Jameson's notion of "allegory," in which a bifocal analysis treats the local instance as meaningful in itself but also and simultaneously as the figure for a utopian transformation of society as a whole; and even Noam Chomsky's theory of deep structure and surface structure in sentences, and the descendants of that theory in structural narratology. This is not the place to work out the "ethics" of all these schema, but it is interesting to note a certain homology between the theory of appropriate action and other theories that claim a comparably global applicability. It is to that most global of imperatives, language, the primary extension of the subject into otherness and of otherness into the subject, that we must now turn.

2

LANGUAGE AND ETHICS, FROM THE BEGINNING

Is not even this "thing" what it is and the way it is in the name of its name?

    Martin Heidegger, *On the Way to Language*

Symbols in fact envelop the life of man in a network so total that they join together, before he comes into the world, those who are going to engender him 'by flesh and blood'; so total that they bring to his birth, along with the gifts of the stars, if not with the gifts of the fairies, the shape of his destiny; so total that they give the words that will make him faithful or renegade, the law of the acts that will follow him right to the very place where he *is* not yet and even beyond his death; and so total that through them his end finds its meaning in the last judgement, where the Word absolves his being or condemns it. . . .

    Jacques Lacan, "The Function and Field of Speech and Language in Psychoanalysis"

[Language acquisition is] a didactic assignment that no human being can bypass.

    Paul de Man, "The Resistance to Theory"

1. Language and the Decay of Value

"Actions," Stanley Cavell says, "unlike envelopes and goldfinches, do not come named for assessment, nor, like apples, ripe for grading." Cavell is complaining here about the "formalism" of Kant who, he says, "found too little difficulty in saying *what* 'the' maxim of an action is in terms of which his test of its morality, the Categorical Imperative, is to be applied." The motives for formalism are clear—to encourage the sense that we can get an unmediated and undistorted view of the act itself, the act-without-otherness, so that our judgments will be accurate and just. Cavell, however, argues that formalism suppresses the "problem in saying what it is which is under scrutiny" (*CR* 265). What is, or ought to be, under scrutiny is not, according to Cavell, the elusive act but rather the language-using subject himself, whose values, cares, and commitments are legible in his utterances in a way that the object of reference is not: ethical knowledge, Cavell insists, is a "knowledge of *persons.*" But the knowledge Cavell seeks can only be obtained through an attention to the "problems" that persons have describing things. Finally, Cavell's argument, like Kant's, turns on a certain view of language. For if we are to see language as a medium of self-disclosure, a source of reliable information about persons, then the referential function in which Kant placed such trust must be downgraded or bracketed in favor of "rhetoric" or "style"—*le style, c'est l'homme.* For both Kant and Cavell, then, the case for ethics must be made through language. They differ not in focusing on the act or on the person, but in promoting different functions of language—reference in Kant's case, rhetoric in Cavell's.

Cavell's initial point is, of course, debatable. The sentence of Heidegger's placed at the beginning of this section suggests that actions, or "things," *do* come named and graded, that the essence of the thing is determined in the name, or in "the name of its name." Indeed, the relation between things and names is notoriously difficult to describe, part of the problem being that the relation itself is just one more "thing," and the description one more "name." In this sentence, Heidegger nearly suggests that the thing has no independent material existence apart from its name; while Cavell implies that actions exist in essential completeness before they are named. These are, one might infer from the available evidence, positions that neither would be likely to defend in these forms. The effort to determine the "ethics of language" seems to have the effect of leading the most rigorous thinkers to abandon their principles. Nietzsche's memorable pronouncement that "there are no moral phenomena; there are only moral interpretations of phenomena," for example, demystifies "morality" by aligning it with interpretation—but does so by invoking uninterpreted raw "phenomena," and implying that interpretation is not itself a phenomenon—again, not an argument commonly associated with Nietzsche's name (*Beyond Good and Evil* §108).

Can there be any account of the relation between words and things, language and its other, that does not carry with it some unwanted residue of implication? Kenneth Burke attempts such an account by replacing Nietzsche's "phenomenon" with "motion" to indicate that which has not, or not yet, fallen under linguistic formalization. For Burke, language is "'the critical moment' at which human action takes form, since a linguistic factor complicates and to some extent transcends the purely biological aspects of motivation" (*Grammar of Motives*

318). But again, the notion of "pure biology" suggests an untranscended animal substrate more reminiscent of, say, the fiction of Jack London than of Burke's urbane inquiry. Moreover, the idea of a "critical moment" repeats the gesture made less conspicuously by Nietzsche and Cavell of installing a narrative in the place of a description. The relation that is simultaneous between language and its other seems to demand a temporal account that actually posits what it sets out to deny, the essential discreteness of word and thing. The very terms for "what is represented"—"action," "phenomenon," "thing," or "motion"—imply that any representation is a misrepresentation, a radical transformation of the nonlinguistic into the linguistic. Arguments about language appear to be under some imperative to resist themselves.

It would, however, be more accurate to say that language resists *it*self, and that this internal resistance produces, especially in "rigorous" thinkers, a resistance to consistency. Manifesting itself as confusion or incoherence, this resistance, recalling certain features of ethical discourse discussed in the previous chapter, actually points to the convergence of language and ethics.

Thus an attention especially to the resistances of language does not distract from, but invariably indicates, ethical issues. It is frequently argued that Modernism and Postmodernism display their anti-ethical and therefore antihumanistic prejudices most decisively in their substitution of the category of "language" for the category of "man." But this charge does not survive a review of the dominant thinkers of the last century, among whom are included not only Heidegger and Freud, but Wittgenstein ("To imagine a form of language is to imagine a form of life"); Foucault, whose career moves from discourse to power to ethics; Lacan, whose account of the subject in linguistic terms is also an account of ethics; Lyotard, who discusses authoritarianism as a use of the descriptive mode; and Derrida. For all these, language is not just an autonomous formal system but rather a medium whose formal elements permit an unformalized excess to become legible, a medium saturated with otherness, and thus with ethics.

In the case of Nietzsche, that excess is human conflict, whose resolution converts the evaluations of the powerful and victorious into facts. *On the Genealogy of Morals* in particular responds to what Anthony Cascardi calls the "challenge of modern moral theory," to "provide a nonarbitrary basis for making judgments about values while recognizing the fact that reason is powerless to dictate specific ends" ("Genealogies of Modernism" 210). Such judgments, Nietzsche asserts in the first essay of the *Genealogy*, are the fossils or tombstones of power, and therefore anything but arbitrary. The very terms "good" and "evil" memorialize some concrete situation of domination and subsequent mystification. In fact, as power is sedimented and established, ethical judgments, themselves effects of dominance, become subject to what Nietzsche calls "forgetting," a process of ideological evaporation through which the interests of a self-preserving power become, simply, facts. Interest becomes invisible and disappears into nomination, into ontology; adjectives resolve into nouns and verbs. But the emphasis of the analysis on the fading of force into language should not obscure the fact that the real target of analysis is, for Nietzsche as for the other thinkers named above, "a form of life."

Jameson praises Nietzsche on precisely this point, for having cast the ethical "ideologeme" in terms of a "concrete subtext" of conflict, but argues that this subtext remains "mythic" (*PU* 117). Ethics, he says, should be seen not as a direct expression of a hypothetical ethnological circumstance, but rather as an imaginative response and resolution to an actual historical moment, when the feudal nobility became conscious of itself as "a universal class or 'subject of history.'" This universalization of the nobility did not, of course, eliminate conflict; and thus the problem arose of how to designate the enemy—no longer the barbarian, but rather another feudal lord—as evil, "when what is responsible for his being so characterized is quite simply the *identity* of his own conduct with mine, the which—points of honor, challenges, tests of strength—he reflects as in a mirror image" (*PU* 118). Romance solves this problem by producing a narrative in which the insolent evil knight, at the point of death, asks for mercy by revealing his name, "at which point, reinserted into the unity of the social class, he becomes one more knight among others and loses all his sinister unfamiliarity" (119). Thus a protracted ordeal is telescoped into a single incident, in which the ethically marked other dissolves into an unmarked sameness. The relic of a world in which evil was literally visible, decisive ethical evaluation fades once imposed, giving way to modernity and the solidarity of the bourgeoisie.

Once again ethics has precipitated self-betrayal. For by contracting history into an anecdote, Jameson implies that "ethics itself" can be overcome, forgotten, or transcended: it happened once, Jameson implies; it can happen again. Nietzsche's "mythic" argument suggests, by contrast, a continuous historical process by which evaluations are converted into facts. Primary and primordial, evaluations are "older" than facts, which represent the senescence of domination. Descriptions, in which the element of evaluation is no longer legible, are to explicitly evaluative statements as the Appalachians are to the Rockies, smoother and more homogeneous because of their greater age. As Matthew Arnold states (quoting Joubert) in "The Function of Criticism at the Present Time," *"c'est la force et le droit qui règlent toutes choses dans le monde; la force en attendant le droit."* And Arnold stresses the point: *"Force till right is ready."* What Nietzsche adds is the argument that the steady imposition of force eventually produces right, that is, a willingness to accept force as right. Always contestable—and contestable in the name of right—description still bespeaks power; the idiom of fact is like the landscaped terrain of an ancient battlefield, or the fertile soil around a dead volcano.

The Modernist emphasis on language must not, then, be opposed to history; for language seen from this perspective is the surest index to history, to a silent history that continually effaces itself. Much ethical theory would, in fact, profit from being recoded as an allegory of, and indirect testament to, this conception of language in history. Take for example R. M. Hare's claim that "secondarily evaluative words" such as *lazy* do not in fact commit those who use them to "substantial moral evaluations." One may, Hare says, use such words "in a purely descriptive sense without evaluative commitments" so that "the adoption of the moral commitment is in principle separable from the adoption of the word" (*MT* 17). What "principle" could it be that permits the use of evaluative words without evaluations, if not the principle of forgetfulness, which determines the historical conversion of value into fact? It is possible that even Nietzsche underestimated the force of forgetfulness, seeking to confine it to a determinate phase of struggle, after domination has been established, when in fact the struggle for secondarily evaluative words goes on all the time. Values and facts, force and right, do not have the same generational relation as that, for example, between baroque and rococo; they rather operate in resistance in any period, any culture, any utterance, as phases of the one continuous process that dominates not just the history of what Hare calls "moral words" such as *ought, good, should,* but history itself, inasmuch as the central fact and theme of history is decay—the laboratory, as Marx said, of life in history as well as in nature. In terms of language, this decay means that at any moment, anywhere, evaluations are fading into facts, shedding signs of their evaluative origins, assimilating. Thus ethics cannot be regarded as one ideologeme among many, or as a stage of psycho-historical development that may be superseded or recalled. Ethics is instead a word for this decay, this fading, this transformation.

If, during times of crisis, the course of evaluative decay is interrupted and dominance comes under question, facts suddenly appear as opinions, right as force; and the name—effective security measures, antipersonnel device, just cause, a match made in heaven, national interest, for your own good—must be renegotiated. At such moments, we suddenly have a choice where before there had seemed to be only necessity. Cowardice or prudence, offensive or defensive, mercenaries or freedom fighters, candor or insensitivity, benign neglect or callous indifference, humility or self-abasement, tool or weapon, torture or intelligence-gathering, murder or assassination, efficiency or ruthlessness, adhering to an ethic of the good or sparing ourselves the pain: when consensus dissolves, the name appears to be underdetermined by necessity but overdetermined by interest, a virtual compost of evaluation. The crisis is resolved, however, not by the raw imposition of a force that does not bother to mask its forcefulness, but rather by the forceful imposition of principle: language users must be convinced rather than persuaded of the rightness of the name. The recognition of the name's wrongness promotes a "Kantian" presumption of freedom to call the thing what it ought to be called; but the process of evaluative decay also produces an "Aristotelian" awareness of *philia,* the filiations and rays of mutuality and responsibility that structure our relations with others. An ethical attention to the question of nomination leads, then, in opposite but complementary directions: towards the ideology of autonomy, free choice, a stable object world, right naming; and *also* towards the ideology of cultural-political determinism, an ideology of the anti-ideal, in which the subject herself is more named than naming. The law of language is that things must be given their proper names—*and* that no name is truly proper.

I have pursued the Nietzschean argument this far in order to suggest one way in which the Modernist emphasis on language, often discussed as an avoidance of the question of ethics, might be seen instead as one particular approach to ethics; I have, moreover, tried to emphasize the depth and complexity of the questions opened up by what might seem a limited inquiry into some features of language. It is, admittedly, easy to limit the inquiry and to gain some appearance of precision. But the proper approach to the subject of ethics and language must be based on the premise that neither ethics nor language truly has a limit, that the two cannot be decisively marked off from each other. The power and adequacy of any speculation on this subject will grow to the extent that it sheds a dependence on a certain kind of precision.

As an example of such precision, consider Hare's main premise, that there is a special "moral" subset of language in words such as *good, right, just, wrong, worthy, must,* and *ought,* which are distinguished by their "affective" or "emotive" character from the language of verifiable fact. For Hare, the issues and energies of ethics converge on a severely limited linguistic field. One danger of this assumption is that ethics will be marginalized as "soft" in a world dominated by hard facts. But Hare has used the idea of a special ethical language to argue, in *The Language of Morals* (1952), *Freedom and Reason* (1963), and *Moral Thinking* (1981), that what he calls moral statements are distinguished for their hardness, forming a distinct kind and use of language that reflect the uniquely imperative quality of moral judgments. Hare defines his project, accordingly, as the no-nonsense interrogation of the meanings of moral words in order to "generate logical canons which will govern our moral thinking" (*MT* 20). On the basis of a few words, especially the "modal imperatives" such as *ought* and *must*, whose "logical properties" (i.e., that they are "prescriptive and universalizable") "exhaust their meaning," Hare hopes to construct a general theory of ethical reasoning (*MT* 3; see also Cavell, *CR* ch. 12). This general theory centers on *must*, which is in one sense a commandment (If you must do something, then do it); and in another, a "lawlike" necessity (If he must be in the garden, then he is in the garden) (*MT* 23). *Ought* is, for Hare, merely a puny and envious *must*, an embarrassment to the logician, who ought to—or rather, who *must*—forget it: *ought,* Hare says, "is to be used in our reasoning *as if* it were always fully prescriptive, and *as if* its prescriptions were not to be overridden, though we humans do not always so use it" (*MT* 24). (One sign of "rigor" is the pejorative use of "human.")

Without repeating the argument for the centrality of the *ought,* I want to argue that a strictly limited attention to a few "special" words that operate in an utterly predictable and uniform way occludes the larger and less easily specifiable relations between language and ethics. One symptom of this occlusion is a pattern of wavering in Hare's work. In his early work, Hare argued that when logic and fact-finding had done their work, then an element of "pure evaluation or prescription" entered the scene to dominate the moment of choice. In the more recent *Moral Thinking,* however, Hare swings around to what seems to be the opposite extreme with the claim that while we do have freedom to reason, the rules of reason in ethical questions are so rigid that "we shall, if we are rational, exercise our freedom in only one way" (7). Do we have virtually unimpaired freedom, or virtually none? Do we make our decisions on the basis of pure evaluation, or rigid rules? Why would Hare, whose writings give little sense of a man given to radical self-doubt, undo himself in this way—unless there is no real difference between these sterile alternatives, unless a pure choice without reasons, pressures, or resistances were essentially identical to no choice at all, and identical precisely in their nonexistence?

Bracketing off the "human" from the "rational," Hare's work dramatizes the need for, among other things, a more comprehensive and nuanced understanding of the relation of fact to value within language, and, more generally, of language to ethics. Bernard Williams makes a start by drawing attention not to the modal imperatives but to the much larger number of "those 'thicker' or more specifically ethical notions" such as "*treachery* and *promise* and *brutality* and *courage*," which he says are both descriptive and prescriptive, "world-guided" and "action-guiding." These terms, he says, suggest through their unsystematic impurity the dispositions and the sense of fact of some particular, local system, some way of life (*ELP* 129). Thick concepts (*coward, lie, gratitude, liberal, betrayal, fascist, honor, phony, friendship, red-blooded, respectable, responsibility, indolence*) simply cannot be made descriptively or evaluatively pure. But while sidestepping one pitfall by acknowledging that in certain terms at least, fact and value coalesce, Williams has, in a way that ought by now to be predictable, tumbled into another, and deeper. For by concentrating on a larger but still limited number of individual words, he discourages attention to the more pervasive pressures exerted both by and on the individual through language use itself. He has, in fact, radically understated his case by suggesting that only a few words can claim "thickness." A descriptively "thin" word would, however, have to apply only to one object, even to a single instant of that object's existence; and an evaluatively "thin" word would designate an assessment without an object. Neither would be in the dictionary. A proper understanding—a "thick" understanding—of ethical "thickness" would extend the idea to all of language, with descriptive or evaluative factors constantly wrestling with their others. Language itself must be seen as an ethically thick compound if we are to understand how constant and irreversible is the wedding of facts to values, objects to assessments, in our utterances, thoughts, and perceptions.

2. From Agency to Relation

But what is "all of language," or "language itself?" Where is the boundary between language and its others? How can one talk about language without making it into a noun, an agent, another person? Perhaps one reason Hare and Williams prefer to meditate on a few words is that they want to retain the conception of language as a discrete thing, a tool, an instrument under the control of the subject. So long as we are talking about the use of a small number of words, the subject is in charge. But when ethics is permitted to seep out beyond the borders of modal imperatives, or of thick concepts, to stain language use as such, then evaluation becomes limitless, the subject has no clean tools to work with, the very distinction between the speaker and the spoken becomes questionable, and the speaker can even appear to be just a highly determined instance of language in action. In fact, such a reversal of agency is deeply rooted in the history of ethical discourse. Hume states it explicitly in the *Enquiry Concerning the Principles of Morals,* where he asserts that "the very nature of language guides us almost infallibly in forming a judgement" about ethical qualities; "as every tongue [a natural language, not an individual speaker] possesses one set of words which are taken in a good sense, and another in the opposite, the least acquaintance with the idiom suffices, without any reasoning, to direct us in collecting and arranging the estimable or blameable qualities of men" (27).

Hume actually seems to ignore most of language in his discussion of language's "nature." His radically reductive binary account of "estimable" and "blameable" qualities (of "men") eliminates all considerations but the lexical; nor does it allow for evaluative factors to be confused, conflicted, undecidable, unintentional, tentative, or unconscious. But the very omissions that make his idea of language so defective impart to language itself the power to guide the human subject, almost like a Levinasian other, "without any reasoning."

Elsewhere, Hume seems even more convinced of the authority of language. In the *Treatise of Human Nature,* Hume records his astonishment at the dynamics of the promise, in which the verbal formula imposes itself on the entire situation, in "one of the most mysterious and incomprehensible operations that can possibly be imagin'd, [which] may even be compar'd to *transubstantiation,* or *holy orders,* where a certain form of words, along with a certain intention, changes entirely the nature of an external object, and even of a human creature" (*Treatise* 233–34). The example is especially pertinent because it concerns the promise or debt, which Kant and Nietzsche took to be the primary instance of ethical consciousness—the origin of bad conscience, the interiorization of obligation, the germ of accountability and even of memory itself, the birth of futurity. What disturbs Hume is the observable fact that the different "natures" of language and human beings seem at one moment to be separate and at the next—the "critical" moment, the "ethical" moment—to be virtually identical, in the sense that the snake and the fish could be said to be identical at the moment when the snake swallows the fish.

One effect of the power-of-language argument is sharply to limit the autonomy of the agent, who is humbled before "a certain form of words" as before the law. Since Hume, this "operation" has come to seem less and less "mysterious and incomprehensible." It takes on a thoroughly demystified form in, for example, the work of Benjamin Whorf, who posited a "far-reaching compulsion" affecting cultural and behavioral norms and even ideas of time, space, and matter from the "large-scale patterning of grammatical categories, such as plurality, gender and similar classifications [such as] tenses, voices, and other verb forms" ("Habitual Thought" 137). The "forms of a person's thoughts," Whorf said, "are controlled by inexorable laws of pattern of which he is unconscious" ("Language, Mind, and Reality" 252). Our very perceptions, Whorf claimed, registered the "sway of pattern over reference," and could only be regarded as projections onto the face of nature of the rules of our language ("Language, Mind, and Reality" 261). This once-provocative argument has become conventional through reiteration. Edward Sapir's claim that human beings are "very much at the mercy of the particular language which has become the medium of expression for their society"; or Heidegger's statement that "language is more powerful than we, and therefore weightier"; or Lacan's assertion that the subject is the "slave of language"; the numerous ways in which recent literary criticism has privileged the text at the expense of authorial intention—all these seek to reverse a traditional master-slave relation between the subject and "its" language (Sapir, "Linguistics as a Science" 69; Heidegger, *Way to Language* 31; Lacan, "Agency of the letter" 148). However conventional, such a reversal of agency is neither necessarily true or benign. Not, certainly, in the case of Paul de Man, who often distinguished between the "linguistic" and the "subjective" as a way of marking the peculiarly "inhuman" imperatives of the former. De Man's distinction was even appropriated by Geoffrey Hartman to explain de Man's 1940–42 journalistic writings in the German-controlled Belgian newspaper *Le Soir:* contributing an anti-Semitic article to a collaborationist publication, Hartman wrote, de Man found himself "betrayed" and even "trapped by an effect of language, an ideological verbiage that blinded critical reflection" ("Looking Back on Paul de Man" 21, 22). At this point the danger of the power-of-language argument that had begun with the inquiry into "language itself" or "the very nature of language" declares itself. Such an argument runs the risk not only of permitting convenient displacements of responsibility but also of reaffirming the concept of agency—attributed now to an *un*accountable and *un*principled language—which was the target in the first place.

There are risks even when language is depicted as an ethically positive force. Consider, for example, the work of Charles Taylor, who argues in *Human Agency and Language* that a uniquely self-evaluative human being is disclosed by virtue of "three things that get done in language" (263). The passive voice here is admirably circumspect, but it is overridden in the account of the three things, which, very briefly, are: (1) Making articulations. Taylor also describes this as "formulating things," "bringing something to explicit awareness," and "drawing boundaries," and indicates by all these that language enables us to apprehend some object, act, or quality in contrast to others. (2) The founding of public space. Language, Taylor claims, places matters before *us,* enabling "a common vantage point from which we survey the world together" (259). This public space is always contested but never erased, and never absolutely possessed by any one. (3) Permitting the formulation of standards. The standards Taylor has in mind are not utilitarian or functional, but standards considered and evaluated as themselves. A cat will eat some food and not others, and so exhibits a standard; but it exhibits no sense that standards are worth having, that some standards are more important than others, or that standards command respect in themselves. Expressing "essential human concerns" that can be formulated only in language (263), standards reflect a uniquely human capacity to formulate "second-order desires," desires to have certain desires as opposed to others; and thus, Taylor argues, language fosters ethics and a distinctively human being.

Taylor is not wrong, nor even forgetful. He is simply wishful, repressing symmetrical, equally demonstrable cases that language smudges or compromises distinctions; that it confuses or compromises a public space that is instituted by other means; and that it distracts us from standards as such. Taylor nearly suggests that mere language use will bestow on its users a liberal humanist virtue, making them clear-headed, sharing, and principled. In short, he applies without evidence or empirical warrant the language of agency to language itself in order to represent as a necessary consequence of language use a particular set of *oughts.*

Habermas makes an even more specific argument for the ethical power of language, claiming that language's "ethos of reciprocity" stands as "the foundation of morality in general" ("Arnold Gehlen" 122). For Habermas, in this essay at least, the symbolic structure of language works in a specifically Kantian direction, predisposing its users towards a socialized "duty" and away from hedonistic "inclination," modelling the process of acculturation in general. The externalization of impulse that occurs in language necessarily fosters a psychological "reflexivity" that promotes the individuation that eventually unfolds into full-feathered moral consciousness.

Habermas's are among the most sharply formulated and optimistic claims for the ethical power and scope of language, and among the most idealistic as well. Although he tries in this essay (and with more success elsewhere) to avoid characterizing language as an agent in nearly conscious pursuit of certain goals, Habermas nevertheless describes "the ideal speech situation" as an ethical ideal as well: in this ideal situation, a perfect reciprocity, a perfect "mutual consideration and respect," emerge from "mediation through discourse, that is, through a public formation of will that is bound to the principle of unrestricted communication and consensus free from domination." The possibility, which he claims is immanent in all communication, of a process ideally and absolutely free from coercion, domination, or interference, is, he insists "the single principle of morality" ("Arnold Gehlen" 119).

Indeed, by this point in the argument Habermas has become a polemical moralist, not an analyst of ethics. The freedom from restriction in the "ideal speech situation" supports a highly restrictive view of the ideal moral situation. For as Habermas's critics over the years have not failed to point out, it is all too apparent that any definition of the "ideal speech situation" or the "single principle of morality" could be used to justify the suppression of those elements that could be charged with comprising the counter-realm of "distortion" or "restriction." What constitutes a deviation from communicative rationality? Metaphor? Irony? Black Standard English? Anything issuing from an institution, a governmental agency, a corporation? Who decides whether mutual respect is being respected? And how can one achieve an ideal freedom from coercion when so much of communication falls under the heading of influence or persuasion? Can one always tell the manipulative from the nonmanipulative? What is the formal difference between convincing and persuading, or between "strategic" and "communicative" uses of language? And what evidence does language yield that "unrestricted communication" rather than coercive "domination" is not just an aspiration but a norm? The "ideal speech situation" corresponds not only with a restrictive morality, but with a restrictive view of language. Running even greater risks than Taylor's work, the example of Habermas demonstrates how specific and how specifically moral (as opposed to ethical) the claims about language can get.

The most urgent contemporary interrogation of the agency of language is taking place in feminist discourse, where the Humean premise that language *has* a nature has led many directly to the conclusion that this nature is inequitable, exclusive, and oppressive (see Lakoff, Kaplan, Olsen, Daly, Kramarae). For many feminists, the very features that Taylor and Habermas would count among language's virtues must be counted instead among its crimes. In the words of Nancy M. Henley, "language ignores, it defines, and it deprecates women. As a result, women and girls are hurt both psychologically and materially by it" (3). Many of the most hardwired linguistic determinisms cite Dale Spender's *Man Made Language,* which pictures the

"English lexicon" as "a structure organized to glorify maleness and ignore, trivialize or derogate femaleness" (42). English in particular, Spender charges, "has been literally man made" and through such means as the coding of "motherhood" as an exclusively positive term, has served as "one of the means by which males have ensured their own primacy" (12). A more sophisticated (i.e., academic) deterministic argument focuses not on lexical patriarchy but rather on the way in which, as Mary Poovey puts it, language "privileges identity, singularity, and linearity" ("Feminism and Deconstruction" 55). Following the urgings and examples of Cixous or of Irigaray, who argues that a feminine "morality" produces a language unlike men's, many have sought ways of "disconcerting language" (or even, as Mary Daly says, of "castrating" it) by exploring an alternative language "based on the body," in the hope of overturning this primacy and achieving representation (Daly, *Beyond God the Father* 9).

The question many feminists confront is whether there could ever be either a nonsexist or a specifically feminist language. But to answer this question in any way presupposes that language itself is capable of agency, and this is precisely the point that the most reflective and, I believe, empowering analyses eventually surrender. Deborah Cameron, for example, begins by laying out arguments that "language is a weapon," that "language is part of patriarchy," and that "language is pervaded by sexism" (*Feminism and Linguistic Theory* 1, 3, 4). But her conclusion rejects all these positions as well as the biological essentialism on which they are based. To concentrate on the "deceptively simple word *language*," she writes, enables feminists to escape responsibility and the patriarchy to escape blame. Other factors—"sociofamilial relations," the "division of labour," the physical environment, and even "individual genetic make-up"—are more instrumental than language in sustaining the psycho-social system feminists wish to resist (170). The task of feminism, Cameron concludes, is to "destroy the pernicious belief that we have to be controlled and oppressed by our language" (173). One of the most influential attempts to do just that was Julia Kristeva's early article on "The Ethics of Linguistics," where Kristeva attacked not language but linguistics for its "aura" of normative "*systematics*." Our ideas of language have, Kristeva wrote, been perverted by the powerful institution of linguistics: "As wardens of repression and rationalizers of the social contract in its most solid substratum (discourse), linguists carry the Stoic tradition to its conclusion" (24). The strategic move that has gained the support of many feminists was Kristeva's refusal to yield language up to the oppressor, her insistence that language was not only a system but a process as well; and that the system of language, although laced with boundaries, in-

corporated the potential for "upheaval, dissolution and transformation" (25). If the feminine has been marginalized by systematics, then
other resources of language can be mobilized and exploited to reverse
this marginalization. The goal, sketched out in Kristeva and developed more fully in Toril Moi's *Sexual/Textual Politics* is to "aim for a
society in which we have ceased to categorize logic, conceptualization
and rationality as 'masculine', not for one from which these virtues
have been expelled altogether as 'unfeminine'" (160). For Kristeva,
Moi, and others, effects of oppression—effects of agency—are produced *in* language, but not *by* language.

This position is by no means uncontested, however, and the continuing debate testifies not only to the difficulty of the questions
posed by feminism but also to a general uncertainty about the "nature"
of language. Although attractive for social or political reasons—honorable reasons connected to the desire for justice—linguistic determinisms fail to respect the aberrance of language in a world conceived (in
language) in terms of nouns and verbs, agents and actions. The curious fact is that there are no words to talk about the nature or effects
of language, which, though constantly on display, yet eludes its own
descriptions, perpetually sliding beneath its own signifier. Nor does it
help to say, as James Boyd White does, that language is "reciprocal: it
acts on us, and we on it"; for this merely confuses the issue even further by equating the action of language with that of a human subject
(*When Words Lose Their Meaning* 8). A subtler language of agency than
the one language provides is needed in order to describe what it is that
"gets done" in language. Richard Rorty has praised Donald Davidson's
"willingness to face up to the *contingency* of the language we use,"
which is to say, his willingness to conceive of language as *not* having
an intrinsic nature, his willingness to surrender the resources of language in order to describe language (*Contingency, Irony, and Solidarity*
9). But language itself compels this willingness, this surrender; the
powerful mimetic faculty of language is powerless to mime language
because language is never "itself," is never simply a medium, a faculty,
or a system, and cannot be observed or represented. In a sense, *language* is a word for that for which we have no words, that which is
constantly spoken, but never truly spoken about.

This may be what Heidegger meant by saying that "the essential
being of language cannot be anything linguistic"; or that "our relation
to language is vague, obscure, almost speechless" (*Way to Language*
23–24, 58). Representing everything but itself, language presents but
conceals itself in "communication," "understanding," "words," "meaning," even "humanity." Language is the "transcendental signified,"

and it is remarkable that the poststructuralist critics who exalted language while denying the possibility of a transcendental signified never thought to say so. Language is the site of so many operations that are critical to a human form of being that it is extremely difficult to get hold of what, after all, we are talking about when we talk about language. Activated by individual acts of will and intention, language seems a supplement to a world essentially complete without it; and yet the world is already saturated with language, and it is pointless to try to imagine, as linguistic determinists do, a world that is newly altered by language, as though language belatedly imposed itself from the outside. Something less than an agent and more than a medium, at once "nowhere" and "everywhere," language is neither "responsible" nor "neutral," neither fully active nor entirely passive; its power is at best, or at least, a kind of pseudo-power to inform and shape the norms, values, objects, and states that acquire form and shape in it.

We must, in assessing the ethics of language, resist above all the temptation to work from a limited set of words, a restricted use, a particular form. Such reductions may, as we have already seen, yield clear *moral* conceptions of what language ought to do or be, but will in doing so falsify and reduce the richness of language that is properly indicated by *ethics*. It takes audacity even to call clarity a temptation, but if language is ethical—a point of consensus among all the writers discussed so far—it is precisely because it—language itself, not isolated words or sentences—resists all moral clarities.

The point can only be demonstrated indirectly, by showing how arguments based on a restricted conception of language always, in the moment of their greatest integrity, cross or exceed themselves. One final example of this excess is provided by Levinas, who, in the very passage quoted in the previous chapter, in which he draws a distinction between the ethical and the moral, resorts to what seems an essentialism. The distinction is between *saying* and the *said:* "Insofar as ontology equates truth with the intelligibility of total presence," Levinas tells an interviewer, "it reduces the pure exposure of saying to the totalizing closure of the said." The two, he argues, are altogether different: "Language as *saying* is an ethical openness to the other; as that which is *said*—reduced to a fixed identity or synchronized presence—it is an ontological closure to the other" ("Dialogue" 28–29). But what to do with the fact that every act of saying must produce a said? How to account, in Levinas's terms, for the necessary reciprocal conditioning of openness and closure, the ethical and the unethical? In light of this reciprocity, can we still regard openness as both a linguistic essence and as an ethical aspiration? Isn't it rather a metaphor, a (closed) figure for some desirable quality Levinas would like to promote, projected onto language? Levinas often, as Derrida points out, seems to be "betraying his own intentions" ("Violence" 151). But Robert Bernasconi has recently argued that Levinas's key terms are typically imbricated, over the course of an extended text, with their others, so that, for example, "the terms of the title *Totality and Infinity* are not related to each other antithetically," for totality "bears the infinite within it" ("Levinas and Derrida" 194). In this instance, perhaps it would be generous, then, as well as correct to point out the position at which Levinas might ultimately have arrived if the interview had extended further into the night, perhaps all the way to dawn, that reduction and closure are inherent to the openness he prizes.

The larger argument is, again, that no *moral* argument can be referred solely to the nature of language. The predicament with which language confronts all moralists is that there is no purely formal, clean, risk-free solution to ethical problems. Those who turn to language in hopes of discovering either the offense or the expiation discover that language is both less and more than they had thought: less, in that language, by "itself," is nothing; and more, in that regardless of what attributes language can be said to possess, it can also be said to possess others as well.

One useful implication that might be drawn from Levinas is that, from the point of view of ethics, the salient feature of language is its otherness to whatever can be said, intended, placed, observed—its simultaneous ubiquity and unlocatability. From this point of view, another word for "language" might be "relation" or "relatedness." Language, we could say, is not a thing or even a system of relations between things; rather, what relates things can be called "language." "There is," William James argues in the course of explaining the "stream of consciousness," "not a conjunction or a proposition, and hardly an adverbial phrase, syntactic form, or inflection of voice, in human speech, that does not express some shading or other of relation which we at some moment actually feel to exist between the larger objects of our thought" (*Principles of Psychology* 251). One of the more austere efforts to describe language as relation was made by Bertrand Russell, whose Theory of Descriptions held that linguistic terms in "denoting phrases" acquired meaning not through natural properties of reference but only through logical arrangements encoded in the form of the sentence. In the sentence "The deepest bell in the campanile is flat," the phrase "the deepest bell in the campanile" refers to nothing at all until placed in the context of the whole sentence. And when this sentence is put into logical form, it becomes the following: something is the deepest bell in the campanile; everything satisfying that description is flat; if anything satisfies that description it is identical with the first thing. As Stanley Cavell comments on this decoding procedure, "what emerges is that the brunt of reference falls wholly upon logical terms such as 'everything' and 'something' in conjunction with the variable pronoun 'it,' the whole complex being bound together by the cross reference of pronouns and the logical relations of conjunction and implication ('if-then') and identity. Such terms and relations seem to be fundamental to all language, and their meaning obviously does not depend on there being any particular thing in the world" (*Themes out of School* 208). According to the Theory of Descriptions, "language itself" can be assimilated to "relation itself."

As might be expected, Cavell is unimpressed by such a performance, which seems to take us away from any useful knowledge of persons. But Russell's claim that language can be analyzed entirely in terms of relations between markers can provide a foundation for an understanding of the ethics of language. For the unrestricted relatedness *of* language can be seen as a model for our relation *to* language, and, *through* language, to others and to the material and immaterial world. Heidegger views the human relation to language as a "betweenness," a "correlation" in which the reduction of the human to the status of commodity is resisted. "The word 'relation,'" Heidegger writes, "does want to say that man, in his very being, is in demand, is needed, that he, as the being he is, belongs within a needfulness which claims him." For Heidegger, man is man only in relation; and relation is accomplished only in a dialogue; and a dialogue is true only when language speaks "to those who seemingly are the only speakers—men" (*Way to Language* 32, 52). As even this minimal précis suggests, the relatedness of language does not exclude persons; indeed, relation "speaks" to persons in their very speaking.

Heidegger's complex argument turns on the forceful speaking of language to those who use it. From both the outside and the inside—that is, from within one's "own" speech—a sense of necessary relation between things is engendered and articulated. The mere use of language requires an understanding, no matter how uncertain, provisional, or nonbinding, of a kind of relatedness that Heidegger, for one, identifies as essentially human. "Thus *our* saying," he writes, "remains forever relational" (135). And: "In order to be who we are, we human beings remain committed to and within the being of

75

language, and can never step out of it and look at it from somewhere else" (134). The idea of language for Heidegger, an idea which is not only ideal but actual and concrete, entails the fundamental ethical concept of commitment—a commitment, we could legitimately infer, to relation.

We are approaching, almost as an oasis, the position not that language produces determinate effects, but that the nebulous phenomenon of ethics is indeterminately but crucially implicated in the nebulous phenomenon of language. The model for such an argument is Kant's effort in the *Critique of Pure Reason* to explain why certain propositions (of, for example, mathematics, geometry, and causality) seem incontestably true. Kant argued that our minds are structured in such a way that any perception we have exhibits certain features, especially concerning time and space; so that, as Robert Nozick puts it, "the statements formulating these features not only are true but must be true" (*Philosophical Explanations* 546; hereafter *PE*). Nozick extends the argument by asking whether ethical truths could have the same force as those of geometry and causality: "Could ethical truths hold as the result or side effect of some process wherein we structure and cognitively organize the world, or ourselves, or the relationship between ourselves and the world?" If so, then the structuring that "brings ethics in its wake" must be inescapable, that is, "something we would not choose to escape, even if we could." Noting that ethics "binds us in the first person," Nozick advances as his candidate for this deep structuring the fact of "being an I," in particular a reflexive "I" (547). The question that will lead us further on is how we achieve this *bound and reflective personhood,* to which the only adequate response is: through language.

The most obvious and profound way in which a reflexive "I" is structured in language is through that primary instance of relation, the first person pronoun—the common property of every mortal and mutable subject, the most immediate reference point for subjective experience, the linguistic residue of Lacan's "mirror stage," and, according to the paleolinguists, included in every human language. As we have already seen, language itself, language considered as external to the subject, is a vaporous and uncertain thing. We cannot even specify the basic rules governing intelligibility, for many "poorly formed" statements work quite well in the right context ("Where y'at?"), and many "well formed" statements work not at all ("Colorless green ideas sleep furiously"). But actual utterances can be described in exhaustive detail; and this suggests that language doesn't just "contain" an "I" as one of its words, but is in some sense actually gathered and focused in the speaking or writing "I," which serves as a kind of primary word organizing the entire vast domain.

Embedded in the concept of the deictic "shifter" whose meaning is peculiar to each subject, yet peculiar in the same way—universally unique—is a shadowy ethical or "pre-ethical" concept of potential relatedness and commonality based on a structuring of experience performed by all, but by each in his or her own way, on his or her own terms. Some see the "I" as virtually an ideology. Mary Daly, for example, urges that the feminist "castrating" of language should begin with the "phallic" "I," which must be "broken" or "cut" to display "the woman-breaking effects of language" (*Gyn/Ecology* 327; see also Wittig, *The Lesbian Body* 10–11). The view from the patriarchy, however, is that the "I" is already split. Lyotard comments that the Kantian concept of the "person" "in fact signifies that the same entity occupies the legislating instance, that of the I in the *I am able to,* and the obligated instance, that of the you in the *You ought to*" (*Differend* 126). This splitting of the subject through the exchange of pronouns, and not the arrogant seizure of a singular and self-mastering identity, is what "signifies autonomy" (126). Other pronouns, and other ways in which the subject is cut, broken, castrated—but also reconstituted and empowered—are implied by the universality of the "I." From *another* point of view, *a point of view in some ways equivalent to mine,* "I" am also a "you," potentially a "one," an "it," and even part of a "we" and a "they." The first person pronoun instructs us on the conditions and possibilities of "being an I," while the other pronouns provide the "moving parts" that Nozick claims are essential to self-conscious "reflexivity," the "process by which, in the third person, [the self] structures another self as having its own reflexive first person" (*PE* 549). All mine, the "I" is the linguistic basis of "autonomous" individual identity; but the fact that the "I" is shared with all others serves as the linguistic basis for intuitions and ideologies of connectedness and collectivity.

An apparently neutral capacity to use pronouns brings in its wake an ethically engaged capacity to imagine an other to the self and an otherness within the self. These are the very foundations of the *ought,* of the law that I take responsibility for although it does not originate in me, and which I urge on others as binding upon them. Nozick speaks of "moral push" and "moral pull" as the forms of ethical force: "My value fixes what behavior should flow from me," he says; and "your value fixes which behavior should flow toward you" (*PE* 401). Ethics is "harmonious," Nozick adds, when the push is at least as great as the pull, when "you" fully deserve the treatment "I" give you—when, in short, the hypothetical understanding of the other necessarily indicated by these pronouns is actually in force. Ethically and cognitively speaking, the pronomial issue is identity: the self as it names and understands itself, as it names and understands other selves, as it criticizes, transgresses against, regulates, and transcends itself (see *PE* 71ff; 547–51; 662n.31).

The system of pronouns provides, then, a fundamental if not ideal ethical basis for diverse moral codes, all of which can be derived from the generous matrix of the "I." Both Bentham's law, "Everybody to count for one, nobody for more than one"; and the Kantian categorical imperative to "act only on that maxim through which you can at the same time will that it should become a universal law" can be read as extreme and rigorous reflexes of some of the recognitions awakened by the "I." To follow Bentham means to cast yourself as just one among many; to follow Kant might mean to cast yourself as the hypothetical subject of all possible experience, and to consider all others as transformable into yourself. In a restricted but definite sense, the pronouns themselves anticipate Bentham and Kant and require us to recognize their positions as possibilities for us.

But the domain of the pronoun is even more spacious than these examples by themselves would suggest; indeed, it can contain virtually any example. Lyotard contrasts Kant with Levinas on the point of their radically different casting of pronouns. For Levinas, "the I does not even know if the other is also an I, nor does the I know what the other wants from the I nor even if the other wants something from the I, but the I is immediately obligated to the other. This is what the I's displacement onto the *you* instance marks: You ought to" (*Differend* 113). The "secret" of ethics, Lyotard writes, lies in "the asymmetry of the pronouns" (114). In some respects a Kantian, Habermas also rejects Kant's handling of pronouns. The categorical imperative, Habermas charges, requires an ethical model of "global subjectivity" based on "the arbitrary individual positings of a multitude of absolute individuals" ("Arnold Gehlen" 118). In the idea of unrestricted intersubjective communication, Habermas might like to imagine that he has invented an entirely different moral principle, but his radical alternative to Kant simply elaborates one more possibility of exchange and relation implicit and inscribed, as it were, in the "I." Even Levinas's radical ethics converge with Kant's, and with Bentham's, and Nozick's, in its derivation from the system of pronouns. An alternative to conceiving language in terms of agency, pronouns lead us to consider language as relation. Their use *raises the issue* of self-understanding and intersubjective relation that each moral system will structure in its own way, and leads on to the possibility of other forms of linguistic determination in ethical thought.

3. Language as Resistance

If thinking on language has traditionally proceeded by moral as well as empirical or speculative procedures—the identification of "temptations," the urging of "resistances"—the present argument is traditional; for it has produced its own set of temptations. First, language as an alien latecomer to an innocent, nonlinguistic world, an autonomous formal system of representing the already-there. Second, the severance of language from history. Third, language as containing a specifically "moral" subset of words, or of competing moral "languages." And fourth, language as agent, which is to say, language "itself," a discrete entity that produces identifiable effects. The principle of resistance is the same for all cases: language as "relation," reflecting, discovering, expressing, defining, and engendering—yet without autonomy or agency—the relatedness of things as well as of subjects, a relatedness within which such concepts as obligation, responsibility, respect, care, and freedom can arise.

What is given in language is not the content of ethical consciousness or a guide to ethical decision-making. These hopes for language do not survive an encounter with what has been described as "a brute empirical fact," the "unreflective character of natural language use. People simply say things without, in general, working out what it is they are to say and how it is to be said; others, and they themselves, just understand what was said without, in general, working out what has been said and how it was said" (Platts 9). Considering the astonishing number of calculations and acts of selection that must be performed to produce the simplest utterance (not to mention the 115 muscles that must be coordinated to produce speech), linguists such as Benveniste and Saussure have held that, no matter how rich or precise our intentions, most aspects of language use are "unintentional" and beyond the reach of conscious determination. "The reality of language," Benveniste says, "remains unconscious" ("Categories of Thought and Language" 55; see also Levelt). Language provides, rather, a model or program, a way of becoming accustomed and, in effect, committed to ethics. "In" language, we might say, the subject acquires, however unconsciously, a formal understanding of certain kinds of recognitions or judgments, and makes the decisions that bring ethics in their wake.

One of these decisions concerns the issue of materiality. Language is form, and formed, and thus non-ideal; materiality is a linguistic imperative. The heavily ideological question is, which form of materiality, writing or speech, expresses language's essence? Which is most intimate with language's proper function or true nature? The question can be decided and justified either way, and hence decided only "on principle." When language is seen to be doubled—in other words, when the *is* of the case splits into otherness—the question about the essence of language must be decided by an *ought*.

At this point, we have a choice ourselves, for the question of writing and speech has been powerfully conceived in two ways. In one, Jacques Lacan characterized writing as the Other that has suffered repression. It is especially significant that, despite his haphazard methods of composition and his pronounced preference for the spoken word, Lacan's seminar on ethics, the *Éthique de la psychanalyse*, was the only one he wished to compose, to revise, to write (*Encore* 50). For writing is not only the other of the spoken word, but also the mark of the "radical heteronomy that Freud's discovery shows gaping within man," the virtual sign of the "self's radical ex-centricity to itself." It is this ex-centricity that Lacan identifies with the Kantian ethical law, and this law that Lacan boldly identifies as repressed desire ("Agency of the letter" 172, 171). Perhaps the most compact way of describing the difference between Lacan and Derrida on writing is to say that while Lacan argues that ethics functions by a repression that is exemplified by writing, Derrida says that writing is typically the victim of a repression undertaken in the name of ethics. But the most compact way of indicating their common ground is to point to the predominance in the arguments of both of ethical factors.

More insistently and persuasively than anyone else, Derrida has developed the position that writing inhabits language, and consciousness itself, like the shadow of death—the death of intention, of presence, of subjectivity—frustrating logocentric or phonocentric pieties, expressed in Plato, Rousseau, Husserl, Saussure, and others, about the ideal identity of language and living consciousness. Piety's response to this frustration is not passive: as Derrida points out, logocentrism constantly seeks to neutralize or eliminate the otherness of "absence, dissimulation, detour, differance, writing"; and it typically does so by mobilizing ethics as the agency of suppression. "The ethic of the living word," Derrida charges, "would be as respectable as respect itself if it did not live on a delusion and a nonrespect for its own condition of origin, if it did not dream in speech of a presence denied to writing, denied by writing. The ethic of speech is the *delusion* of a presence mastered" (*Of Grammatology* 139).

"Ethical" thought, Derrida continues, "dreams" an opposition between qualitatively different and unequal things. But such a dream, which has troubled the sleep of Western philosophy from antiquity to the present, is not itself ethical—that is, not proper, not right—because it displays a "nonrespect for its own condition of origin." Out of respect for an originary writing, and all the qualities of distance and deferral associated with it, Derrida makes an ethical resistance to "ethics." The patient, intricate, and radical argument that unfolds in *Of Grammatology* suggests that the difference *between* writing and speech is haunted and undermined by a logically prior difference *within* each term. Both speech and "the vulgar concept of writing," Derrida claims, derive from a single "origin" in a speculative "arche-writing" that contains without privilege elements of presence and absence, ideality and materiality. Indifferent to ethical distinctions, the arche-writing is yet the original site of differences that are susceptible to "ethical" (mis)interpretation; and hence it is also "the origin of morality as well as of immorality. The nonethical opening of ethics." Ethics is "opened" in the violent conversion into external difference of a set of internal differences which are "rigorously suspended in order to repeat the genealogy of morals" (140). But in Derrida's analysis, the arche-writing closes, or at least undoes the opening of, ethics as well. For, as he shows, any logocentric or phonocentric attempt to repress writing in favor of metaphysical conceptions of intuition or voice will refer back to the arche-writing in which speech and writing originally coexisted; and this very origin will undermine such attempts even as it underwrites them, precisely *by* "underwriting" them. The return of the (written) repressed will be inscribed as a rigorous necessity in all metaphysics, a fact that cannot be written off.

Derrida points not only to a double investment, a resistance within language between its two material modes, but also to a certain complexity in the ethical relation to the other, the relation most commonly conceived in terms of subjective feelings of obligation to or respect for other *persons*. Converting such conceptions into linguistic terms, Derrida introduces an element normally invisible in ethical discourse by exposing the "nonrespect" displayed by speech towards its other. This suggests that within ethics an altogether "nonethical" contentiousness prevails, in which speech—the linguistic token of presence, singularity, personhood, intention, choice, and in general the difference between speakers—scorns its "condition of origin," writing, the linguistic token of absence, derivation, iterability, belatedness, and in general an indifference to, and therefore an equality of, subjects. As a counter to this nonrespect, deconstruction first experimentally reverses the relation between the two terms, disclosing the possibility of an "ethics of writing" that displays an equal and opposite nonrespect

81

for its other, the "living word." And second, deconstruction displaces the opposition itself by demonstrating that neither speech nor writing is so utterly itself as to be uninhabited or unmarked by the other. More specifically, Derrida insists that while writing and speech may exclude each other in a crudely literal or "vulgar" way, they cannot exclude the qualities associated with the other.

Many, including perhaps Derrida, at least in *Of Grammatology*, might feel that this conclusion leaves ethics in a condition of ethical disrepute. But if the procedures of deconstruction seem themselves mechanically nonevaluative and therefore anti-ethical, and if its arguments seem to render even "respect itself" nonrespectable, still deconstruction no more transcends or discredits ethics than does Jameson's Marxism. Indeed, both the reversal and the displacement are in Derrida's terms themselves manifestly ethical gestures, the first predicated on a justifiable nonrespect for an arrogant "presence," and the second on an equally justifiable nonrespect for the opposition presence/absence, and, more generally, for the binary opposition itself. Derrida thus moves serially through an ethic of the living word, of writing, and of the deconstructed binary opposition.

But in order to assess what Derrida has done, we must disentangle the two terms that Derrida equates, morality and ethics. Ethics begins in a neutral original otherness, a condition of resistance requiring a decision made on principle; this decision occurs in the second-stage process I have called morality. Dictating a specific choice between alternatives, morality produces an other that is privileged, and an *other* other that is banished, suppressed, delegitimated, and yet displayed as a possible and, in other contexts or circumstances, equally justifiable alternative. Derrida's real contribution in his account of the non-ethical opening of ethics is twofold: he has, through the concept of the arche-writing, envisioned language logically prior to the moralisms of speech and writing; and, just as important, he has demonstrated the inescapability of ethical factors in an analysis of language.

The question of the material base of language underlies another imperative: language must indicate something; it must be determined by something "outside" itself. The question to be decided on principle is, What ought language to be determined by? Should it be obligated by objects, intentional states, or concepts; or ought language's reference remain internal, a reference to language itself?

What is misleadingly thought of as a "referential" argument (misleading because language always refers, but does not always refer to the nonlinguistic) would urge that the true or essential missions of language are to designate or mime a real or possible "world," making it perceivable, knowable, useful; to reinforce our optical sense of particularity; to register the weight, contours, and density of the "real"; to give voice to the mind; to be verifiable. If language were not dutiful in this respect, partisans of reference would claim, no other duty could be enforced or even stipulated. But as language respects its referent, then all other duties become possible. This is, at least, the premise of Kant in the essay on "perpetual peace," where reference is set to work on behalf of reason against the forms of inclination prevalent in politics. Without being mentioned as such, the idea of a faithful referential function is nevertheless crucial to the central notion of *Publizität*, which is for Kant the test of ethicity: "If my maxim cannot be *openly divulged* without at the same time defeating my own intention, i.e., must be kept *secret* for it to succeed, or if I cannot *publicly acknowledge* it without thereby inevitably arousing everyone's opposition to my plan, then this necessary and universal, and thus a priori foreseeable, opposition of all to me could not have come from anything other than the injustice with which it threatens everyone" ("Perpetual Peace" 135–36). Kant's intentions or "plan" may be in dispute, but the adequacy of reference at all levels—the "maxim" of the intention, the description of the planned act, the representation of the consequences—is unquestioned; and it is, in fact, only the untroubled adequacy of reference that enables people to form the proper opinion of the plan at all.

What troubles the advocates of reference—including, eventually, Kant—is that reference does not fully deliver the goods, much less the good. No matter how earnest the effort of the speaker or writer to claim a worldly solidity for his utterance, language cannot even represent the entire referent, but only that dimension of the referent that *can* be represented. Paul Ricoeur has assigned to this dimension the title of mimesis$_1$, a capacity or inclination of things to be represented, a mode of pre-articulation or pre-understanding within things themselves. As a way of understanding mimesis$_1$, we could think of the current inquiry into the ultimate nature of matter, "superstring theory." The mathematics of superstring theory apply to, and work only in, ten dimensions—the four to which we (and our languages) are accustomed, and six to which most of us are not. These six inarticulate and inarticulable dimensions could be considered phases of being permanently excluded from ordinary language, tokens of an inalienable otherness from representation, an interior silence and invisibility. Nothing can *be* fully in its representation, and it is precisely this otherness, the unyielding and inaccessible darkness of the matter, that both commands and limits representation, that makes of representation a duty to be urged and an obligation to be followed, lest language, pursuing the implications of its inabilities, simply shear off from the world and become the ideal metadiscourse that philosophers in their youth—Russell, Wittgenstein, Ryle, Goodman—periodically attempt to design.

But the strongest argument for considering extralinguistic reference as a duty, a question to be decided on principle rather than as a necessity, lies in language's stubborn and intrinsic refusal to yield itself wholly, to realize a perfect respect for its referent by dissolving entirely. Arising from within reference, from within the task of indication, another imperative demands that language refer to itself. The conflict of *oughts* produced by a dual referential imperative can be apprehended, with its unmistakably "ethical" inflections, in John Searle's attack on the "detached anthropological standpoint" which enables people to *mention* words such as "promise" without "commitment," so that "words no longer mean what they mean": "The retreat from the committed use of words," Searle charges, "ultimately must involve a retreat from language itself" (*Speech Acts* 198). It is not good enough for language simply to refer; for language to be "itself," which is to say, honorable, unwilling to "retreat," it must refer to something other than language itself. The argument would be unnecessary, of course, if language users had no opportunity or inclination to use language in this way—as Searle himself does in his example—and if language were not actually, and inherently, capable of referring to "language itself."

In citation, we can see how even reference might fail to respect a worldly "other." This failure can also occur through renaming or reclassification, in which something is discovered to be the referent of multiple, incompatible names. One of the first texts to address this problem in relation to ethics has already been mentioned, Hume's *Enquiry Concerning the Principles of Morals.* Here, Hume announces that his method will be to appeal to the inner sense or feeling of morality, "which nature has made universal in the whole species" (26), through language, whose "very nature" is an "infallible guide." A more detailed reading of the *Enquiry* could easily demonstrate that the magnificent confidence of this beginning is not sustained, as Hume encounters difficulties, even within his chosen examples, in deciding the most basic questions. He takes up these difficulties in the final appendix to the *Enquiry,* "Of Some Verbal Disputes," where he begins by conceding that the English language provides no absolutely precise way of demarcating virtues from talents, vices from defects. Anything that could be described as a moral achievement could, he recognizes, also be described as an organic condition, an aptitude, a knack. From this recognition, Hume is swiftly led to consider the differences between social, intellectual, and moral virtues; between qualities of head and heart; between the voluntary and the involuntary. Distinctions are elaborated without resistance from the referent—virtue, talent, whatever—but with massive resistance from Hume, who is manifestly disconcerted by the "caprices of language" he has stumbled upon (148).

Hume seems at this point to be sliding towards de Man's position that language "already speaks about language and not about things. . . . All language is language about denomination, that is, a conceptual, figural, metaphorical language. . . . The paradigmatic linguistic model is that of an entity that confronts itself" (*AR* 152–53). Grappling with a capricious, metaphorical language, Hume finally, and simply, abandons the *Enquiry*'s initial premise about the infallibility of language as ethical guide in a conclusion that is both obstinate and dispirited: "it is of greater consequence to attend to things than to verbal appellations" (156).

As unconvincing as Hume's dogged retrieval of "things" may be, it forcibly recalls the dual character of reference, which "speaks about" both language and its nonlinguistic other. What seems to Hume a dilemma has in fact been translated into rigorous argument by Cynthia Chase, who maintains that reference is not accomplished in the apprehension of an entity, but in "the indication of a particular object, which *signifies* its reality or perceptibility precisely as its belonging to the class of things that can be perceived or pointed out" ("Witty Butcher's Wife" 996). Chase emphasizes the linguistic functions of signification, indication, and classification, but still preserves a place for the "particular object," the Humean "thing," a place de Man is less willing to save. What we "see" in reference is, according to Chase, a double image of the "thing itself" and the class of nameable things—really, the class of names, or "language itself." Things must be named if we are to be guided by language in the exercise of our moral sensibility; but to name something is necessarily to class it, and to class it is to cut the cord of matter, to choose between possible names, to consider the resources of language at the expense of the thing.

Even without considering the more problematic cases where the representation produces uncertain or conflicted evaluative plus or minus signs, then, Hume had reached a certain limit of reference in the inability to tell *what* a thing is. What he had called the "plain foundation of preference" had to be based on a plain foundation of reference; but the "capricious" proliferation of classificatory possibilities enabled by the general phenomenon of reference erodes the ethical confidence that had initially been based on reference. The very entities one might evaluate or choose between can become obscured in a blizzard of representations—many warranted, many more possible—that drive the philosopher to appeal to raw, anonymous "things." Within the last fifty or sixty years, Hume's dilemma has been reenacted within the theory of reference itself. "Referring," according to Anna Whiteside, "is shifting ever further from the concrete referent of the linguists and Ogden and Richards. Reference is now relative, encompassing both referent and signified, since it goes beyond specific meaning for a particular readership, to show that meaning is but one meaning in relation to many others." Beginning with a sense of reference as the relationship that holds between the expression and what the expression stands for, linguists now, according to Whiteside, stand on the brink of a conception of reference as "unlimited semiosis" (187). This otherness within reference between the solidity of classified acts or things and the dissolution of solidity in reclassification suggests that language does not in fact have the ethical function Hume wanted to claim for it.

The real ethical function of language is confirmed rather than dissimulated by the undecidability of reference. For the "concrete referent" of Ogden and Richards (and Hume) delivers a stable object world, a world of determined "things" to which the "very nature of language," as Hume defines it, could serve as infallible guide; while the "unlimited semiosis" of contemporary linguistics (and Hume) foregrounds the "underdetermined" character of all names. From Hume's discussion, an aggressive reader might learn about choices that are both determined and free: insofar as the name is uncontested, language guides; but insofar as the name is negotiable, language users—themselves extravagantly overdetermined, but convinced of their autonomy—must choose freely, in accordance with principle. Thus language activates a circumstance, the interplay of obligation and freedom, that dominates explicitly ethical decision-making.

This intricate and intimate relation between "language" and "ethics" may help explain the often incongruous-seeming animus that drives academic discussions of language. Most recent literary theory and much modern thinking on language can actually be read as an ethically-motivated attack on reference. Saussure's "arbitrariness of the sign," Derrida's "differance," Lacan's "incessant sliding of the signified beneath the signifier," Ricoeur's "metaphor," Kristeva's "intertextuality" and "abjection," Jameson's "political unconscious," Barthes's "*jouissance*," and de Man's "rhetoric" all have as their common target the dislodging of naive notions of reference and the kind of ethical earnestness these notions generally imply. And while all could be regarded as doubles of the counter-referentiality Hume had discovered within reference, it is typical in these attacks for reference to be pitted against its other. It is as though a rogue function of reference had risen up, acquired a name of its own, and stood opposed to reference itself—which could now claim for the first time to *be* "itself," having been purged of its "conceptual," "reflexive," or "self-regarding" dimension. But now, having become itself, reference has to struggle to maintain its purity or integrity. The academic battle over the essence of language is not occasionally but characteristically cast as a battle of values or principles: between honesty and duplicity, respect for the world and narcissistic indifference to it, primordiality and derivation, discipline and hedonism.

Such stark alternatives compel choice. Language constantly presents the hearer or reader with choices that must be made on the basis of inadequate information, decisions underdetermined by the arguments. If we read, for example, that God speaks in tongues of flame; that the black bat of night has flown; that the joint is jumping; that expenditures outran income; or that where id was, there shall ego be, we must decide a question that the statement does not decide by itself, whether the statement is referential or rhetorical (or: literal or figurative, ordinary or deviant, rational or irrational, "prose" or "poetry"). An *ought* must negotiate the claims of two justifiable *is*'s. This dynamic is played out in the work of de Man, in which such terms as "undecidability" and "unreadability" indicate the necessity of choice without grounds. An "unreadable" text—and all "texts" are unreadable— leads, de Man writes, to "a set of assertions that radically exclude each other. . . . They compel us to choose while destroying the foundations of any choice" (*AR* 245).

Even before the 1987 revelations concerning de Man's early journalism, many readers felt that de Man's work not only resisted ethical issues but actively represented an anti-ethical position (see Corngold; and Norris, "De Man Unfair to Kierkegaard"). De Man's invocations of language as "pure performance," language as agent of superior force or of the "internal necessities" of itself, suggest a rapt attention to language at the expense of a diminished "world" whose very existence is dubious: "The entire assumption of a nonverbal realm," de Man writes, "may well be a speculative hypothesis that exists only, to put it in all too intentional terms, *for the sake of* language" (*AR* 210). De Man's insistence on the rhetorical character even of philosophical utterances certainly would have seemed to Hume, for example, to constitute a dramatic loosening of the grip of language on the world, a desertion of the expedition by the guide—especially since rhetoric is conventionally considered somewhat more akin to lawyers than to the law, identified, as de Man says, with "persuasion, eloquence, the manipulation of the self and others" (*AR* 173). For those who believe in the ethicity of reference, an imperial rhetoric is disastrous, for rhetoric seems to owe everything to its own machinery and next to nothing to the world beyond the word, except insofar as that world is word-like.

If there is, as Derrida has famously said, nothing outside the text, that could be a large exception. But a rhetorical world is hard to imagine, for it would be a world without things as reference produces them, a world endlessly vulnerable to abrupt slippages, rearrangements, impossible combinations, and mutations. Rhetoric relentlessly unravels the individualizing work of reference, bodying forth—as Northrop Frye says of literature—"a world of total metaphor, in which everything is potentially identical with everything else, as though it were inside a single body" (*Anatomy* 136). Undoing the stability of reference, rhetoric seems the linguistic form of what Kristeva has called "abjection," a psychically rudimentary state of undifferentiation. From this perspective, rhetoric represents the paralysis of knowledge in the ungroundedness of choice, a token of uncertainty, disjunction, and upheaval. Nothing, it seems, could be clearer than the distinction between reference and rhetoric, nothing clearer than that we must choose between them, and nothing clearer—especially given the necessity of choice—than the ethical advantage of reference over rhetoric. How, after all, could we choose anything if everything is potentially identical? De Man himself well understood the crisis provoked by the threat of undifferentiation, and described "the urge to protect, as the most pressing of moral imperatives, [the] borderline between both modes of discourse" (*Rhetoric of Romanticism* 85).

De Man's tone here and in other such passages has been understood to be ironic by those eager simply to erase reference and replace it with rhetoric, and consequently to erase the entire notion of the moral imperative of language. A recent article in a collection entitled *Reading de Man Reading* illustrates the form of what may become a canonical misreading. In it, Bill Readings argues, with some support from certain passages in de Man, that reference is "a figural necessity of the fiction that language is the vehicle of a communication"; that the literal is "the trope of a language that can erase its own metaphoricity"; and finally, that "the referent" is itself "in its most rigorous sense . . . a metaphor" (Readings, "Deconstruction of Politics" 229). Having established to his satisfaction that metaphor is the fundament, the "rigorous" truth of language, Readings moves without resistance to a celebration of Lyotard's equally facile substitution of the *ought* for the *is*, the "political" for the "real," of judgment without criteria for a pseudo-universal justice. No empirical real in language, no nonideological or nonpoliticized discourse. The world really is a plurality of readings: hence the necessity "for what now seems the only chance for a rhetorical politics that *works,*" in the replacement of a "terroristic" "politics as practiced by the social subject" (who believes in reality) by a "politics as practiced by the deconstructed or the ethical subject" (239).

But de Man does not authorize such erasures. First, while he does urge a resistance to reference, his resistance is itself "moral," a resistance to the "seduction" or "temptation"—terms he uses almost compulsively—of reference's "confusion of linguistic with natural reality" (*Resistance to Theory* 11). A second point apparently, but only apparently, contradicts the first. Despite his resistance to reference, de Man does not simply reverse the polarities of a certain linguistic moralism. Especially at the most characteristic and powerful moments of his later texts, de Man insists on a principle of omnidirectional resistance as both an intrinsic feature of language and as the principle of relation between reader and text (see Kamuf, "Pieces of Resistance"). This resistance militates against any reversal of traditional hierarchies that merely replicates the opposition it seeks to deconstruct, reversals like the one advocated by Readings. Christopher Norris describes just such a "tempting" misreading of Derrida's comparable treatment of metaphor "as saying simply that this theory has got things upside down; that metaphor is there from the start, since 'literal' meaning (the *letter* of the text) is itself nothing more than a kind of aboriginal trope." This simple overturning neglects, as Norris points out, "a further and crucial stage in Derrida's argument," in which the circle is broken (*Derrida* 82). "It is not," Derrida says in this further stage, "a matter of inverting the literal meaning and the figurative meaning but of determining the 'literal' meaning of writing as metaphoricity itself" (*Grammatology* 15). In this elegantly contorted sentence, applicable to de Man's premises as well as to his own, Derrida suspends both rhetoric and reference, metaphor and the literal, in a relation of undecidability, a *properly* ethical situation where the necessary choices are rigorously underdetermined.

Stressing the act of "determining," Derrida all but states that rhetoric and reference are not different kinds of language, but rather different interpretive practices; or as one commentator says, different "laws" whose competing claims must always be worked out pragmatically, and yet, since they *are* "laws," on principle. The referential function may be the "law" of language, the function that "alone comprises the directions for meaning and thus makes language into language at all"; but this outward-looking law "is not the only law, for its validity is continuously contested by the other law: that of language's figurality" (Hamacher, "LECTIO" 185–86). With language jointly ruled by opposing laws, there is a permanent opening for deconstruction: the "literal meaning" of any utterance can always be shown to be "metaphoricity"; but metaphoricity can also be characterized as parasitic on reference, as arising from the ruins of reference, or as merely novel reference.

According to the law of reference, the word tempts and the world resists; according to the law of rhetoric, it's the other way around. The resistance to each is structurally implicated in the other that it resists. With language, one is always at a juncture; the path continually splits into doubled *oughts* that lead outward towards "the world," with its impacted demands, conflicts, and consequences, and inward towards the absolute neutralities of the internal being of "language itself." We must choose, and yet no choice can eliminate, for the chosen-against, as well as the chosen-for, is a "law."

This principle is so powerful that it finds a way to subvert and coerce even arguments that seek to oppose it. In a recent essay, Elaine Scarry argues eloquently for seeing language as a special system capable of soaking up the materiality of the world, embracing and celebrating the bodily realm. Scarry advocates a referential "materialism" as the engine of an ethically desirable "intervention": "Only language endowed with the referential substance of the world," she insists, "has the force and weight to impinge on that world" ("Introduction" xxv). Against the generous abundance and magnanimity of worldly reference stands the puny "weightlessness" of language that, having "lost its referential aspirations," "bears very little reference to anything beyond itself" (xxii, xx). This category of disgrace includes most "conversation about literature," which effects a "thinning out" of the "personhood" of those who indulge in it (xxi). The next step in this argument should—it seems—have been to urge those who aspire to "thick" personhood to confine themselves to referential statements. But just at the point where the argument urges the superior morality of reference, just as one might expect to be told to stick to discourse about flesh, football, tractors, the argument suffers a slippage of the kind one might associate with rhetoric. Although language *ought* to refer, it does not always do so; indeed, Scarry writes, the "advantage" of language in "supplementing 'the sensuously obvious'" often derives directly from its "referential freedom or fluidity" (xx). Language intervenes or "impinges" on the world, acting on and altering what it represents, precisely through its nonreferentiality, through which it builds its own insubstantiality back into the world, modifying the world's recalcitrant and reactionary heaviness. Reference may have "weight," but "force" is proper to rhetoric. Her own discourse, with its portrayal of language's "aspirations" and effects, is necessarily rhetorical, and so the argument dramatizes its central contradiction: that rhetoric, initially depicted as a dubious and impotent other to reference, turns out to be the active principle in language's "interventions." Considered as process rather than as a conclusion, the argument brilliantly exemplifies the truth of resistance.

In the course of the discussion of de Man, we saw how one of his readers, Readings, held that figurality, by destroying the illusion of the real, established the rule of the ethical. Another, Hamacher, held that reference and rhetoric constituted the two "laws" of language, but that "the referential and, moreover, the ethical function of language is thwarted by its figurative function" (186). So ethics is identified bluntly as rhetoric by one reader and just as bluntly as reference by another, with de Man himself pressed into the service of both ethics and the corruption of ethics. But if Derrida and de Man are claiming that there is no other to resistance, then it must be precisely such collapses of resistance that they resist above all. These collapses can be identified as *moral* choices, choices that Derrida especially acknowledges must be made, and are in fact made constantly, with real effects in the real world; but that de Man especially insists cannot be made rigorous or absolute. Establishing the *ethics* of language in the necessity of principled choice, deconstruction deconstructs the morality, or moralities, of choice itself.

Sometimes de Man opposes the disjunctive and unpredictable force of rhetoric to the normative force of grammar, whose "semi-automatic" patterns and "impersonal precision" constitutes a "merely formal" and virtually mechanical element (see *AR* 16, 294, 298–99; see also Bennington, "Aberrations"). The recognition of the copresence of grammatical and rhetorical aspects of language may occasion, as de Man says, an experience of "vertigo," but this copresence could also be seen as a linguistic version of the Kantian subject, a creature constituted by inclination but hailed from within by the formal law. "Grammar," if this analogy holds, would represent the "conscience" of language, the imperatives by which language is bound simply by virtue of being language. The extended law of grammar has a long reach, covering all the structural conventions of language, from the rules of sentence formation to the deep structures posited by Chomsky, through literary genres, conversational conventions, institutional discourses, all the way up to the "obscure set of anonymous rules" governing the "fellowships of discourse" discussed by Foucault. Mechanical, random, and impersonal, grammar is structured like the unconscious of a system of human expression. But by its primary function within the sentence of distinguishing the subject from, and relating it to, the predicate, grammar establishes another dimension of the ethics, or perhaps pre-ethics, of language.

Especially in this century, grammar has been under suspicion. Heidegger accused it of promoting a "metaphysics" based on a false conception of agency that could be corrected only by the "liberation of language from grammar" ("Letter on Humanism" 194). For many other writers, grammar is complicit with gender trouble. Virginia Woolf imagined a "woman's sentence" that would liberate expression from the linearity and logic of the simple declarative. More recently, Mary Daly has identified as one of the "spooks of grammar" the kind of "agent deletion" that occurs in specifically "ethical" sentences in which a truth is stated without reference to any person whose interest that "truth" supports: "These issues are necessarily linked . . ."; "It is thought to be the case that . . ."; "This is surely intolerable . . . ," and so forth (*Gyn/Ecology* 324 ff.). And in a well-known text, Julia Kristeva marked a resistant, fugitive linguistic force opposing the regularity of syntax, a kind of "music" indicative of "primary processes" and "the maternal body's vague, autoerotic jubilation" (*Desire in Language* 167).

The key terms of anti-grammar polemics are traceable to Nietzsche, who devises a narrative in which gender, metaphysics, grammar, and ethics are linked in a lurid scenario. According to Nietzsche's notorious argument, the notion, crucial to ethics, of the free and accountable subject arises from "the seduction of language (and of the fundamental errors of reason that are petrified in it)." (I have written about these errors in another context, so part of what follows condenses and adapts a more detailed reading; see *Ascetic Imperative* 203–19). Concentrated in the grammar of the sentence, the error Nietzsche condemns "separates the lightning from its flash and takes the latter for an action, for the operation of a subject called lightning." Presupposing a fictive free agent, "a neutral substratum" behind every act, grammar "doubles the deed," positing "the same event first as cause and then a second time as its effect" (*Genealogy of Morals* 1.13: 45). Facts notwithstanding, grammar forces one to regard the agent as accountable for his actions because he was free to do otherwise.

Nietzsche can explain the enormous appeal to "the weak," those ancient perpetrators of the "slave revolt in morals," of these grammar-induced notions, which would have empowered them to think, "We are weak because we have decided to be, in the interests of 'morality.' " But, at least with the model of the subject to which he is committed in the *Genealogy*, he cannot really provide an historical or psychological, much less a prehistorical or prepsychological, explanation of how or why "the strong," those primitive creatures of blind force, whose force was exemplified and perpetuated in their naming of the world, could have been "seduced" by a system they could never have comprehended, much less valued. For all that grammar could have implicitly proposed to the strong was the new and grotesque notion that they *need not* exercise their strength in acts of rape, pillage, arson, and murder; and to them, this could hardly have been an attractive prospect. In fact, seduction would appear to be exactly the wrong metaphor to apply to the linguistic enthusiasm of the weak, too; for they would have no initial resistance to the idea, no reason not to embrace immediately and wholeheartedly a system that appeared to confer on them the power of choice and self-determination—the power of power itself. Perhaps Nietzsche himself was seduced by the seduction metaphor as a way of explaining the inexplicable fact that an ethic of weakness triumphed against the interests of those in power.

Rather than question the aptness of Nietzsche's metaphor of seduction, however, we ought to question directly his concepts of strength and weakness. For in his account, language acts as an ethical force—a suddenly oxymoronic concept since for Nietzsche ethics is an implement and expression of weakness, and force the mark of strength. Language cannot do otherwise than promote a "weak" accountability, even though the inability to do otherwise is itself "strong." Moreover, from the moment we use language—even to employ the rudest signs in the most tentative, semiconscious, and imprecise way—we ourselves cannot do otherwise than to accept this ethic of the weak who believe in the ability to do otherwise.

Nietzsche argues that language makes the weak strong and the strong weak; but it is both more accurate and more suggestive to say that language makes people strong and weak, implicating them in the "ethical" circumstance of *being obligated to make free choices.* It is language, in fact, that is powerfully implied but missing from the account of "will" in *Beyond Good and Evil.* Here, Nietzsche describes will as "above all something *complicated,* something that is a unity only as a word." In all willing, he writes, there is "a plurality of sensations, namely the sensation of the condition we *leave,* the sensation of the condition towards which we *go,* the sensation of this 'leaving' and 'going' itself, and then also an accompanying muscular sensation which, even without our putting 'arms and legs' in motion, comes into play through a kind of habit as soon as we 'will.'" Willing is above all an emotion of command: "A man who *wills*—commands something in himself which obeys or which he believes obeys," so that the single word *will* indicates both command and obedience. Rather than the anti-ethical subject-in-action of the *Genealogy*, Nietzsche here pictures the willing body as itself "a social structure composed of many souls," both ruled and ruling. Thus conceived, it falls "within the field of morality: that is, of morality understood as the theory of the relations of dominance under which the phenomenon 'life' arises" (*Beyond Good and Evil* 19). When we ask, "Under what circumstances does the human animal become 'complicated' in this way?" the answer is provided by the *Genealogy:* under the circumstance of language, which presupposes and enforces a subject both strong and weak, commanding and obeying.

Ethical issues disturb the surface even of discourses that aspire to a strictly neutral or scientific account of language. Discussing the "nature of the linguistic sign"—the sign considered in itself—Ferdinand de Saussure verges on the discovery of a displaced ethical circumstance, the structural imbrication of freedom (in the arbitrariness of the sign) and necessity (in the "immutability" of language, the fact that it is fixed, not free). What de Saussure calls the "stacked deck" aptly describes language "itself," but only—I would argue—because it also describes the ethical subject: "We say to language: 'Choose!' but we add: 'It must be this sign and no other'" (*Course in General Linguistics* 58). The ethical circumstance commands an even greater narrative urgency in Roman Jakobson's "Two Aspects of Language and Two Types of Aphasic Disturbances," a text that builds on Saussure's work, not least in its strenuous attempts to distinguish between the regularities of language itself and the untheorizable contingencies of use. As they did Saussure, these very attempts plunge Jakobson into a meditation on ethics in his discussion of what he calls the "ascending scale of freedom," according to which the freedom of the speaker is precisely zero in the combination of elements into phonemes, but increasingly great in the combination of words into sentences, sentences into utterances, and so forth (242). Since any instance of language will obediently use given phonemes, but will combine these phonemes more or less freely, we could, on the basis of Jakobson's work, conclude that the language user is always in the paradoxical but routine ethical circumstance of being both radically free and radically bound.

Our freedoms extend all the way down, and our obligations all the way up. We choose our words, of course; and these choices indicate and define our character and commitments, our view of the world, our "persons," as Cavell says. Moreover, we could also, in a more restricted sense, be said to "choose" to speak in sentences, to employ conventions and idioms. And in a greatly diminished but still real sense, we choose to use language rather than to communicate in some other way or not to communicate at all. No matter how universal or innate the language faculty, we must expend effort to learn a language, and we are responsible for the directedness of our effort in carrying out what de Man calls a "didactic assignment." We say what we want. And yet, hedged in by the myriad conditions of intelligibility, by the rules of grammar, the dictionary, as well as by the audience, the subject, or the truth, our statements are determined. In our most deeply personal as well as our most automatic, merely appropriate, and pro forma utterances, we are not responsible for what we say. We say what we must.

Language provides, then, a powerful, because largely unconscious, model of the dialectic of freedom and obligation that defines ethics, an inescapable indoctrination in a fundamental principle: that to be ethical is to rule and to be ruled. The ethical subject is free and accountable, but submits to the law as to necessity. In just this way, the linguistic subject names the world, but uses the sounds and marks tradition has bequeathed to it; expresses itself, but manipulates the codes and conventions of "expression" available in its linguistic culture; imposes its living will onto the world, but submits its will to the mortification and drift of the arche-writing; speaks itself, but is spoken to; invents ceaselessly, but plays by the rules. Within language, the subject discovers its most intimate and immediate models of activity and passivity, its most compelling forms of resistance.

4. Language from the Ethical Point of View, with Examples from Wittgenstein and de Man

If language indicates a doubleness in ethics, ethics also discloses a doubleness in language. This doubleness is Wittgenstein's subject in the pivotal 1929 "Lecture on Ethics," where he repeatedly describes the language of ethics as a "temptation." We are constantly tempted, Wittgenstein says, to think and speak ethically; by which he means to use the properly relative, specific, and factual terms of language as though they were absolute. The innocent phrase "the right road to Grantchester," for example, implies an absolute rightness apart from any particular goal, such as covering the distance in the shortest time or taking the most scenic route. The problem Wittgenstein addresses is that evaluative terms do not modify or restrict themselves: until someone says different, the right road is right for all purposes and under all circumstances. The referential generality of certain kinds of language has sometimes been seen as having a positive ethical value, as when Hume claimed that language grants the power to "correct the momentary appearances of things, and overlook the present situation" (*Treatise* 244). But Wittgenstein insists that the ethical dimension of language is transgressive and "nonsensical," that it "bewitches" the mind and "run[s] against the boundaries of language" itself. Insofar as we consent to this bewitchment, Wittgenstein says, we are "running against the walls of our cage," a cage that protects as well as restrains. A "book on Ethics which really was a book on Ethics," he warns, "would, with an explosion, destroy all the other books in the world." Assuming that at least a few of these imperiled volumes serve useful functions, the language of ethics becomes a dangerous, even an ethically questionable, thing.

The temptation does not arise precisely from within language but from "certain experiences" that "constantly tempt us to attribute a quality to them which we call absolute"; and this constant temptation, corresponding to a "tendency in the human mind which I personally cannot help respecting deeply" and "would not for my life ridicule," leads us to desire the ethical "misuse of our language." The tendency is so ingrained that it's not clear that we could resist it if we wished; and so admirable that it's not clear that we should wish. But what is above all unclear is the position of ethics; for while resistance to temptation is by definition ethical, Wittgenstein describes as ethical the temptation to transgress, raising the question of what would authorize the resistance.

In fact, Wittgenstein seems to have confused the position of everything. According to his argument, a certain use of language is not, strictly speaking, a temptation, but the sign of assent to a temptation that is centered in "certain experiences." But language must also be a sign of a temptable "tendency in the human mind." We could, in other words, locate both the tempting externality and the transgressive internality in language, which would then become a figure both for that which beckons from beyond the cage and that which is hopelessly imprisoned within it. But what of the prohibition? That, too, must be centered in language, which registers its protest at the assent to temptation by becoming disordered and "nonsensical." Language now becomes a figure for the cage itself. Wittgenstein has, with incomparable and, it seems, unconscious efficiency, suggested a view of language as the site of the entire ethical drama of resistance, including the resistance to ethics.

Trying to criticize a particular use of language, Wittgenstein paralyzes his own critique but comes to the edge of a larger and more important discovery about language and ethics. In the "Lecture," as in the *Tractatus Logico-Philosophicus,* Wittgenstein is confident about the ability of language to represent the specific, objective, real things of the world. At the same time, however, Wittgenstein tries to produce an account of why some representations are truer, more accurate, more comprehensive than others. Following the track of what one of his most astute recent readers calls "an inner impetus toward an ideal" within representation itself, Wittgenstein concluded that some uses of language could *show* or reveal *das Mystiche*, whose telos is not thought but will, or practical action in the service of the Good (Edwards, *Ethics without Philosophy* 21). At this early point in his career, Wittgenstein holds that the ethical force of language lies in promoting its own abolition in worthy action. Thus various representations point to the world through description; but representation *sub specie aeternitatis* points beyond the world and indeed beyond language towards the mystical. Language's signals are crossed in the *Tractatus*, as they are in the "Lecture on Ethics," where ethical language arising from a structural tendency in the human mind is still language misused.

What Wittgenstein needed at this point was a conception of language capable of accommodating without contradiction the relative-factual-descriptive and the absolute-evaluative-prescriptive. He needed to realize that the irresistible tendency to conceive one's particular experience in absolute terms is reflected in an equally irresistible force of generality even in the humblest instances of description. He needed, in a word, to understand that what he called the ethical use of language was not a misuse, but a necessary and entirely proper use; and that language did not in any simple sense resist ethics, for both language and ethics are structures of resistance. Within a few months of writing the "Lecture," Wittgenstein was, however, beginning to resist ethics in a new way, for he was telling friends that "language is not a cage," and was moving rapidly toward the conception of language as nonrepresentational game or instrument expounded in *Philosophical Investigations* and *On Certainty*. This conception liberated him from the imprisoning thought that language was essentially a rational and descriptive system of nomenclature, but it did so by eliminating the category of ethical "misuse." Taking seriously Wittgenstein's professions of respect for the forces that produce this misuse, we could say that all Wittgenstein really needed was to de-pathologize the analysis of the "Lecture on Ethics," to recognize that the most emancipatory as well as the most respectful conception would be of language as a cage from which one may escape at any time. Necessarily indicating the concrete, language just as necessarily discloses the categorical. Letters themselves are categories, and if we cannot grasp language as a system of categories, a prime instance of the categorical imperative—as the "Wild Child" studied by Pinel at the end of the eighteenth century could not—then we are outcast from the linguistic community, and truly in the wilderness.

The persistence of the idea that ethics constitutes a disturbance, a perturbation, a confusion of language is impressive, not least in the memorable meditations it provokes. The increasingly famous passage in which de Man voices this suspicion is worth quoting at some length:

> Allegories are always ethical, the term ethical designating the structural interference of two distinct value systems. In this sense, ethics has nothing to do with the will (thwarted or free) of a subject, nor *a fortiori*, with a relationship between subjects. The ethical category is imperative (i.e., a category rather than a value) to the extent that it is linguistic and not subjective. Morality is a version of the same language aporia that gave rise to such concepts as "man" or "love" or "self," and not the cause or the consequence of such concepts. The passage to an ethical tonality does not result from a transcendental imperative but is the referential (and therefore unreliable) version of a linguistic confusion. Ethics (or, one should say, ethicity) is a discursive mode among others. (*AR* 206)

De Man's "two distinct value systems" recalls Wittgenstein's distinction between the concrete and the absolute, as his "confusion" recalls Wittgenstein's "nonsense," and perhaps anticipates and informs Hillis Miller's "unreadability." But de Man does not see the "discursive mode" of ethicity as a "misuse" of language, nor, most emphatically, does he see it as particularly worthy of respect. Indeed, the entire passage seems determined to rule out the very possibility of value and especially of the evaluating subject. Ethics is a "structural interference," a "category," an "aporia," a "discursive mode among others." Imperative only insofar as it is "linguistic," ethics is a byproduct of a rigorously nontranscendental, inhuman, and even mechanical process. The essence of the argument resides in the very opposition, maintained and reinforced throughout de Man's late work, between the "linguistic" and the "subjective."

De Man does not compromise on this improbable opposition. "What makes a reading more or less true," he says elsewhere, "is simply the . . . necessity of its occurrence, regardless of the reader or of the author's wishes." Reading is a form of corrective coercion, a chastening and purging, an "argument," as he says, because "it has to go against the grain of what one would want to happen in the name of what has to happen" ("Foreword" xi). The very construction of this distinction, however, is a deconstruction. For if reading *has* to go "against the grain" of desire, it is determined in every way by desire, which it crosses, checks, or regulates. The impersonal and inhuman law of "argument," like the law of ethics, bears a necessary and constitutive relation to the willing subject, whose resistant mass shapes and

defines "what has to happen." Even de Man finds subjectivity an irresistible temptation, impossible but necessary. His initial error, then, is
to portray a resistance as an opposition, and to imagine an undifferentiated and essential language that his own analysis refutes.

But understanding this passage entails more than simply identifying "errors." For the very principle of the passage seems to be self-
refutation. His target is not just "ethics" but Kantian ethics, in which
a willing subject rationally and freely chooses to obey a transcendental
law. But de Man's own definitions deconstruct the opposition between
the systems he proposes and opposes. In the passage quoted at length
above, de Man says that ethics can be defined as "the structural interference of two value systems." He identifies those two systems not as
the subject and the law, desire and knowledge, being and duty, the
individual and the community, the particular and the general, but as
the system of value expressed in judgments about right and wrong
and the system of truth expressed in judgments about truth and falsehood. At the technically-definable moment when these two systems
intersect, there ethics happens. But in this passage, ethics is itself
doubled, for the Kantian imperative is enlisted to legitimate an anti-
Kantian position, so that it is impossible to say where de Man actually
stands vis-à-vis Kant. On the page before this passage, de Man had
proposed as a "paradigm for all texts" "a figure (or a system of figures)
and its deconstruction" (AR 205). With a minimum of ingenuity, this
paradigm, too, can be adapted to the Kantian ethical subject, which
could be described as a system constituted of inclinations together
with the law that overrules them.

Indeed, it is Kant who appears to be the deconstructor and de Man
who appears to be the victim of naive metaphorical mystification. For
by situating the law within the subject, as the ground of its "deeper"
or "truer" interests, Kant claims that insofar as we are rational beings,
desire turns on itself, preferring necessity to inclination, deep to shal-
low: what we "want" includes what we do "not want." We could, on
strictly Kantian grounds, posit an "arche-reason" that contains without privilege reason and inclination, with both caught up in a strictly
undecidable exchange of values and priorities. Thus the anti-Kantian
argument has to go against the grain of what de Man might want to
happen in the name of what has to happen; it is Kant, after all, who
deconstructs the opposition of the law and the subject, and de Man
who argues for the undeconstructability—for what Levinas might call
the "absolute foreignness"—of language and desire, the law and the
subject.

"Death," de Man wrote, "is a displaced name for a linguistic predicament" (Rhetoric of Romanticism 81). By the same token, language

might be a "displaced name" for an ethical predicament. Certainly, de Man's own ethical predicaments have become increasingly legible in the last few years, as readers have seized on precisely the kind of marginal moments in his texts to which de Man was so uncannily sensitive in the texts of others, discovering in the extreme ascesis of his style, his passionate refusal of passion, either an anguished melodrama of revelation and concealment, contrition and cover-up, or a continuation of his totalitarian temptations, with "language" simply taking the place once held by "Germany." The more that is known about de Man, the more pressing and problematic becomes the most fundamental question: What *is* de Man's work after all? A form of linguistic fascism, an elaborate shelter for a guilty conscience, a series of scrupulous and rigorous readings, or a brazen display of his own triumphant virtue ("man," "love," "self"—these I have renounced)? "De Man's work" is itself crossed by the conflicting value systems of truth-and-falsehood and right-and-wrong; against the grain of his desires, it has necessarily become "ethical."

De Man omits from his account of ethics many traditional elements, including free rational choice by a conscious subject, an autonomous moral law, and communal norms. Still, his essential point is that there is more to ethics than the discourse of ethics has allowed, and that this "more" should be called "language," figured as the negation of subjectivity: de Manian ethics occurs through the "structural interference" of the subject's desires and language. This opposition must be deconstructed into a resistance, but remains an arresting suggestion of a nontranscendental source of the ethical law.

We seem to have come a very long way from language as friendly and infallible guide to ethical judgment, but in a sense we have been arriving all the time. Out of the ashes of Hume's attempt to discover in language a guide to specific moral evaluations has risen another and better hypothesis: that language, at the level of generality we have been considering, does not solve our problems, instruct us in or lead us toward the good, or tell us what we should aspire to; language rather provides us with model, program, map—our best *example* of ethical thinking, and our point of entry into an ethical world. What language "infallibly" does is to serve as the medium in which we become adept at ethical thought.

A general account of the ethics of language must focus on structures of resistance and otherness. Examples would range from the countless lexical binarisms, to the binarisms that include language as one of the terms, such as image/text or perceiving/interpreting, on up to those larger conceptual oppositions such as human/nonhuman or nature/culture in which language figures as the decisive factor. But they would also include the oppositions through which language can be analyzed, and, since the postulation of an opposition is the accepted mode of discovery in language and literary theory, these are myriad: reference/rhetoric, writing/speech, strength/weakness, generality/specificity, form/meaning, form/usage, combination/selection, irony/allegory, paradigm/syntagm, signifier/signified, metaphor/metonymy, expression/indication, sense/reference, performative/constative, grammar/semantics, grammar/rhetoric, literal/figurative, occasion-meaning/applied timeless meaning, illocutionary/perlocutionary, *langue/parole*, well-formed/deviant, syntax/phonology, literary/nonliterary. Resistance, whether figured "strongly" as a clear distinction between entities, or "weakly" as a kind of dotted line drawn within an essentially unified field, appears to be a virtually inevitable way of thinking *about* language. Not surprisingly, strong and weak resistances are also primary ways of thinking *with* language, which thus provides a powerful, and powerfully "natural," model for the very idea of an ethical "world" in which choices must be made on the basis of shared, or shareable, principles.

An ethics modeled by and on language would, it now appears, have to be based not on one imperative but on two. According to what might be called the imperative of difference-between, we must choose and act on a principled basis, recognizing inequalities and distinctions. But the fullest and final expression of this "categorical" imperative is war, the ultimate form of difference between entities conceived as monologic blocks; and as Kant says, there ought not to be war. War violates and so calls forth a counter-categorical imperative to realize human solidarity in a perpetual peace—a peace that would be encouraged by the sense that differences-within eroded the rigid distinctions on which choice—ultimately, war—was based. The inertia of an unresisted principle of internal differentiation would, however, require the correction of its other. Perpetual war and perpetual peace: each the unethical ethical resistance to the other.

"Language" remains an abstraction. It attaches itself, however, to many concretenesses, including the most familiar ethical concept of all, conscience. The two are so inextricably linked that Rorty, for one, feels that an argument made about one is virtually an argument about the other. "I shall try," he says at the beginning of *Contingency, Irony, and Solidarity*, "to show how a recognition of [the contingency of language] leads to a recognition of the contingency of conscience" (9). But the connection is solid even in accounts that stress noncontingency. In the Kantian version of conscience, the moral law divides the subject, obligating precisely through its insistent otherness, its refusal to tell us anything about ourselves. The law speaks from a position beneath or beyond consciousness or ego-ideals, and yet assumes the form of a voice telling us on every occasion that we ought to act in such a way so that the maxim of our act could be accepted by everyone in comparable circumstances. A linguistic imperative in that it speaks and speaks of language (maxims), the law still says nothing, its speech characterized by a reticence that is not just indeterminacy. The law—the law in itself, not the various rules, prohibitions, or habits followed by all—will not tell us what to do, and will never instruct us in specific situations. Instead, the law simply instructs us to submit our actions to general descriptions that can be both understood and endorsed by others who do not share our interests, circumstances, or prejudices. In short, the law enjoins us to use language as a communicative instrument serving all but possessed by none, one that exceeds and "transcends" the private subject—to use language not as an end only but as a means also.

To conceive of conscience as the possibility of language rather than as actual words is to approach an understanding of Heidegger's curious discussion of the *Anruf* of conscience in section 58 of *Being and Time,* where he says that the inner voice comes from within and yet calls "from afar unto afar." The Heideggerian conscience surprises, decenters, and disconcerts a subject otherwise lost in "Oneness." Perhaps most disconcerting of all, the call of conscience summons the subject to duty without really saying anything: "The call asserts nothing, gives no information about world events, has nothing to tell." The law does not specify; its speech is purely formal and without content, the speech of language itself.

Conscience emerges from and defines an interior distance, calling across a gap in the subject, a space wherein the subject differs from itself and requires "communication" to make itself known even to itself. The conscience serves as the quasi-audible reminder of an inalienable internal otherness that requires and engenders signs. Lacan's suggestive description of this internal otherness turns on the idea of repression, through which, as Lacan says, the subject becomes self-aware, entering the domain of symbolic forms. For Lacan, the voice of duty simply is repressed desire, and it speaks to a subject constituted by repression. The law does not enjoin or exhort us to repress our desires; rather, as John Rajchman explicates Lacan, "we have an inner voice of conscience because we are constituted as subjects through a primal repression of our desire; our conscience derives from that repression" ("Ethics of Modernity" 51). What appears in Kant, Heidegger, and Rorty as an alliance between conscience and language becomes in Lacan an identity, one that answers to the strongest possible formulation: conscience is language without words.

The bare idea of language without words may seem needlessly provocative, even mystical; but it is in fact the very basis of Noam Chomsky's revolution, which is generally credited with converting the field of linguistics from a classificatory enterprise into a scientific one. Many aspects of this revolution remain in dispute, but the fundamental points are not, and these display a striking relevance to the subject of language and ethics. For what Chomsky proposed was that language learning was different from other didactic assignments in being enabled by a language faculty possessed by all, "a perfect knowledge of universal grammar," as Chomsky writes, "a fixed schematism" used by everyone in acquiring language ("Linguistics and Philosophy" 88). A capacity for identifying and understanding deep syntax and transformational rules, this faculty is, Chomsky argues, incontrovertible evidence of the presence in the brain of an unlearned and unconscious structure. Chomsky's emphasis on syntax at the expense of semantics, form over meaning, enables him to divert attention from language directly to the structures of the human mind. And it is this diversion that not only qualifies linguistics to be a science—a branch of cognitive psychology—but which places Chomsky in the rationalist philosophical tradition of Leibniz and Descartes, the proponents of innate ideas.

Magnificently daring as this latter claim is, it strategically overlooks crucial differences between the "ideas" posited by Chomsky and those posited by Leibniz and by Descartes, who never claimed either that innate ideas were unconscious or that language was an innate idea. To see Chomsky as a rationalist also effectively obscures an even more remarkable lineage. For Chomsky's account of the language faculty recalls nothing so powerfully as the categorical imperative. Like the universal language faculty, the categorical imperative is innate, unconscious, universal, rationalistic, noncontingent, formalistic, and peculiar to the human species. Moreover, both are dedicated to the act of evaluation—in Kant's case, to the evaluation of actions; and in Chomsky's, to the evaluation of sentences. And both resist specificity. While various rules have appeared to be generally applicable, none has so far proven to be universal, encouraging the hypothesis that it is not particular rules that constitute universal grammar but rather rule-governedness itself. Chomsky is not, as some have claimed, the last great Cartesian, but rather a great, and hopefully not the last, Kantian.

This theory receives a kind of support in the fact that the ritual form of dissatisfaction with Kant has repeated itself in the counter-revolution against Chomsky. Since Hegel, Kant has been attacked for what has been described as the inhuman, sterile, and even perverse formalism of his idea of ethical reason. Surely, the anti-Kantian argument goes, real human beings are not slaves to some dehumanized and autonomous imperative of Reason that tells them to think of themselves as universal subjects; and since we exist only as particular subjects in particular circumstances, the categorical imperative does not exist. A similar blood-and-sand anti-Chomskyan argument has protested against the severe formalism and complexity of his system. Chomsky suffers, his critics have charged, from a fundamental misunderstanding of the means and ends of language. Language is not form, but a combination of form and meaning, according to the generative semanticists; and not just form and meaning, but deeds, according to the speech-act theorists and pragmatists (see Bresnan; and Searle, *Speech Acts*). No absolute line can be drawn between syntax and semantics, or between form and meaning; and therefore an autonomous deep syntactical structure does not exist.

The frequent vehemence of these disputes is misleading, for the actual point of disagreement is relatively trivial. Kant does not claim that human beings are wholly determined by the dictates of pure practical reason, any more than Chomsky argues that language is entirely composed of pure syntax. Rather, they have posited reason and syntax as elements of human understanding, and have made a series of assertions about what they might look like. On the other side, nobody really argues that the transformational rules Chomsky has developed describe nothing at all, nor does anyone seriously assert that human beings are incapable of thinking in a way that strongly appears to be independent of their circumstances or inclinations. Everyone agrees that autonomous formal systems of reason and syntax can be theoretically posited and their operations described, with some empirical evidence; and everybody would also agree that these systems are not in practice really autonomous, but are rather invariably conditioned, by inclination and capacity for Kant and semantics for Chomsky. The question that divides Kant and Chomsky and their humanistic opponents is rather the character of the relation between the autonomous system and its other: does the embeddedness of autonomy in its other compromise autonomy as a theoretical construct, or as a practical factor? And this is a different, and somewhat smaller, question than is generally advertised.

The principle on which, I am claiming, everyone agrees is the structural interference of two value systems, which de Man singles out as the mark of ethicity itself. As a footnote—the only one—I should add that this interference may help explain why Chomsky apparently feels no distress over the fact that his work in linguistics—supple, infinitely adaptable, incomparably detailed—seems to have an "inhuman" lack of affect; while his politics—rigid, uncompromising, insistent—are generally seen as "humanistic." For we can see in his linguistics and in his politics, and in their relation, the unmistakable resistances of ethics, the encounter of the "human" with its other.

3

FROM CONVERSION TO ANALYSIS

Come on, come on; and where you go
So interweave the curious knot,
That ev'n th'observer scarce may know
Which lines are Pleasure's and which not.
> Ben Jonson, *Pleasure Reconciled to Virtue*

Become what you are!
> Nietzsche, *Thus Spake Zarathustra*

1. Conversion, Pain, and Pleasure

At the end of the *Protagoras*, Socrates bullies his opponent into a series of damaging concessions, and finally into a hugely annoyed silence. "What, Protagoras," Socrates demands, "won't you say either yes or no to my questions?" "'Finish it yourself' said he" (360D). Socrates finishes it by announcing what had gradually become obvious, that he had succeeded in getting Protagoras to exchange positions with him:

> It seems to me that the present outcome of our talk is pointing at us, like a human adversary, the finger of accusation and scorn. If it had a voice it would say: 'What an absurd pair you are, Socrates and Protagoras. One of you, having said at the beginning that virtue is not teachable, now is bent upon contradicting himself by trying to demonstrate that everything is knowledge . . . which is the best way to prove that virtue *is* teachable. . . . Protagoras on the other hand, who at the beginning supposed it to be teachable, now on the contrary seems to be bent on showing that it is almost anything rather than knowledge; and this would make it least likely to be teachable' (361A–B).

W. K. C. Guthrie's "Introduction" to the Penguin edition follows the line of most of the commentary on this dialogue in affirming that it is a "dramatic masterpiece" with "lively, accurate portraiture" and "a lively description of scene and actors"; that its conventions are similar to those of the novel; and that "we read the whole dialogue like the text of a play" (7). But the dialogue's very "literary" excellence "perplexes those who would extract its philosophical lesson" (8). According to Guthrie and a long tradition of readers, the fact that the dialogue is an "artistically constructed whole" rather than a "systematic treatise" can only mean that if Socrates' "philosophical ideas" are present in the discussion, they are "surprisingly well disguised" (8, 24, 8, 8).

Recognizing the force of this approach, I would suggest that (a) both the "literary" coherence and the "philosophical" incoherence crystallize in the process of reversal noted by Socrates, and (b) that this process, far from confusing the issue of ethics, illuminates it in a way that far exceeds even the spacious parameters of Socrates' "philosophical ideas."

At some point, in some way, all discourse that can be called ethical argues that something falls under an imperative to become other than what it is. Numerous such arguments have already been mentioned—Hume's account of the transformation of the subject through the act of promising, Habermas's claim that language guides the speaker away from inclination and towards duty, and Kenneth Burke's statement that language converts "motion" into "action." But the list of possible examples defines the category of ethical discourse itself, and this brings to light an implicit and unargued premise: that conversion is the mark of the ethical.

In one recent instance of ethical implication, Stuart Hampshire resurrects Spinoza's argument that reflection serves an ethical function by "converting" passion into thought, reversing the associated affect from pain to pleasure. Reflecting on even our most painful experiences, Hampshire notes, our thinking becomes more comprehensive, more coherent, more peaceable as we are "converted from egocentricity to detachment." Reflection turns impotence into mastery, pain into pleasure, encouraging the belief that we possess our emotions rather than being possessed by them. To "understand" jealousy, hatred, fear, envy, rage, is, if we follow Hampshire's line, to cease to experience them as such; just as to become aware of the antifeminist tendency of much ethical discourse might produce for some intellectuals the satisfying sense that their own perhaps latent antifeminism was thereby nullified, even transformed into a generous, enlightened, and yet sober realization of the justice of feminism's claims in a hostile world. Thus Hampshire claims for reflection a positive ethical agency as our best and indeed only means of self-liberation from passion, passivity, and egocentricity. There may, Hampshire concedes, be "emotional distractions that will stand in the way of clear and detached thought," but these will be no match for the sheer pleasure of reflexive self-improvement (*MC* 51). "Sustained pleasure," he asserts, "is the mark of virtuous activity" (52). And one can only experience such pleasure, or "natural happiness," when one "is identified through one's own thought with the rational order of things," an identification that promotes "a sense of power and of movement, and also of escape into the open and away from triviality" (58). In such buoyant moods, philosophers dream of a process of ethical conversion or "escape" that orients us towards a future in which we might not only respect but be the other; in which we might become other than an irrational, emotional, unhappy, distracted, impotent, static, and trivial being—in which, perhaps, we might become a "man."

In the terms I have been arguing for, such a dream is moral, with all the worldly specificity characteristic of morality. But if we thought of conversion as an ethical—that is, necessary and neutral—process that might go either way, we would have to be sensitive to conversion's other, to a reversibility in conversion's reversals, to the convertability of conversion itself. Interestingly, Hampshire's own argument effectively discloses an other side of conversion through a subtle tonal instability. When he writes that "the correction of the intellect is an operation of thought upon itself" (48); or that "the first commandment of a moralist, is the order actively to exercise the power of reflection, and to question immediate beliefs and sentiments" (55); or that "to have the power of reflective thought is to have the power of thinking about one's own thinking, in an indefinitely complex spiral of self-correction" (62), we can see that pleasure might not be reflection's constant companion. Each of these sentences describes something that might more appropriately be called pain, whether that of surgery, domination, or vertigo. One can see from Hampshire's own account of reflection why Richard Wollheim might describe self-examination as "a malign phenomenon" (*Thread of Life* 162). On reflection, the pleasure and power Hampshire advertises so enthusiastically seem to accrue entirely to that part or function of the mind that operates, exercises, and corrects; the other part, the reflected-upon self, is simply the victim of its gaze, a prisoner of an internalized Panopticon, more sunk in impotence and narcissism than ever.

Kant, the great exponent of reflective self-dividedness, is not surprisingly therefore, also the great theoretician of ethical pain. But even in Hampshire's anti-Kantian account, the pleasure of reflection does not endure for long; rooted only in part of the subject, such pleasure is derived from the reflective faculty's delicious awareness that it is *not* the passive and dismal creature on which it reflects, but is rather some other, distantly spiralling sort of being. The conversion of the subject in reflection does not eliminate the sense of subjection that Hampshire describes as the target of ethical correction, but it does split up the parts of the self as though they were orphan siblings in a nineteenth-century novel, with one consigned to the gloomy workhouse of the observed and the other assuming the privileged invulnerability of the observer.

Even in the most sanguine account, then, ethical conversion produces pleasure and pain both, the border between them being no more secure than that between the reflective and reflected-upon aspects of the subject. To recognize this must make us suspicious of reflection itself, at least as Hampshire represents it. Since it works through mechanisms as fundamental as self-correction, self-criticism, self-awareness, and self-interpretation, perhaps what Hampshire is really talking about when he speaks of reflection is not an event at all but simply the inescapable condition of human consciousness, as seen by a powerfully transforming utopian sensibility. If this is so, if reflection is not a singular event but a constant and necessary feature of human thought, then insofar as we are self-aware, we are always positioned somewhere in the infinite spiral of self-correction, with some "thought" transcending and neutralizing some "passion," to be transcended and neutralized in its turn. Antifeminism might be considered a "thought," with many reasons and justifications, until such time as one becomes able to see it as a self-protective reflex over which one has no conscious control. At this point, one recognizes oneself at once as the slave of passion and as the thoughtful master of one's (suddenly former and lower) self, continuing in this conviction until it is itself revealed by reflection to be a slave rather than a master of some other interest or unconscious need. Indeed, there is no better historical evidence for this process than the fractious and boring history of ethics itself, a history Alasdair MacIntyre partially summarizes in this way:

> So the Evangelicals of the Clapham Sect saw in the morality of
> the Enlightenment a rational and rationalizing disgust for self-
> ishness and sin; so in turn the emancipated grandchildren of
> the Evangelicals and their Victorian successors saw Evangelical
> piety as mere hypocrisy; so later Bloomsbury, liberated by G. E.
> Moore, saw the whole semi-official cultural paraphernalia of
> the Victorian age as a pompous charade concealing the arro-
> gant self-will not only of fathers and clergymen, but also of
> Arnold, Ruskin and Spencer; and so in precisely the same way
> D. H. Lawrence "saw through" Bloomsbury. (AV 71–72)

Relentlessly unmasking virtue to reveal arbitrary will, self-interest, and complacency, the sequence of ethical theories confirms the suspicion that nothing in the nature of "thought" differentiates it from "passion" except its position in the spiral.

I am not arguing that there is no such thing as thought or passion. Just the opposite: insofar as thought is self-critical and self-interpretive, it constantly produces something like these terms. But what must be stressed is that while self-criticism may well engender the sense of power and possession that Hampshire describes, it can only do so at the cost of a corresponding sense of impotence and transgressiveness that he presumes can simply be left in the dust, relegated to a nonfunctional part of the self. Additionally, our skepticism about the salutary effects of reflection must spill over from reflection to the larger category of conversion, focusing especially on claims of irrevocable enlightenment or decisive awakening. If reflection is a fundamental and constant feature of human consciousness, then conversion is happening all the time, and no particular value can be attached to that fact. I am arguing, therefore, not against conversion but rather against a conception of conversion that is at once limited and grandiose. The template of conversion should be laid not just over sporadic, abrupt life-changes, but rather over all of ethical, i.e., self-aware, life, the transformative effect intensified at times, and continuously refashioned, but essentially constant.

Conversion is a "continuous event," a concept that may become less paradoxical if we think of Foucault's definition of the event as a reversal, an overturning effected by the "reversal of a relationship of forces . . . the entry of a masked 'other' " ("Nietzsche, Genealogy, History" 154). I have argued elsewhere that this definition makes most sense if the "other" is considered to be masked *as* an "other," concealing precisely its identity with that which is being entered. In Foucault's context, this codicil would help explain why the other is able to enter in the first place; and in the context of the present discussion, it clarifies the conservative backlash of conversion which, however dramatic and even melodramatic some of its effects may be, is internally inhibited in being produced by more of the Same. But the most interesting effect of this modification of Foucault's account is that it spreads out the diachrony of the event and converts it to endless synchrony, a process of continual revolution in which a fragment of Same masks itself as Other in order to gain access to itself, so that it can convert itself into an Other, a new monolith which in the absence of opposition thereby becomes Same, beginning the entire process over again. The event of conversion is itself convertible into a process.

We can cast this dauntingly abstract model into somewhat more concrete terms by seeing it as a generalized account of an argument such as Hampshire's, in which a portion—the "reflective" portion—of a subject originally understood to be in "pain" cracks off from the whole and masks itself in order to subvert and overturn the entire subject, converting it into a state of wholeness and pleasure. The reflective part wears the comic mask of pleasure (power, mastery, invulnerability), but, as I have been arguing and as Hampshire concedes in numerous small ways, not only derives from pain but continually produces pain in a process theoretically without limit.

So far, I have been speaking of *pleasure* and *pain* as though I knew what they meant, with a confidence typical of ethical discourse. Thomas Nagel, for example, uses pleasure and pain as a "simple case" of the kind of "objective" or "agent-neutral" value that rivals and structures the subjective "view from within." According to Nagel's "transcendent" view, "pleasure is impersonally good and pain impersonally bad" (*View* 156–62). But the susceptibility of these terms to being caught up in reversals and conversions indicates that they might be more volatile than Nagel and others suppose. The question is crucial because if the history of ethics has a center, a fundamental preoccupation, it is the relation of pleasure and its other. The essential process described and prescribed by ethical discourse is conversion, with pleasure either as its target or its telos. "Ethics itself" is indifferent to the particulars. An argument is "ethical" insofar as it projects some conversion of the subject, through a practice, from a condition of pain to one of pleasure or from pleasure to pain. As examples of the first mode, we can list Aristotle, Spinoza, Bentham, Mill,. Hampshire, Gilbert Ryle, MacIntyre, Rorty, and Bernard Williams; as examples of the second, Augustine, Kant, Freud, Levinas, Hillis Miller, de Man, and Lacan. Whatever their disagreements, all of these zero in on the problem of pleasure and its other as the defining ethical issue.

What, then, is pleasure?

I have put this question in the same stark form as Augustine's question about time in book 11 of the *Confessions* because his immediate response serves equally well as an introduction to the problem of pleasure: as long as nobody asks me, I know perfectly well; but when I am confronted with the question, I no longer know anything for certain. At the merest touch of interrogation, the question of pleasure virtually explodes into the shrapnel of other, smaller and sharper questions. Is pleasure a sensation, a feeling, or an emotion? Is it a bodily or a mental state; is it confined to one or the other? Can it ever be experienced in a pure form? Is it a kind of consent to life in the body, or an expansive, outward movement of the self into the world? Why does pleasure always seem to have an opposite? And how is it that its opposites—pain, work, indifference, *jouissance*—bear no consistent relation to each other? Do we always know when we experience pleasure? Can we experience it at the moment of its cause, or only after-wards on reflection? What relation does pleasure bear to the sublime? to languor? to helplessness? to control? to habit? to an increase or decrease in tension? What is the difference between feelings of plea-sure and pleasurable feelings? Is pleasure connected to activity or to desire? Can pleasures be quantified or ranked? Are there bad plea-sures? Can one be mistaken about pleasure? Is pleasure always attrac-tive, pain invariably aversive? Are pain and pleasure "ultimate ends," as Hume said, that cannot be further justified? How can pleasure be justified at all? What is the difference between allegedly simple plea-sures—eating oysters; making a perfect tennis shot; watching one's child, unspanked after all, absorbed in play; running one's eyes over the parti-colored wings of a Florentine Gabriel; the flush of sexu-ality—and the "ethical" pleasure to which Aristotle and his descen-dants summon us?

Perhaps the most innocuous thing to say is that pleasure is an ex-perience that leads us to reflect not only on the cause but also on the sensation of pleasure itself. Pleasure is marked by an awareness of a certain engagement of ourselves with something. That something can be virtually anything at all; pleasures can be simple, ethical, perverse, intellectual, altruistic, etc. This might suggest that we apply a simple and rather vague concept to a number of highly particularized expe-riences. But the concept is not simple. Even these listless and indif-ferent sentences indicate that a minimal condition for pleasure is a "de-centering" distinction within the subject between experience and reflection. In this account, pleasure de-centers, while pain centers the subject, reducing it to pure sensation. So "incontestably and unnego-tiably present" is pain, according to Elaine Scarry, that it "may come to be thought of as the most vibrant example of what it is to 'have certainty'" (*The Body in Pain* 4). It *may* "come to be thought of" in this way; but then again, it may not. Lacan makes precisely the opposite case in claiming that the break with the pleasure principle in ethics came about by the systematic decentering of the subject. According to Lacan, therefore, pleasure centers and pain decenters. We may well wonder whether we can maintain that the pleasure/pain relation cen-ters ethical discourse, when we cannot even say whether centering is a pleasurable or a painful experience.

What we are beginning to see as an instability within pleasure it-self helps account for its compulsive engagement with other terms. Robert Nozick talks about the "transformation" and "transfiguration" of pleasure "from above" by a principle of "harmonious hierarchical development"; Fredric Jameson, about the "proper political use of pleasure" as a foretaste of utopia, a political and historical construction in the "systematic revolutionary transformation of society as a whole" (*PE* 508, 509; "Pleasure" 73). But they collaborate in a view of pleasure as something to be converted, to be gone beyond, something that awaits its principle, something that cannot remain itself.

Thus, we might now say that while ethical discourse is centered *on* the subject of pleasure, it is not centered *by* it. The *Protagoras,* and Socrates himself, gain in terms of artistry but lose in terms of clarity when Socrates undertakes a "defense of hedonism," arguing that courage, for example, is simply a projective "knowledge" of the fact that, as cowards are despised, it is "better and pleasanter" to enter the battle—a position that, as Guthrie notes, is "regarded by many as the direct antithesis of what Socrates is likely to have taught in real life" (360A, 9). But philosophy typically goes ambivalent on the subject of pleasure. The attitude of Aristotle towards pleasure is notoriously unstable, the argument of book 10 of the *Nichomachean Ethics* conflicting with that of book 7. Nor does the subsequent history of ethics achieve any real clarity on the issue, not even in Bentham, who is always prepared to sacrifice everything to clarity.

Bentham begins *An Introduction to the Principles of Morals and Legislation* with the declaration that "nature has placed mankind under the governance of two sovereign masters, *pain* and *pleasure*. It is for them alone to point out what we ought to do, as well as to determine what we shall do" (1:i). Measurable in terms of intensity, duration, fecundity, and so forth, utility is "that property in any object, whereby it tends to produce benefit, advantage, pleasure, good, or happiness, (all this in the present case comes to the same thing)" (1:iii). An action conforms to the principle of utility when it augments the happiness of the community more than it diminishes that happiness. And actions conforming to utility manifestly "ought to be done" (1:x). So absolute is the power of the principle of utility that when one attempts to combat it, "it is with reasons drawn, without his being aware of it, from that very principle itself" (1:xiii). Nothing, then, could be simpler or more self-evident; which raises the question of why the entire second chapter is devoted to "Principles Adverse to That of Utility," which Bentham calls, respectively, "asceticism" and "sympathy and antipathy." Apparently forgetting or repressing his earlier argument that utility could never be combatted or opposed, Bentham provides for just this possibility with a surprising all-or-nothing declaration that "any one who reprobates any the least particle of pleasure, as such, from whatever source derived, is *pro tanto* a partizan of the principle of asceticism" (2:iii). So there is an other to utility; but mercifully, it is confined to the delusional violence of individuals against themselves, and has never been applied to "the business of government": "We read of saints, who for the good of their souls, and the mortification of their bodies, have voluntarily yielded themselves a prey to vermin: but though many persons of this class have wielded the reins of empire, we read of none who have set themselves to work, and made laws on purpose, with a view of stocking the body politic with the breed of highwaymen, housebreakers, or incendiaries" (2:viii). The principle of sympathy and antipathy recalls the Humean idea of the inner moral sense in its retreat from "any external standard" (2:xiv) to the interior or psychologistic. A strictly private principle, a principle indeed of privation, the principle of sympathy and antipathy cannot in the end even claim to be a principle at all. It is "rather a principle in name than in reality: it is not a positive principle of itself, so much as a term employed to signify the negation of all principle" (2:xii). So although the principle of utility is all-dominating and all-encompassing, it is shadowed by "principles adverse to utility," privatized, masochistic urges standing decisively beyond both pleasure and principle.

If anybody who "reprobates any the least particle of pleasure" is a "partizan" of asceticism, and if anybody who places any credence in his own sense of right and wrong is a partizan of the principle of sympathy and antipathy, then who is left to serve the unchallenged principle of utility? Bentham seems to have set up conditions for utility that exclude everyone who is a "one" from pursuing it, while insisting that everyone not only ought to but does in fact pursue it. The responsibility for this situation does not lie solely with Bentham himself, but with the definition of pleasure with which he is working, a definition of pleasure as that which is and ought to be desired. What Bentham cannot admit is any complicity or interference of pleasure with pain, or any discrepancy between means and ends. From a distance, the saint who exposes himself to vermin might be seen to be pursuing pleasure in some other world, but this pleasure is vigorously repressed by the saint himself, who therefore appears from a utilitarian perspective as misguided, perverse, or deluded—as do all those who do not concede that every single "particle" of every single action that they take is determined by the principle of pleasure. Utilitarianism must define as delusional anyone who acts from a motive not perfectly consistent, not perfectly public. Curiously, the portrait that emerges from this account is that of an impossibly self-interested creature—so self-interested, in fact, that he would refuse to undertake what psychoanalysis determines as the most primitive gesture of self-interest, the repression of the pleasure principle in the interests of survival.

Against the grain of Bentham's discourse, the discussion has shifted into the key of psychoanalysis, which can be considered historically as an attempt to re-pose, from the opposite point of view—beginning, that is, from the premise of both the fact and the value of pain— the problems encountered by philosophy in dealing with pleasure. The anti-utilitarian, anti-philosophical tendency of psychoanalysis becomes most manifest in the work of Lacan, an anti-Bentham or anti-Hampshire for whom even *jouissance* is, according to his chief disciple, "not pleasure; it is rather closer to unpleasure" in that it "doesn't work for the good of the individual. If it is a good, it is one which goes against any well-being," even approaching the death drive (J.-A. Miller, "Interview" 8, 9). Like Jameson's History, Lacanian discourse is "always profoundly extremist, so to speak, and it hurts" (8).

The source of Lacanian pain is the unconscious, "the radical heteronomy that Freud's discovery shows gaping within man," an Otherness that "can never again be covered over without whatever is used to hide it being profoundly dishonest" ("Agency of the letter" 172). Such phrases seem to open the possibility of "honesty" and an end to "ignorance" and "*méconnaissance*" in a free welcome extended by the subject to the Other—an end to pain. But the Otherness cannot be known, for it gapes "within man" and consequently within understanding itself. The palpable form of the unconscious but imperative Otherness, the "law that has formed [humanity] in its image," is language ("Function and field" 106). Correlatively, the unconscious is the language or "discourse" of the decentering Other, of whom Lacan says, "*It speaks*" ("The Freudian thing" 125). The medium of desire, language is for Lacan so definitive of a human being that he can say that "man's nature is woven by effects in which is to be found the structure of language" ("The signification of the phallus" 284). Thus "man's nature" dictates skepticism as a form of respect for the Other. But skepticism produces its own results and positivities, so that man's nature is continually faced with a virtually irresistible temptation to believe in skepticism as a foundation, imagining, for example, that the statement "I know nothing" represents a positive cognitive achievement. A mode of perpetual advance, skepticism must be commanded to attack its own unguarded rear, ordered to renounce whatever it has gained. Skepticism thus becomes not only a fact, a fundamental feature of human consciousness, but a value, an aspiration, a negative ideal, a "mode of sustaining man in life, which implies a position so difficult, so heroic, that we can no longer imagine it" (*Four Fundamental Concepts* 224). Skepticism is, then, both the necessary condition and proper attitude, the *is* and the *ought,* of a linguistic being, that is, a being with an unconscious, that is, a human being. As Lacan says in a well known pronouncement, "The status of the unconscious . . . is ethical" (*FFC* 33).

It speaks; and speaks, as Lacan adds, "no doubt where it is least expected, where there is pain." The entire argument, the entire model of the mind, the very notions of language and desire and consciousness themselves, are founded on the experience of a pain that is not merely described but encouraged and valued as authentic, true, and productive. Insofar as the goal of psychoanalysis is "the advent of a true speech and the realization by the subject of his history in his relation to a future," the constant object of analysis is, as Lacan warns a therapeutic profession in danger of forgetting this essential fact, the promotion of an ethic based, like every "human formation," on "the restraining of pleasure" (*Ecrits* 88; *Discours de clôture des Journées* 145–46). The attraction for Lacan of Kant lies precisely in what Lacan takes to be Kant's decisive split with the post-Classical ethical posture of "transcendent love," a centering and harmonizing force in place of which Kant proposed what might be called a "Modernist" ethic of decentering and fragmentation, of renunciation precisely of all the goods we can know and value, no matter how worthy they may be. Overriding Kantian comments on, for example, "the sweet sense of having done right," Lacan argues that the Kantian Law anticipates the Freudian unconscious, obligating the subject just because it does not appeal to anything that can be represented as good, or even represented at all. The Kantian Law commands, in Lacan's words, "the sacrifice, strictly speaking, of everything that is the object of love in one's human tenderness—I would say, not only in the rejection of the pathological object, but also in its sacrifice and murder" (*FFC* 275–76). Kant *avec* Sade.

If an ethic of pleasure seems uncritical and even fatuous, an ethic of murder may seem theatrical and flamboyant. Both can be accused of bad faith because of their suppression of the masked others on which they are based. But like Bentham and Hampshire, Lacan displays his own suppressed others in marginal and inconspicuous ways. Lacan may have tried to discredit Kant's autonomous rationality by revealing its similarity to Sade's delirium, but neither is altogether discontinuous with the pleasure principle. As Lacan himself comments, "The ascetic who flagellates himself does it for a third party" (the first two presumably being "the ascetic" and "who") (*FFC* 183). The simple presence of an other—a hearer or reader of one's language, a witness to one's actions, or even (why not?) oneself—can convert the madness of self-flagellation into a complex and self-conscious form of virtue, power, and pleasure.

Nowhere is this more evident than in the case of Lacanian converts who flaunt pain, neglecting in their simplicity and exuberance to re-press the pleasure of the flaunting as carefully as Lacan himself does. When Lacanians speak of "the intolerable truth of our discontent," the very truthfulness of the discontent makes it tolerable: any truth is tolerable, as long as it's true. Gregory S. Jay's discussion of the impact of Lacan on pedagogical practice provides a more extended example. Taking aim at the "subject of certainty" (*sujet supposé savoir*), Jay pro-poses that the facile pleasures of the "conventional" pedagogic model of the passive "consumption" of knowledge should be replaced by a more severe and sober awareness of how truths are "performed" or "produced." When we renounce the "technological, quantitative, ab-solutist or correspondence model of truth," we will, Jay asserts, be pitched into an "ethical" situation in which we will be responsible for what we know. But the discomfiting consequences of seeing knowl-edge under the sign of the *ought* are themselves renounced in the very next sentence, which reclaims the reassuring scientific, or scientistic, *is*: "Here, on the contrary, is a laboratory for discovering the rules by which truths have been produced, the value systems these truths have supported, and the historical consequences of such discourses and in-stitutions." It is no wonder that students rush to the lab with "relief and excitement"; for "here" they can "see" truths without having to believe them, the whole spectacle redounding to the credit of the pro-fessor who knows and generously shares "the rules" ("The Subject of Pedagogy" 798). An undergraduate "rebellion" against authority com-bines with a traditional epistemology to produce a distinctively Ameri-can *jouissance*. Whatever else it may be, however, this argument is not a necessarily degraded or degenerate form of Lacan's rigorous origi-nal; it is, rather, an exceptionally blunt confession of the pleasure and power of Lacanian ascesis, without which no renunciation would be worth the pain, and indeed without which pain would not even be pain. For what the inquiry into pain and pleasure has yielded so far is that if anything is certain and definite, it is that pain and pleasure cannot be certainly and definitely opposed, with the otherness of the other excluded on principle. The Benthamite principle of pleasure mirrors the Lacanian principle of pain in giving way, finally, to some-thing beyond anything principle can account for, to something be-yond principle itself.

2. Psychoanalysis and the Ethic of the Mind

It is a curious thing how philosophical discourse turns psychological when it turns to pleasure, and equally curious how psychoanalytic dis-course on the same subject turns philosophical. No matter how unwilled or automatic this conversion appears, however, it encounters and even produces resistance. In the *Post Card,* Derrida begins his unsurpassable analysis óf the canonical psychoanalytic text on pleasure, Freud's *Beyond the Pleasure Principle,* by citing Freud's antipathy to philosophy, evidenced by his unwillingness to read, or at least to admit that he had read, Nietzsche, whose "guesses and intuitions," Freud said, "often agree in the most astonishing way with the painfully laborious findings of psychoanalysis," and who, consequently, "was for a long time avoided by me on that very account; I was less concerned with the question of priority than with keeping my mind unembarrassed" (*An Autobiographical Study* 60). Among Freud's letters to his friend Wilhelm Fliess are a number of revelations that might have proven embarrassing to the author of this passage, such as the disclosure that the forty-year old Freud was very much concerned with the "priority" of philosophy. "I knew no other longing than that for philosophical insight," he confides to Fliess about his early years, "and I am now in the process of fulfilling it, as I steer from medicine over to psychology" (*Letters* 180). On January 1, 1896, Freud confesses that he now entertains a positive "hope of reaching my original goal, philosophy" (159). Most embarrassing of all might have been the publication of a letter dated February 1, 1900, in which he reveals to Fliess that he has just spent a good deal of money on the collected works of the overmastering Nietzsche, hoping "to find the words for much that remains mute in me" (398). If Freud is "mute" before reading Nietzsche, he is mute about Nietzsche afterwards. As the elderly author of *Beyond the Pleasure Principle,* Freud represses his middle-aged enthusiasm for philosophy as though philosophy were but a child's game whose juvenile pleasures embarrassed the scientific adult, like a naked baby picture.

Freud's accounts of therapeutic procedures confirm the necessity of repression. "The cure," he writes in 1915, "must be carried through in abstinence. . . . one must permit neediness and yearning to remain as forces favoring work and change . . ." ("Observations" 165). For this work, the analyst requires a "coldness of feeling" comparable to that of a surgeon who "pushes aside all his affects and even his humane compassion and posits a single aim for his mental forces—to carry through the operation as correctly and effectively as possible," a posture Lacan describes as "being a saint" (Freud, "Recommendations" 115; Lacan, *Television* 15). Both in his therapeutic and in his scholarly practices, Freud portrays himself as a man of sorrows, a martyr to science, scornful of ease, willing to undergo any renunciation in the service of the truth. Indeed, the fact that a particular position requires renunciation seems to certify its truthfulness. A passage in the sixth chapter of *Beyond* in which Freud chronicles the progress of psychoanalytic science underscores this point. At an early stage in the development of libido theory, Freud says, "Everyone assumed the existence of as many instincts or 'basic instincts' as he chose, and juggled with them. . . . [Psychoanalysis] kept at first to the popular division of instincts." Such a casual and nonrigorous assumption of popular clichés could not be called truly scientific; but "the next step," the step into science, "was taken when psycho-analysis felt its way closer towards the psychological ego." Certain "far-seeing minds" had projected this next step, but they had "failed to explain" the basis of their projections. "Advancing more cautiously, psycho-analysis observed" certain regularities, and "by studying" children, "came to the conclusion" that the ego is the "true and original reservoir of libido" (45). Analysts are now "venturing upon the further step" of characterizing the sex instinct as Eros, but are now "faced by another question" concerning their conclusion that all instincts derive from the libido. "It was not our *intention* to produce such a result" (46), for analysts had been prepared at one point to regard self-preservative instincts as being among the death instincts; "but we subsequently corrected ourselves on this point and withdrew it" (47).

Every one of the "next steps" is depicted as a renunciation, which could be seen not merely as a frequent *effect* of veracity, and not even as a *test,* but nearly as a *guide* to the truth. Hence Freud's embarrassment at the possibility that he may have merely repeated the speculations of warm-blooded philosophers free to think whatever they pleased. It is actually a double embarrassment: Freud would not want to be thought indolent or nonrigorous; but neither would he want simply to confirm through hard labor a truth readily accessible all along. Hence the repression, late in life, of "philosophy," a repression undertaken in all probability in innocence of the fact that this repression itself was eminently "philosophical." Freud's portrayal of himself and his discipline in ascetic terms actually reenacts such portrayals in the history of philosophy, a history whose proudest moments foreground the quest for the truth at all costs, even when the truth is the "direct antithesis" of what one wants. This history is allegorically forshadowed by the reversal of positions in the *Protagoras*, and it is epitomized by Kant's dismissal of the then-current "apocalyptic tone" in philosophy, the rhapsodic style of those who, as Derrida summarizes Kant, "scoff at work, the concept, schooling . . . to what is given they believe they have access effortlessly, gracefully, intuitively or through genius, outside of school" (Derrida, "Of an Apocalyptic Tone" 9). Renouncing not the conclusions of philosophy but rather the ease of its methods, Freud repeats philosophy's own renunciation of pleasure.

Interesting in itself, Freud's ascesis becomes even more striking when seen as the constantly reaffirmed duty of the scientific researcher and author of a book that begins by asserting, with a confidence virtually Benthamite, that "in the theory of psycho-analysis we have no hesitation in assuming that the course taken by mental events is automatically regulated by the pleasure principle" (*BPP* 1). If the theory posits pleasure, a "lowering of tension," as the organism's central and indeed only goal, the scientist (or scientific "organism") keeps raising the tension by directing his attention to repression, "reality," and death. The scientist insists—almost, it would seem, as a matter of principle—on the agonizing labor of his own methods.

Does psychoanalysis itself lie beyond the principle on whose dominance it insists? On what principle does psychoanalysis insist, after all? The most obvious way to approach this question would be to ask what the text says about its subject. But to this simple question Freud has no simple answers. As Derrida comments, "The definition of the pleasure principle is mute [like Freud before and after Nietzsche] about pleasure, about its essence and quality" (PC 276). Pleasure does not simply *remain* elusive throughout Freud's investigation, but rather *becomes* elusive as it is braided in elaborate and subtle ways with its others. Freud is candid about the polemical function of the book in combatting Jungian "monism" ("Our views have from the very first been *dualistic*, . . . Jung's libido theory is on the contrary *monistic*"), but the cost of insisting on a dualistic determination of all mental events while arguing at the same time for the unchallenged reign of pleasure is nothing less than a "paralysis," as Derrida puts it, with respect to the most rudimentary definition of his subject, which becomes not an observable entity but an equation with two unknowns (*BPP* 47).

The nature of pleasure, and the laborious pain of Freud's argument, are best brought out by a skeletal and pedestrian account of the positions taken serially throughout the text. Freud initially proposes that pleasure be imagined as a diminution in the "quantity of excitation" in the organism as opposed to an unpleasurable increase in excitation (2). Unpleasure has two potential sources: the "reality principle," to which the therapist appeals; and repression, with which the therapist contends. But neither of these has anything more serious than a lover's quarrel with the pleasure principle. The reality principle, for example, "does not abandon the intention of ultimately obtaining pleasure, but it nevertheless demands and carries into effect the postponement of satisfaction, the abandonment of a number of possibilities of gaining satisfaction and the temporary toleration of unpleasure as a step on the long indirect road to pleasure" (4). In other words, the reality principle simply slows the pleasure principle down by routing it through elaborate and often puzzling "détours" that, by avoiding the dangers that lie on the major arteries leading to pleasure, actually preserve the organism so that it may continue to pursue pleasure. Derrida notes that the reality principle "imposes no definitive inhibition, no renunciation of pleasure," but acts as the pleasure principle's "delegate, its courier, its lieutenant, or its slave" (282). But while the opposition between pleasure and reality is thereby renounced, an alterity "even more irreducible" is opened up: "Because," as Derrida writes, "the pleasure principle—right from this preliminary moment when Freud grants it an uncontested mastery—enters into a contract only with itself, reckons and speculates only with itself or with its own metastasis, because it sends itself everything it wants, and in sum encounters no opposition, it *unleashes* in itself the *absolute* other" (283). The unpleasure produced by the reality principle, then, does not unseat the pleasure principle, but actually confirms its mastery by erecting an "absolute" otherness within that preempts any other otherness that might lie without. Pleasure is thus distanced from itself, but, and for this reason, is always and forever only itself, encountering no opposition that is not already its own.

The challenge to the dominance of the pleasure principle seemingly represented by repression is similarly coopted. As Freud explains repression here, certain instincts that the ego finds incompatible with its evolution into "more highly composite organizations" are rejected and held back at a lower level of development (4). Left structurally unsatisfied, these banished instincts struggle, once again "by roundabout paths," towards pleasure. To the extent that they succeed, the conscious ego experiences the success as unpleasure. Creating "*perceptual* unpleasure," pleasure that "cannot be felt as such," repression provides a way of explaining pain as a complex instance of the pleasure principle (5).

The consequences of this account of repression extend from the pleasure principle all the way up to the most disciplined and highly organized mental processes. Converting positive terms into their others, repression, as Derrida says, "upsets the logic implicit in all philosophy" (289). The pretense of philosophy, as of science, is that its formulations cast no shadow of implicitness, that the meaning of its terms is exhausted by their surfaces. To suggest that a philosophical discourse "represses" conclusions other than those it announces, as I earlier tried to do with the discourses of Hampshire, Bentham, and Lacan, for example, is to "upset" its logic. And to suggest that ethical discourse consists of the demonstration that terms—for example, pain and pleasure—are repressed, that they can and ought to be liberated through conversion, is to suggest that an entire area of philosophy is dedicated to upsetting the logic of philosophy by promoting a logic of upset. If all these suggestions are true, then philosophy must have a certain stake in repressing "ethics," in keeping it "implicit"; perhaps sensing this "unconscious" of philosophy, Freud insisted that science must repress philosophy in order to maintain its own distinctive logic.

The analysis of repression also prepares for Freud's reluctant reconsideration of the possibility of a pleasure that is itself felt as unpleasure in the form of primary masochism, a possibility called "mysterious" in the second chapter and "positively mystical" in the sixth (8, 48). Indeed, the argument itself becomes mysterious and extraordinarily devious at this point. In the practice of therapy, repression creates the need for analysis; but, while appealing to the more advanced or mature reality principle, analysis, based on the retelling of one's traumas in narrative form, itself marches under the banner of a "more primitive, more elementary, more instinctual" "compulsion to repeat" (whose repetition of Nietzsche's "eternal return" might have been embarrassing to its discoverer) (17). This compulsion is precisely what analysis seeks to overcome, not by elimination but by repetition: analysis repeats the repetition compulsion it seeks to repress. Moreover, analysis seeks to cure repression by reimposing it. The initial and most famous example of the repetition compulsion in this text vividly suggests a principle of marching-in-place. The *"fort-da"* game in which an eighteen-month old child makes a spool disappear and then reappear is described both as a reenactment of repression (or, as Freud says, of "the child's great cultural achievement—the instinctual renunciation (that is, the renunciation of instinctual satisfaction) which he had made in allowing his mother to go away without protesting" [9])—*and* as a game in which the child becomes master of a situation over which in reality he had had no control whatsoever—the disappearance and reappearance of his mother. Staging pain for the purpose of producing pleasure, the child repeats and advances, represses a desire and fulfills it, renounces and gains.

The discussion of the repetition compulsion itself repeats Freud's gesture of proposing an other to the pleasure principle and then describing it in terms that disclose the fact that it is no other at all. The compulsion to repeat, or "primary process," seems a serious candidate for a true otherness because of its great psychic antiquity; it seems to lie beyond the pleasure principle because it rules, or had ruled, before the pleasure principle established itself, "before the purpose of dreams was the fulfillment of wishes"; even "now" it frequently "overrides the pleasure principle" by reproducing, for example, the psychical traumas of childhood (27, 16). The most fundamental force in the mind, then, is in principle unassimilable to the pleasure principle, its "freely mobile" processes harkening back, like repetition itself, to the mind's prehistory, and actively resisting being "bound" by any secondary process (28).

Still, somehow, everything Freud says about the retrograde primary process suggests that it has eyes in the back of its head, for it appears to look forward as well. Does not repetition indicate, produce, and belong to the future as well as to the past? The basic premise of therapy confirms this suspicion, for the reorienting of the subject towards a free futurity depends upon the binding of the traumatic memories generated by the primary process. Even while working against repetition (especially "when at the end of an analysis we try to induce the patient to detach himself completely from his physician" [30]), analysis proceeds and succeeds only through the agency of a repetition which it represents as prior, automatic, unconscious, inferior to itself. Like other "great cultural achievements," analysis repeats in the style of work what is, in other forms, merely child's play, random goings and comings; correlatively, play is an "effortless"—and hence subversively valueless—reworking of the highly valuable task of renunciation.

The convertability of work and play suggests that the rigor of the distinction might be open to question. In fact, a closer look at the primary process posited by analysis reveals that this process is pre- and self-bound; for as Freud, with no apparent sense of incongruity, reminds his reader, repetition produces, especially in children—and especially in games like *fort-da*—"secondary" effects (or effects of secondariness): "repetition, the re-experiencing of something identical, is clearly in itself a source of pleasure" (30). The free working of the unbound primary process thus binds the subject—whose freedom, Freud insists, can only be attained by the secondary binding of the primary process. The untrammeled freedom of the freely mobile compulsion to repeat produces mastery and pleasure, mastery as pleasure, while the binding of this compulsion to the "conservative" goal of pleasure has the effect of freeing the subject. Both primary and secondary processes seem overdetermined and redundant: the putatively autonomous repetition compulsion yearns to advance to its own overcoming, while the questing pleasure principle yearns to return, to descend to its own dissimulation. We can thus speak of a repetition within the repetition compulsion of the pleasure principle, and of a symmetrical repetition within the pleasure principle of the repetition compulsion.

The pleasure principle is decidedly not looking itself, for it has, we notice, somehow become (1) earnest, hardworking, and orderly; (2) nostalgic, constantly reaching back for childhood memories to bind;

and (3) masochistic, seeking out ancient sources of pain. Derrida regards the discussion of repression as the key moment in the undoing of philosophy and logic in *Beyond*; but, for reasons that will emerge only gradually, I believe that a more powerful case in this respect can be made for the repetition compulsion. For the time being, I will simply note that while repression introduces the possibility of pleasure as pain, the primary process suggests not only that possibility but other undoings, other otherings, as well—compulsion as principle, freedom as binding, primary as secondary, past as future. This confusion of terms and times unleashed by the repetition compulsion reaches a strange but inevitable climax when Freud, describing the "attribute" or "urge" of instincts "*to restore an earlier state of things,*" gives this state the momentous name of death (30).

"Analysis" provides, of course, the implied frame of reference, the site at which the primary process, with its sense of "possession by some 'daemonic' power," is courted and converted by the pleasure principle into its other (30). But what of Freud's own analysis? Has it truly attended to the other? What would a faithful representation of the primary process look like, how would it proceed? Two possibilities, two imperatives, emerge. As a work of analysis, a "secondary" work, Freud's text must attempt to bind the primary process to its argument, to enclose it within its grasp. And it does; the argument about the primacy of the pleasure principle, announced in the very first sentence of the text, proceeds more or less undeflected, working through the resistance of the primary process, and beyond as Freud "pursue[s] to its logical conclusion the hypothesis that all instincts tend towards the restoration of an earlier state of things" (37). In this sense, the analysis "represents" the primary process, containing its volatility within the strict and narrow path of discursive rationality, employing it as an obedient illustration of the primacy of the pleasure principle.

But another imperative makes an equal but opposite demand to "represent" the subject in the sense of standing as its representative. This imperative commands that the analysis itself become "unbound" in mimetic emulation of the primary process. Remarkably, Freud appears to have been as scrupulous about the second imperative as he had been about the first. All the undoings of logic tracked above, but especially the gradual revelation of the secondariness of the primary process and the primariness of the secondary process, can be recuperated as forms of obedience to this representational imperative. A discourse dedicated to establishing the "original" otherness of the unbound repetition compulsion to the pleasure principle then proceeds to show how this opposition cannot be maintained, in the process *repeating* its own failure to establish the otherness of other psychic forces (e.g., the reality principle and repression) to the pleasure principle. In its failure, the discourse becomes unbound, raising tension and relinquishing mastery—a stunningly brilliant, multi-leveled representation, in this second sense, of the primary process at work.

The question is not, what is a true representation? but rather, which principle of representation will be followed? Either the analysis can reduce the tension created by the other, insisting on its "own" undisturbed dominance at the expense of denying the primacy of the primary process; or it can seek to exemplify the other, surrendering the primacy of secondariness on which all analysis is based. The truth can and therefore *ought* to be pursued on two divergent paths. The representation of the unbound pitches the discourse into a crisis of representation that awakens a stubbornly problematic question of duty, or rather of duties, each of which complements but disqualifies the other. Like Lacanian "skepticism," the unbound primary process represents an irresistible temptation, a prohibition both maintained and transgressed.

The entire problem of representation merely repeats the initial problem encountered by the analysis of the pleasure principle in the first pages of the text, where the reality principle is offered as a first explanation of pain. There, it was argued that the constant experience of reality as pain does not force a retraction of the hypothesis about the domination of the pleasure principle, because we can imagine the reality principle as what Derrida calls the pleasure principle's "representative, slave, or informed disciple" (282). Thus while the pleasure principle is, as Freud says, "proper to a *primary* method of working on the part of the mental apparatus," it can be seen to employ on occasion a secondary method of representation (4). We are now in a position to ask what principle of representation the reality principle follows. Does it represent pleasure in "reality"—that is, is it some kind of picture of pleasure in the language or colors of "reality?" Or does it represent pleasure "in" reality—that is, is it a form of pleasure, a representative of pleasure in a domain called "reality," as an embassy represents a country in a foreign land? According to one principle, the representation repeats but also represses what it represents; while in the other, the representation *is*—if only by a legal fiction—that which it represents. Which is the primary principle of representation? These questions are of the greatest urgency for a discourse such as Freud's that insists on the analytic truth of its representation as its highest principle. But Freud's answer shimmers with ambivalence, for his analysis, as we have seen, displays both imperatives, and does so even while insisting on its own orderly advance.

We must not get ahead of ourselves. Let us, therefore, return to death, the triumph and defeat of the pleasure principle. If the reality principle is "*its* other," Derrida says of the pleasure principle, the "death drive" is "its *other*" (285). The positing of the death drive constitutes a second wind, a moment of renewal, when the analysis suddenly discovers something that might replace the pleasure principle as the ultimate and unopposable force.

The death drive is the name given to the tendency of all instinctual behavior, which is thereby, strikingly, opposed to the blunt and irrefutable fact of life. But can instinct really be opposed to life? Can death be a "drive" without being alive? With great boldness and delicacy, Freud works through this paradox, arguing that no properly *instinctual* force of "self-preservation, of self-assertion, and of mastery" sustains life in defiance of the deathward drift of the pleasure principle (33). Rather, the "internal" and "backward path" of death is blocked by "external disturbing forces" which maintain a repression of the instinct (32, 33, 30). What we might be tempted to think of as self-preservative instincts are, Freud cautions, really only "component instincts whose function it is to assure that the organism shall follow its own path to death"; the organism does not positively wish to live, but "to die only in its own fashion" (33). The purpose of instinct is, under this formulation, not to live, but to secure private ownership of one's death, to individualize the death drive.

Freud is not content, however, to retain the problematic hypothesis of instincts that contradict the larger instincts of which they are but "components," and he immediately posits another group of instincts, the sexual, which he announces as "the true life instincts" (34). And now, with the great opposition of life (sex) and death, Freud brings all of mental existence into the embrace of a single principle, while accounting for difference and opposition. Although a principle of opposition, and of opposition to the pleasure principle, this new singularity seems remarkably easy to assimilate to the initial hypothesis of an unchallenged pleasure principle, since one side, death, is the ultimate reduction of tension, while the other, sex, constitutes "the greatest pleasure attainable by us" (56). As this mutual investment in the pleasure principle suggests, the two sides are not locked in eternal combat, but work together through "a vacillating rhythm," in which "one group of instincts rushes forward so as to reach the final aim of life as swiftly as possible; but when a particular stage in the advance has been reached, the other group jerks back to a certain point to make a fresh start and so prolong the journey" (35). A rhythm, as Derrida puts it, of "alteration without opposition" (285).

Such vacillation might produce stability, both in the organism and in the argument, as it simply enforces the pleasure principle, on whose dominance the text insists. But it does not. Perhaps sensing that his own argument was about to produce a Jungian monism that would be dissonant with his principles, Freud shifts the terms of this "alteration" in the very next sentence, suggesting that the sex instincts "from the very first" have already embarked upon their work of "opposing the 'ego-instincts'" (35). This new term, which a footnote added in 1925 says is actually a repetition of an old term deriving "from the earliest psycho-analytical terminology," modifies the opposition, perhaps decisively. For while the ego-instincts have been casually substituted as a synonym for the death drive, they might (especially in terms of the earliest psycho-analytic terminology) have been more readily aligned with the resistances to the death drive, with dying-in-one's-own-fashion. Nevertheless, Freud begins the sixth chapter by restating "a sharp distinction" between the "conservative," "retrograde" ego-instincts, which "exercise pressure towards death" through the repetition compulsion, and the sexual instincts, which prolong life and even lend the organism "the appearance of immortality" (38). Thus not only has sex, whose drive towards a lowering of tension has been argued to death both inside and outside psychoanalytic discourse, been opposed to death; but through a kind of synonymic slippage, "ego" has been deployed as the opposite not just of sex, but of self-preservation, self-assertion, and mastery—really, it seems, against the idea of ego itself.

The radical instability of this argument, whose key terms—pleasure principle, fort-da, death instinct, repetition compulsion, repression—have become enshrined for many as the very principles of psychoanalysis itself, cannot be overstated. Nor has Freud finished with his conversions, especially with regard to the ego-instincts, which continue to metamorphose so violently through the sixth chapter that Freud found it necessary to append another clarifying footnote (to the second edition, 1921) in which he tracked the vicissitudes of the term. "It is not so easy," he writes, "to follow the transformations through which the concept of the 'ego-instincts' has passed."

To begin with "we" applied that name to all the instinctual trends

> which could be distinguished from the sexual instincts directed
> towards an object; and we opposed the ego-instincts to the
> sexual instincts of which the libido is the manifestation. Subse-
> quently we came to closer grips with the analysis of the ego and
> recognized that a portion of the 'ego-instincts' is also of a libidi-
> nal character and has taken the subject's own ego as its object.
> These narcissistic self-preservative instincts had thenceforward
> to be counted among the libidinal sexual instincts. The opposi-

127

tion between the ego-instincts and the sexual instincts was
transformed into one between the ego-instincts and the object-
instincts, both of a libidinal nature. But in its place a fresh opposition appeared between the libidinal (ego- and object-) instincts
and others, which must be presumed to be present in the ego
and which may perhaps actually be observed in the destructive
instincts. Our speculations have transformed this opposition
into one between the life instincts (Eros) and the death
instincts. (55)

Of special interest is the turn taken in the middle of this dizzying account, in which the inconspicuous "manifestation" of one of the two
great groups of instincts, the libido, takes over not only the sexual
instinct itself but also the ego-instincts, so that libido usurps the place
initially held by the pleasure principle, as the dominant force regulating mental events. Following the unfurling law of the argument, however—neither one nor two—libido is immediately pitted against its
other, the destructive instincts. And so after a wild career, the argument concludes with the opposition between life and death instincts—the same one, as Freud had already commented, with which
he had "started out" (47). At this point it might be useful to number
the steps of the argument as it ceaselessly transforms, and ceaselessly
repeats itself.

1. Pleasure Principle (PP) is opposed to reality principle (but the reality principle merely defers pleasure).
2. PP is opposed to repression (but repression produces pleasure as
   one of its effects).
3. PP is opposed to the compulsion to repeat (but this compulsion is
   bound by the PP, and is a source of pleasure—indeed, as the
   death drive, it is the instinctual form of the PP.
4. A new monism, the death drive (DD), is opposed to self-preservative instincts (but these are only "component instincts" of DD).
5. DD is opposed to sex instincts, the true life instincts (but both DD
   and sex instincts are implicated in PP, and so cannot be opposed
   to each other).
6. Ego instincts are opposed to sex instincts (but both implicated in
   the libido, and so cannot be opposed to each other).
7. A new monism, the libido, emerges, but is internally divided between ego and object.
8. Libido (ego and object) is opposed to destructive instincts.
9. "Speculation" transforms this opposition into the opposition of
   life and death.

Even the most pedestrian reduction of the text (which concludes with "the words of the poet—'What we cannot reach flying we must reach limping. The Book tells us it is no sin to limp'" [58]) still produces a hold-on-to-your-seat quality of racing, and erasing. Throughout, the key terms are all caught up in a compulsion to rename, a conversional frenzy in which principles split apart into otherness, become their own others, are swallowed whole by their others. And yet the argument goes nowhere, nothing is accomplished or changed, its end is its beginning. Derrida describes the text as "a-thetic" to indicate the "non-positional" or nonprogressive nature of a discourse that, even as it insists it is constantly taking the "next step" towards the "beyond," keeps returning to the place from which it has started out, replicating the "vacillating rhythm," the fort-da, of the behavior it represents.

What could be responsible for such flagrant analytic irresponsibility? What could turn principles against themselves? Could it be anything other than pleasure itself, which has neither essence nor an absolute beyond, so that there is neither pure pleasure nor anything but pleasure? The very term "pleasure principle" is in conflict, for, as Derrida points out, principle itself "makes war on pleasure" (399), a never-ending war of aggression, appeasement, resistance, collaboration, and double agency, a war of all against, and with, all. Is pleasure, the negation of responsibility, then responsible?

Or is it something other than, or beyond pleasure? Derrida sees in the athesis of *Beyond the Pleasure Principle* an uncanny anticipation of the fort-da of the psychoanalytic "movement" itself, which "maintains a relation to its history like none other," every new discovery or statement grounded in a "return to Freud" (303–4). But if the history of psychoanalysis is inscribed in advance in this text, it is inscribed as the other of a far different discourse, which it systematically represses and seeks to put behind it. One of the covert pleasures Freud may have experienced in writing *Beyond the Pleasure Principle* was the polemical displacement of what he regarded as the wishful pieties of ethical philosophy by the "scientific" bio-psychoanalytic analysis of "mental events." For it is finally ethics, not Jungian monism, that Freud attacks in this text, and ethics that psychoanalysis seeks to drain dry, like the draining of the Zuyder Zee to which Freud notoriously compared the takeover of id by ego. Where *ought* and duty were—Freud's work as a whole insists—there shall *is* and pleasure be.

But it is in precisely this respect that Freud's text is most non-progressive, its conversions least final and decisive. For the pleasure principle itself is announced at the very beginning as a law, a constantly challenged—indeed, apparently constantly transgressed—but never overthrown law of the mind, a law that "act[s] so imperatively upon us" (1). Nor is this law a counter-law, an unlawful law. It is the one and only law itself, the law of the inalienable other. The manifold generation by apparently monistic terms of their others repeats the process Kant described as the commanding emergence within a free and fallible subject of the categorical imperative. Moreover, one of the most important of *Beyond*'s predecessors in terms of the compulsive and yet willed imbrication of pain and pleasure is Kant's *Critique of Judgment*, where the sublime—nonobjectified, limitless and yet totalizing, resistant to representation, attractive and repellent—is conceived (with the speculative ease of the philosopher) as a "negative pleasure," a pleasure "only possible through the medium of pain" (99, §27). The pleasure principle is to Freud what the categorical imperative, and the sublime, are to Kant.

Thus it is the active repression of Kant and ethics that organizes this disheveled text, nowhere more visibly than at the end of the fifth chapter—the same one that had announced the repetition compulsion, the death drive, and the sex instincts—when Freud repudiates all objections to his theory that instincts invariably lead down and back. Painful though it may be to abandon the belief in an "instinct towards perfection" that has brought mankind to its "present high level of intellectual achievement and ethical sublimation," the renunciation is imperative. "I have," Freud writes in the dogmatic tone that he unleashes throughout this scientific text, "no faith . . . in the existence of any such internal instinct and I cannot see how this benevolent illusion is to be preserved" (36). No; the benevolent illusion of the instinctual drive towards pain must be renounced in favor of the painful truth of pleasure. The clustering oxymorons signal the proximity of repression, as Freud's account of the apparent instinct towards perfection confirms. The instincts repressed during the development of the ego strive, Freud says, for satisfaction through "the repetition of some primary experience of satisfaction"; but, finding the path blocked by "the resistances which maintain the repressions," advance "in the direction in which growth is still free." This is no more than a simple description of the behavior of all repressed instincts—that is, of all instincts—but Freud treats it as if it were an account of a rare and aberrant case, in which certain "economic" factors produce an ethical "impulsion" that manages to pass for an instinct (36). Freud argues that this impulsion "cannot possibly be attributed to *every* human being," even while he concedes that "the *dynamic* conditions for its development are, indeed, universally present" (36). But why can't it be attributed to every human being? Everybody represses, all repressed instincts struggle for satisfaction, all such struggles meet resistance, and advance always occurs in whatever direction is left open.

It should not be surprising that the only direction left is the ethical, given the fact that repression initially and in fact always serves, however indirectly, the cause of cultural advancement. Freud tries to marginalize ethical consciousness by caricaturing it as an extremist "instinct towards perfection"—that is, not an instinct at all but just one of the more exotic fruits haphazardly produced by the pleasure principle. But this marginalization is manifestly a "benevolent illusion" of science, based, like all such illusions, on repression, in this case the repression of repression itself. Freud's own description of the fort-da hesitates revealingly between the case he is trying to make and the one he represses when he describes "the child's great cultural achievement—the instinctual renunciation (that is, the renunciation of instinctual satisfaction)" (9). What Freud cannot quite keep himself from saying, even while he realizes the awkwardness of his remark, is that renunciation itself is instinctual. Just as pleasure is an "irresistible temptation" for the ascetic analyst, and just as the primary process is an "irresistible temptation" for the secondary process, so, too, is ethics—for Freud as for Wittgenstein—an "irresistible temptation," a prohibited or repressed impulse that has already been "instinctively" assented to.

What Freud's argument really suggests, then, is that advancement towards the higher is not a rare mutation of instinct, nor even *an* instinct; but rather that it is the fate and unfailing destination of instinct itself. In *Totem and Taboo*, Freud makes the scandalous argument that ethics derives from the nonethical in the form of murder and incest and that the categorical imperative can be identified with taboo; here, Freud scandalizes himself by suggesting, apparently against his inclinations, that ethics derives from the nonethical in the form of instinct (see Borsch-Jacobsen). Following Freud's method in "On Negation," we should read *Beyond the Pleasure Principle* and think, not "So, it *was* your mother," but "So, it *is* ethics." For what is being repressed in Freud's insistence on the extraordinary character of ethics is the fact that the most fundamental imperative of mental development—that we repress in order to advance—is both a scientific fact and a moral value, an automatic function of the mind that "the organism" puts to "higher" uses in the generation of "all that is most precious in human civilization" (36). At one point in *Beyond*, Freud pauses to note that the unconscious, as a zone of timelessness, contradicted Kant's theorem that time and space were "necessary forms of thought." If the unconscious refutes the first *Critique*, however, it confirms and even radicalizes the second.

What is "most precious" to Freud is here called "science," in whose name some falsely reassuring and regressive thing called "philosophy" and in particular "ethics" must be repressed. But if ethics is a repetition and management of repression, then the distinction between science and ethics becomes as fragile and relational as that between pleasure and pain. *Beyond the Pleasure Principle* provides compelling evidence as to how fragile this distinction is. For this evidence, let us return for a moment to the pathetic spectacle of the repressed instinct striving for satisfaction through the repetition of some primary experience. Finding the path to an ideal repetition blocked (repetition is always resisted, never ideal), the repressed (and therefore law-abiding) instinct becomes what in a sense it already is, an ambivalent agent of advance, pursuing the path of pain. Two laws, or actually one complex law of advance-and-return, are pursued simultaneously, the law of repetition-pastness-pleasure, and the law of renunciation-futurity-pain. The same *fort-da*, the instinctual renunciation of instinct, operates all the way up to the highest levels of metalanguage. "Science" is what Freud calls the endlessly repeated renunciations that comprise and compromise an argument that limps along, prepared on principle to "abandon a path that we have followed for a time, if it seems to be leading to no good end" (58). In "science," instinct not only seeks but finds both repetition and renunciation through, for example, such advanced and painfully humbling speculations as the hypothesis that the "primary process," the oldest, most elemental process in the mind, is a drive for the "perpetual recurrence of the same thing" (16). On its own description, Freudian science dissolves into its others: as a series of repetitions undertaken in the name of a constantly reaffirmed pleasure, the analysis testifies to the awesome reach and power of instinct; but as a series of painful renunciations that "will permit of no halting at any position attained, but, in the poet's words, '*ungebändigt immer vorwärts dringt*'" (presses ever forward unsubdued) (36), it also demonstrates character, fortitude, virtue, the impulsion to perfection. The entire paradox is crushed into the pun of *ungebändigt*, which means both "unsubdued" and "unbound." The analysis presses forward unsubdued, pursuing its obligations, its cultural duties; but, in repeating itself, remains unbound, unmastered. The argument Freud makes in *Beyond* depends on the possibility of a "beyond," a space unimplicated in otherness; but the argument Freud enacts, the argument *performed*, rejects precisely that possibility.

Several recent readings of Freud have disclosed the same remarkable feature, that the texts are themselves structured by the very mechanisms they purport to analyze (see Weber, *Legend of Freud*; Mehlman; and Chase, "Oedipal Textuality"). Typically, this revelation has been deployed in an attack on "foundationalist" thought, a category that would presumably include ethics as well as psychoanalysis. Whatever their intentions, or pretensions, such attacks often reinstate a foundation in negative terms (So, it *is* a foundation). In *Beyond*, however, instinct and metalanguage not only work each other reciprocally, but are both revealed to be subject to repression, a subjection that produces in each features of primariness and secondariness, regression and advance. Repression marks instinct as scientific and science as instinctual. Ethics—the name for this repression, and the mediating factor between science and instinct, being (for Freud) lower than one but higher than the other—is inescapable, but neither properly foundational nor antifoundational.

Pressing forward on the same path, going beyond *Beyond*, Freud discovered, a few years later, the site of ethics within the mind, "a special agency in the ego" formed during the resolution of the Oedipal crisis. This is the superego, an unconscious within the ego that behaves as though it were repressed, ever seeking impossible satisfactions. It is to the superego, the representative in the mind of the ethical standards of mankind, that a perhaps guilty Freud refers in rebutting charges that psychoanalysis has "ignored the higher, moral, supra-personal side of human nature" (*The Ego and the Id* 25). But like the earlier attempt to discover a "beyond" to the pleasure principle, the "second topography" of superego, ego, and id reaffirms that principle once again in its irreducibly ambivalent form: nothing but pleasure, and no pure pleasure. For the superego, as Freud points out, dictates both pleasurable repetition ("You *ought to be* like [your father]") and painful renunciation ("You *may not be* like [your father] . . . that is, you may not do all that he does; some things are his prerogative") (24). Itself vacillating, the higher, moral, supra-personal side engages in a vacillating rhythm with a lower, sub-personal side. This also vacillates; for the id not only is the reservoir of a rebellious and endlessly fecund desire, but also provides the raw material for the ego ("a specially differentiated part of the id") and the superego (formed by the ego "out of the id" [28]). Thus while the pleasure principle "reigns unrestrictedly in the id" (15), this does not mean either that the id is the home of a pure pleasure or that ethics is pleasure-free.

The relation between pleasure and its other warrants one final comment. In one of the quieter moments in *The Ego and the Id*, Freud asserts that the ego differentiates and comes to understand itself first and perhaps always through the experience of pain (15–16). This pain must be produced by the repression made necessary by the tendency of the organism constantly to seek pleasure. Self-understanding, therefore, and with it all that constitutes human consciousness, can be grasped as an effect of the violent negotiations between forces of pleasure and pain, neither of which can claim priority, neither of which can claim to be more, or less, instinctual than the other.

Perhaps the best way to understand the pleasure/pain relation is to imagine each as the other's repressed unconscious. We could then speculate that repression itself has the status of the fundamental law of human consciousness that Freud attributed to pleasure at the beginning of *Beyond*. Considered as the law of human consciousness, a law operative at every level from the instinctual to the philosophical and even to the scientific, repression indicates a certain feature of all positive terms, especially binary distinctions, that describe "mental events" (paradigmatically, pleasure and pain; but also dynamic and economic, conscious and unconscious, ego and id): that they contain and indeed are determined by (that is, they do *not* "contain") their own others. If, as Derrida says, repression "upsets" the logic of philosophy, it also sets up that logic, including the logic of psychoanalytic "philosophy" insofar as that logic is structured by, and attracted to, repression. The revolting tangle of terms and concepts in *Beyond*, almost horribly alive and mutating on the page, dramatizes this terminal and terminological repression. Most significantly, if we see these terms as themselves repressed, we can then begin to account for the necessity of, and endless possibility for, descriptions and prescriptions of conversion in ethical as well as therapeutic discourse. For conversion would become the center of what we might call the mind's ethic, whose duty is the liberation of the repressed in a given term, a given discourse. Conversion would be both what the mind does and what it ought to do.

Applied to this ethic of the mind, we could call the conversional process *analysis*, stipulating as its central act *repetition:* attending to the other, analysis repeats it, converting it from what it was to what it really is and ought to be. With this view of analysis in mind, we can rethink repetition and repression themselves. As we have seen, the instinctual character of repetition explains the fact that children derive pleasure from all repetition while adults, for whom, as Freud says, "Novelty is always the condition for enjoyment" (*BPP* 29), experience nausea or boredom. Repetition, we could now speculate, confronts adults with their own repressions, making them experience repression's characteristic *perceptual* unpleasure accompanied by unconscious pleasure; while children, whose repression has not been so thorough, experience a perceptual pleasure in the achieved gratification of the primary process, and a lesser degree of unpleasure depending on how far along on the path of pain they have advanced. But repetition is not only the object of repression. In the act of analysis, a game especially enjoyed by repressed adults, it is also the means of repression. Analysis is a willed form of that which resists willing, the compulsion to repeat. Analysis is therefore the repressed version of the repetition compulsion—even the primary process of adult repression itself. For what analytic repression primarily represses is the compulsive or instinctual character of its own operations, the fact that even as it enforces the law, even as it inflicts pain, even as it drives towards the realization of higher laws and imperatives, repression still gratifies the most primitive and rudimentary urge of all. Analytical repetition represses, as it repeats, an instinctual repetition.

This primary form of repetition is, we should recall, self-repressed, consisting only of a distilled secondariness, an urge to repeat independent of any aboriginal thing to repeat. Internally crossed by repression, repetition is not only different from itself, but engenders differences in both the analyst and in the object of analysis. Here Freud's discussion of "the organism's" repetition compulsion is instructive. Analysis presumes and produces an object—call it a "text"—that is opaque and mute, a self-contained but unself-conscious "organism" (hence, perhaps, the "organic" ideal of aesthetic form) that requires the conversional powers of analysis to become meaningful, engaged with reality, more fully itself than it could be by itself. This is in fact, as Stanley Fish has argued, the very definition of the analysand (see *Doing What Comes Naturally* 525–54). At the same time, analysis converts the analyst, for it is only through acts of analysis that an organism becomes something more than an organism. Predicated on repetition, the power of analysis is yet power itself, the mark of acculturation, maturity, mastery. Thus, while the pleasure principle extends all the way down, the primary process reaches all the way up: repetition *is* unconsciousness, it *brings* consciousness out of unconsciousness, and it *is* consciousness.

Perhaps the process can only be understood metaphorically. One such metaphor occurs in *The Merchant of Venice*, when Bassanio seeks to persuade his friend Antonio to lend him some more money to replace that which he has squandered:

In my school days, when I had lost one shaft
I shot his fellow of the self-same flight
The self-same way, with more advised watch,
To find the other forth; and by adventuring both
I oft found both. (1.1.139–44)

Only conscious repetition, a "fellow of the self-same flight" as the primary process, could retrieve that process from the oblivion of unconsciousness and compulsion, or bait the hook of analysis. It is, remarkably, this same psychologically negligible Bassanio whose choice of the lead casket in the guessing-game seemed to Freud so intensely evocative of the subject's adaptation to psychic imperatives. In one of the essays that precipitated *Beyond*, "The Theme of the Three Caskets," Freud argued that in selecting "hazard" over "desert" or "desire," Bassanio had won the prize by the paradoxical gesture of choosing necessity. Neither shrewd nor virtuous, Bassanio yet has an instinct for the essence of analysis and ethics both, the free choice of that which cannot be chosen, the mastery of that which undermines all mastery.

As already noted, an advance-through-repetition marks the psychoanalytic "movement" itself, a representative example of which is Lacan's reading, or conversion, of the passage already referred to that concludes the thirty-first of Freud's *New Introductory Lectures*: "*Wo Es war, soll Ich werden*" (where id was, there shall ego be). To this enigmatic sentence Lacan devotes his most profound commentary:

> —the true meaning would seem to be the following: *Wo* (Where)
> *Es* (the subject—devoid of any *das* or other objectivating article)
> *war* (was—it is a locus of being that is referred to here, and that
> in this locus) *soll* (must—that is, a duty in the moral sense, as is
> confirmed by the single sentence that follows and brings the chapter to a close) *Ich* (I, there must I—just as one declared, 'this am
> I', before saying, 'it is I'), *werden* (become—that is to say, not occur (*survenir*), or even happen (*advenir*), but emerge (*venir au jour*) from this very locus in so far as it is a locus of being). ("The Freudian thing" 128)

What the English translation of Freud represents as a nearly technological and ethically neutral task ("like the draining of the Zuyder Zee"), Lacan describes as a duty, disclosing the ethic that the translation, and even the original, repress: "it is my duty that I should come to being" (129). We are bound not by prudence, nor by human nature, nor by interest, nor by the pleasure principle, but rather by an imperative ethical duty, a duty we might refuse, to *werden, venir au jour,* emerge. Everything hinges on *soll*, whose English form *shall* is capable of implying a wishfulness not quite factual ("I shall not betray my supporters") and a factuality not quite wishful ("I shall arrive at noon"). It is precisely this intricate compromise negotiated by "shall" that enables Lacan to read Freud as an all but ethical thinker who discovered the source of duty but resisted describing it explicitly as a duty. Following the hard code of the scientist, Freud renounced the pleasure of a triumphant repetition of the categorical imperative in favor of instinctual renunciation—that is, the renunciation of instinct—in the formation of an *Ich*; following the hard code of the reader, Lacan renounces the pleasure of a repetition of the obvious or self-evident meaning in favor of a converted meaning, one in which Freud's repressed morality is liberated.

No emancipation without violence. Lyotard even depicts the reader as "the persecutor of the work," holding the text "hostage" insofar as "one thinks one knows" what it means, insofar as one succumbs to "the temptation of knowledge" (*Differend* 14). What is most interesting is not, however, the fact of the violence itself, but the regularity of its displacements, whose principle is formalized in Freud: where x was, there shall y be. Lacan's persecution occurs under this formula, which it specifies as: where text was, there shall meaning be. But the formula determines every stratum of the textual deposit. Freud's depiction of the belief in an ethical instinct as a "benevolent illusion," for example, implies that such a belief is merely a repression of the cold truth, one that had proceeded on the principle of "Where fact was, there shall value be." Exposing such illusions as the self-concealing work of the pleasure principle, *Beyond* is structured on the formula of "Where value was, there shall fact be"—or even "Where philosophy and ethics were, there shall psychoanalysis and pleasure be." Lacan's reading of Freud can only repeat the charge of repression, turning it against Freud's "factual" text itself, which he accuses of being, in fact, a discourse of value. Lacan presumes, that is, that Freud's values had led him to repress ethics, or "duty," in the name of science. According to Lacan, then, Freud's text imposes on the reader a duty to bring out the values that had secretly determined it despite its apparent facticity; and so Lacan proceeds on the principle of "Where fact was, there shall value be." Lacan writes his own text in order to convert a text of value (the text produced by Freud's repression) into a text of fact, one that discloses what the original text, its repressions lifted, actually says: "Where value was, there shall fact be." The duty that Lacan articulates is not, it must be noted, advanced as his own, but as Freud's, simply delivered by a faithful reader. This pretense of deferential repetition cannot, however, quite eclipse the act of persecution, the patricidal urge whose principle is "Where Freud was, there shall Lacan be"—an urge anticipated, we now realize, in a submerged implication of *Beyond:* "Where Kant was, there shall Freud be." The pleasurable play of principles extends, of course, to the present discussion, whose law is "Where instinct was, there shall ethics be."

The Work of the Analyst

1. Freud's account of the effects of the prescientific belief in an "instinct towards higher development":
   Where fact (the reality of sex and death as the only instincts) was, there shall value be.
2. Freud's conversion of this belief:
   Where value (illusions, wishes) was, there shall fact be.

3. Lacan's account of Freud:
   Where fact (Freud's aspiration to scientific objectivity) was, there shall value (his actual articulation of a moral duty) be.
4. Lacan's conversion of Freud:
   Where value (Freud's repression of his own truth) was, there shall fact (the morality Freud actually espoused) be.

3. The Ethics of Analysis

The formula "where *x* was, there shall *y* be" has a long stretch. It can be imagined, for example, as the law, the primary process, of language: where *x* was, there shall language be. Seen under this minimal but comprehensive formula, language exhibits virtually all the behavior Freud attributed to the mind in *Beyond,* including the reality principle (the assimilation of the referent into the system in which the real is determined); repetition (the referent re-presented); repression (the referent suppressed in the dominance of the word); the death instinct (the life of the referent culminating in the inert code); Eros (the joining together of referent and word in a whole that exceeds them); and in particular the pleasure principle, which in the ubiquitous climate of repression must be modified to read: pleasure here (in the mastery and binding of *x*) and pain there (in the loss of *x*'s free mobility, its "instinctual" unconsciousness).

The formula also suggests a temporal succession of moments that might be compared to the Marxian analysis of the sequence of modes of production. Indeed, the Marxian concept adds an element necessary to make both the Freudian analysis and language coherent, the element of a retained trace of internal difference. As Jameson explains it, successive modes of production do not simply annihilate the modes they replace, but exist in a relation of relative and temporary dominance, with the superseded mode retained in a complex whole. Each mode of production therefore "structurally *implies* all the others" so that "the contemplation of any given mode of production . . . must always implicitly or explicitly involve a differential relationship to all the others." Such a structural analysis does not negate the idea of history, but suggests a way of looking at history, "since each 'more advanced' mode of production includes the earlier ones, which it has had to suppress in its own emergence." Differentiated spatially as well as temporally, the earlier modes or moments persist in the later in a "layered, 'canceled' fashion," while "the future modes of production are also at work in the present" ("Marxism and Historicism" 174). In every x, a y gestates; in every y, an x is buried, so that every conversion of an x to a y is in a sense both redundant and self-inhibited, because not only is the new term already, if invisibly, present in the old; but the old term, even when "canceled," remains.

The point of this demonstration is not to reconcile Marx to Freud, but rather to suggest that the principle of conversion that Freud describes as the obligation of psychoanalysis, especially in its therapeutic function, is not limited to psychoanalysis, but applies beyond, in other scenes or contexts as well. The conversional formula, especially in the revised form just proposed, has, as I have already suggested, a particular application to the act of "analysis," as exemplified in the "secondary" text that represents, discusses, and interprets another or "primary" text. In what follows, I will be examining the protocols and procedures through which the analytical text pursues the reality principle. To consider analysis as a predictable process or "formula" of conversion is a risky business, placing in jeopardy the utility—the mastery, pleasure, and truth—of analysis. But the integrity of analysis depends upon its principled indifference to mere utility, even its own; so analysis should have no objection if we pursue the truth at all costs. The initial hypothesis will be that this truth can be profitably articulated in Freudian terms. In trying to order the extravagant scene of analysis, I will be putting to work the very concepts that I have just tried to show in such disarray in Freud's text. I will, in other words, be presuming and implicitly arguing for a latent, repressed orderliness within *Beyond* that illuminates the order of analysis. Admittedly, the essential principle of this order is in an obvious sense also a principle of disorder, a conversional imperative whose dominance within the scene of analysis is so utter and uncompromising that it leaves nothing untouched, nothing simply itself.

According to what could, as a way of stressing a certain monasticism in the history of the practice, be called the "rule of analysis," all texts are repetitions. But within the category of repetition, there are differences. The analytical or "secondary" text, e.g., Lacan's rewriting of Freud's "Where id was, there shall ego be," exists in a particular differential relation to some other text that not only predates it but also remains within it in, as it were, fossil form. T. S. Eliot identifies as the most elementary fact about the work of criticism that it is "*about* something other than itself," as opposed to the "autotelic" primary or "artistic" text that is only about itself ("The Function of Criticism" 19). The secondary text constructs itself as the futurity of the thing it is about, the agent in a kind of time travel, bringing the thing forward from the past into the present by a process of repetition that the thing could not accomplish for itself, being bound to an original context, unable to repeat itself. Although Freud describes repetition as the "primary process," repetition is also the only way in which the secondary process can bind the primary process, so that the very secondariness of the secondary is implicated in the primariness of the primary. In his analysis of the "Rat-Man," Freud noted that when certain obsessional patients think about sex, as they often do, "The thought process itself becomes sexualized . . . the sexual pleasure which is normally attached to the content of thought becomes shifted on to the act of thinking itself" ("Notes upon a Case" 99). Insofar as it is secondary, the secondary text is similarly "obsessive," and conditioned by what it repeats. This conditioning holds for "secondary" processes generally. Lyotard comments that "even a discourse which tries to be as sober as possible, which does all it can to emancipate itself from the theatricality . . . of desire may still be haunted, albeit in a different way, by the 'figure'" ("Figure Foreclosed" 70). This "haunting" is, however, reciprocal. When thought becomes sexualized, sex becomes "cognitive." And when the secondary text brings the primary text into a new context, the "freely mobile" energies of the primary text become bound in a way that emphasizes those of its elements most germane to that context. This binding is the cost and condition of the primary text's continued vitality, the only way of realizing, making explicit, or liberating a certain potentiality that is present but hopelessly locked within the primary text.

This last point is most important because it suggests that the relation of secondary to primary is determined not only by the idea of repetition but also by the concept of repression. The necessary premise of, for example, Lacan's analysis is that Freud's sentence contains, beneath an apparent significance that overlays and obscures it, a true significance that can be detected, elicited, and liberated only by analytical work. The "appearance" that obscures the true significance is produced by what is called "form," those inferred signs of organization or structure that mark authorial intention and agency. Analysis presumes a disjunction, produced by the repression exerted by the will of the author, between form and significance; for if the primary text were not a product of repression, no analysis would be necessary or even possible. A mathematical or scientific text, or any text whose meaning is held to be plain or whose truth to be self-evident, any text whose "form" reveals no sign that it is determined not by the facts but by a human author, cannot be analyzed. If in a certain context such a text were to become analyzable, its value or status as a mimesis of the facts, even its very genre, would change.

The history of science provides countless examples—indeed, it is virtually composed of such examples—of the conversion of a discourse of established truth to a discourse consisting of a systematized displacement, a repression, of certain prejudices or beliefs. Given the passage of time and the advance of scientific knowledge, a discourse that had been held to be a neutral mimesis of truth can always be shown to have a certain form—that is, to have been composed in a certain style, according to certain conventions, reflecting certain wishes, anxieties, denials. One of the most dramatic and telling of such historical conversions involves Freud's discourse, which Freud himself might have called "speculative biology" but which has in recent years been subjected to a kind of reading that operates according to more "literary" or "philosophical" principles. Derrida's reading of Freud in *The Post Card* demonstrates how such a conversion could occur, for Derrida introduces factors that, while not explicit in Freud's text, can hardly be said to be external to it, such as the fact that Freud was the grandfather of Ernst, whose fort-da game he observed; that he was also the father of Ernst's mother Sophie, who died while *Beyond* was being written; that Freud's own terminal illness was well advanced when he "discovered" the death drive; that Freud was passionately concerned to establish his patriarchy both within his family and within the "family" of psychoanalysis. Derrida's reading converts Freudian science, which had taken the form of a secondary discourse in relation to a host of primary discourses—some published, some observed, some internal to the author—into a primary discourse, determined by an elaborate assemblage of urgencies, drives, and pressures, a document above all of repression.

The primary text, then, is represented by the secondary text as the product of a mass of factors connected to a particular author—interests, compulsions, urges, needs, desires, character, situation in various contexts—that might collectively be called "evaluations." Only such "contextual" evaluations could have produced the repression that necessitates and enables analysis. A nonevaluative text would not address an "original context" at all, but would simply stand out of time, like $2 + 2 = 4$. But if the primary text is held to be determined by evaluations, then repression becomes a positive factor, providing the incentive and the material for analysis, the very seed of a secondary act that uproots the text from its embeddedness in the past, repeats it in a changed context that exceeds the active repressive gestures or intentions of the author, unlocks the potential for other meanings than the dominant, apparent, manifest, or accepted one, adapts the text to an infinite future, and thereby effectively *un*binds the repression. The very repression of the primary thus enables its eventual liberation by the secondary.

The relation between analysis and its object can be constructed on the basis of distinctions proper to psychoanalysis, such as primary and secondary, repression and freedom, but also on the basis of distinctions proper to ethics, such as *is* and *ought*, value and fact. When W. K. Wimsatt warns, in "Battering the Object," against the dire consequences of blurring the distinction between text and commentary, or when Jonathan Culler concludes *Structuralist Poetics* with the statement that the "ethics" of structuralism consists of reading codes so as not to be written by them, we can sense the concern of "analysis" itself for preserving principled differences and hierarchies in the name not just of clarity but of virtue. The act of analysis imposes quite specific rigors and duties, and while these may be described in psychoanalytic terms, their ultimate force and point is ethical.

The task of the analyst is to overcome the resistance of a coded, indirect, metaphorical, fragmentary, or occluded utterance, and to produce a version that is represented as being in certain respects truer than the original while remaining true *to* the original. These resistances can be described as "what the text seems to say" as opposed to "what the author intended," as "what the author thought she was saying" as opposed to "what the author in fact said," or as "what the text has been thought to say" as opposed to "the true meaning of the text." But however the difference is constructed, the founding "discovery" of analysis is that of a space between what is and what ought to be.

These differences, like others, are the site of power. However ethically reputable it might appear, the production of the *ought* out of the *is* entails the imposition of a repressive force that, regardless of gestures of respect or humility on the part of the analyst, drives the primary text down into a position of secondary dependence: the truth of the primary can only be delivered by a secondary text that represses the "evaluations" that constituted the primary text. But secondary repression, or re-repression—re-binding or re-mastering—is not just a matter of beating a dead horse, for, it must be repeated, it is essential to a conversional process that actually works to liberate the repressed potential of the primary text.

What of the author of the secondary text? What laws of conversion determine the analyst? If the first requirement of the secondary text is that it represent the primary text, then the analyst must undergo an act of repression in which his self-sufficiency, his autonomy, are humbled and subjected to the imperative of the text. The analyst must be seen to become dependent upon the primary text, foregoing the ease of an infinite self-repetition in favor of the hard task of repression. He must, that is, give the convincing appearance of one who has surrendered the pleasure of unconscious repetition of the same so as to undertake the pain of conscious repetition of the other. This conversion must take the form of a rejection of evaluations—prejudices, beliefs, unresisted statements of all kinds—and a submission to fact, to what the primary text actually says and therefore compels him to say. All analysts submit to fact, but the most exaggerated example in the recent past must be the work of de Man, whose spectacular displays of a pitiless and "rigorous" indifference to any form of desire produced in his analyses an impression of truth which overpowered the improbability of some of the forced and peculiar readings that have been detailed recently by Neil Hertz, Rodolphe Gasché, and others. The presumption of such "rigor" is that a properly epistemological moment precedes, or ought to precede, any intervention of value, including even the values of "ethics."

The primary text does not compel every analyst to say the same things. If it did, there would be definitive readings that really would stand for all time. Rather, it requires analysts to surrender only that which they have; it thus elicits from each analyst different representations that can still claim to be compelled by the text. But without a critical difference, or distance, between what an analyst might have wanted to say and what the text compelled him to say, there would be no primary/secondary distinction, and no analysis at all.

Compulsion, then, marks the secondary as secondary in relation to a primary text that was "free" to organize, to hierarchize, to dominate, to repress just as it wanted to, as in the "free association" Freud encouraged in his analysands. To see Lacan painstakingly working his way through the words of Freud's sentence is to see a laborer bound to the wheel, employing all his strength not to sprint, unburdened, at full speed, but slowly to grind up the primary text so that it may serve the useful purpose for which—the very existence of the secondary text suggests—it has always been destined but has been unable to achieve by itself. When an analytical text does not display this image of forced labor, then it detaches itself from its occasion, flees from its master, and becomes either a defective secondary text or a "primary" text itself.

In all these respects, the secondary text is a theater of pain. But by the iron law of the pleasure principle, all pain is compensated for by pleasure elsewhere, and the secondary text—again only insofar as it is secondary—also provides a scene of pleasure in the binding and mastery of the primary text. Whatever it says about the primary text, and whatever else it suggests about the analyst, the secondary text displays, like a procession of flagellants, a spectacle at once of pain and pleasure, humiliation and triumph.

The situation sketched so far compels yet another visualization— the simplified, yet accurate, representation of the four strata of the secondary text.

The Image of the Primary Text within the Secondary Text
a. What it appears or has been thought to be; the evaluations that structure the repression of the author or of other readers.
b. What it ought to be; the facts, liberated from repression.

The Image of the Author of the Secondary Text
c. What s/he might want to say; values, prejudices, interests, circumstances.
d. What s/he must say; what the primary text compels one to say.

Each pair, a/b and c/d, represents a conversion; and each, therefore, forms a primary-secondary relation within itself. The idea of a conversion to the reduced tension of "pleasure" dominates the a/b relation, while a conversion to the heightened tension of "pain" dominates in c/d. The ethics of analysis thus comprehends both "Aristotelian" and "Kantian" possibilities, which may now be seen as extrapolations from a complex display in the analytical text of the synthetic image of *a person reading one text and writing another.*

Meyer Abrams has argued forcefully against what he calls the "confrontation model" of criticism, according to which the solitary critic observes a text as one observes a painting (*Doing Things with Texts* 78ff.). The idea of a "transaction" between the critic and the language of the text, which is drawn from the general reservoir of language, seems to Abrams more indicative of the collective and dynamic character of all linguistic understanding. The unpacking of the multiple conversions on display in the analytical or secondary text reinforces Abrams's suggestion. To write, and even to read, an analytical text is not just to confront, but also to perform, a complex system of "transactions." In fact, the analytical text simply cannot be observed as if it were a flat, bounded surface, for its surface consists, at a minimum, of a lamination of four distinct yet interpenetrating strata.

To comprehend one is to confront them all. If we wish to isolate one of these dimensions, we must look through a composite image of the other three, even though those other three can themselves only be inferred from the same process.

If we want, for example, to isolate (c), an image of "Lacan himself," we must seek "him" through the evidence provided by (a), (b), and (d). We must attend to what Lacan, or "Lacan," actually says about Freud's text, and thus to the double determination of Freud's text implied by any secondary text ([a] and [b]). What "Lacan" is compelled to say about Freud's text reveals a subjectivity that stands in a certain sense apart from and independent of that text. Seeing (a) and (b) through (d), we can infer a certain kind of person (c) who is addressed and converted in a certain way. In Freud's account of the development of the theory of the libido that was mentioned earlier, the reader could infer a "Freud" who, with his colleagues, might have been content for a time to "juggle" with "as many instincts as he chose," a man (c) like other men bound to the pleasure principle; but also a man (d) who had the integrity to renounce these digressive circus tricks and to take the "next step" when duty and truth called; a man, moreover, who would ultimately reject the "popular division of instincts" (a) in favor of a true, if unpopular, account (b). Each analysis will fill these images with its own content, but any analysis will have to fill them with something.

Necessarily, any competent reading of an analytical text must reflect some awareness, however dim, of all four images. The reading of the analytical text must proceed by assays of bias, by indirection finding direction out, inferring one image from others. A "better" reading will probably reflect a more detailed awareness of all levels than a "worse," but in order for a reading to qualify as competent at all, it must comprehend all four. If it does not, if the inferences are not made, then the reader is not reading a secondary text, but a primary one. This split-level consciousness is not only an *ought* of reading an analytical text, but an *is* as well. It is, of course, possible to write texts in which the distinction between literature and criticism, for example, is "blurred" in the way that Wimsatt warned against; Roland Barthes, Geoffrey Hartman, Rosalind Krauss, and others have actually advocated such blurring as a principle of contemporaneity. Shortly, I will speculate on how such a possibility arises, and what principles it follows. But the possibility of the blurred text does not blur the definition of analysis, which entails a specific conversion of distinct things into their distinct others. In the scene of analysis, there is nothing but conversion. If a general commandment governing every element in this scene—perhaps the general commandment of "ethics itself"—were to be formulated, it could be stated thus: Become what you are (not). The Nietzschean imperative cited at the beginning of this chapter gets it almost right.

So far, I have kept things simple, considering only the image of a single person reading one text and writing another. In the case of Freud, however, this simplicity necessarily falsifies as it represents. Who, or what, is "Freud?" The author of *Beyond* is himself not only determined by the texts on which he reflects and speculates, and by the authors of those texts, but is also determined in multiple ways as the author of *Beyond* and all the other texts past and future, father of Sophie, grandfather of Ernst, founder of psychoanalysis, and so forth, on out to the myriad ways in which he was situated in his culture. Derrida asks the unanswerable question: "What access is there [to the author of *Beyond*] without a spectral analysis of all the others?" (*PC* 323). And if these ghostly others are admitted—as they must be, they are there already—then the binding of the primary by the secondary must entail the taking-in of a theoretically infinite cast of characters who cannot be bound, so that the analytical text becomes unbound in the very act of binding. As if this were not enough, the overdetermination of "Freud" in the primary text must be multiplied by the overdetermination of "Lacan" in the secondary (the author of *Ecrits*, banished member of the International Psycho-Analytical Association, founder of the École Freudienne, practitioner of the "five-minute analysis," a man with allies, enemies, relatives, gender, class, race, history, etc.).

That last "etc." says it all, or rather suggests that one could speak forever and never say it all, never even really begin. But the most serious problem in the present context is not the impossibility of saturation, but the fact that the somewhat mechanical conversion of all elements within the analytical situation seems to go nowhere, serving, at least in the present formulation, no particular purpose. If conversion is a mark of ethicity, it should, it seems, be possible to discern some value, some principle in a discourse structured by conversion.

The first response to this understandable complaint is to recall the distinction between the ethical and the moral. "Ethicity" as a function of conversion is a neutral precondition of value, like the process of being inducted into the army, after which one then undertakes the "moral" acts reflecting positive commitments to particular principles in specific contexts. "Induction" is a conversional "turn" that begins as a civilian act and ends as a military one. Ethics also figures in a sequence, mediating between a formless or nonaligned state and a state in which it is possible to commit oneself to principled decisions. Hence the applicability to ethics of such terms as repression and repetition that can be applied both to "lower" and "higher" processes. But there is another reason why this account of the ethics of analysis may seem permanently, structurally neutral—neutral not just as a precondition to commitment or value but as an incapacity to attain anything like commitment or value. This reason has to do with the account of repetition itself.

So far, repetition has figured in two ways, as a target of repression and as an instrument of repression. In both senses, repetition has been confined to, in Freud's phrases, the "recurrence of the same thing," or "the re-experiencing of something identical" (*BPP* 16, 30). Repetition as recurrence of the same is a principle of stagnant fidelity, of inertia undeflected by any force that comes from "beyond." This is the problem: if the repetition involved in a secondary text, for example, is merely a repetition of the *same* forces that constituted the primary text in the first place, then it is hard to see why or how the secondary could be considered an advance on the primary, and therefore hard to see the need or justification for a secondary text at all. Indeed, such a repetition would violate the very principles of secondariness, including advance, meaning, and liberation. The repetition of the secondary text would, in short, become positively transgressive. An account of the "ethics" of analysis will have to discover some way out of this dilemma, some next step.

Such a step has been taken in Derrida's exploration of "the logic that ties repetition to alterity" (*Limited Inc* 7; hereafter *LI*). The key word for this exploration is "iterability," which Derrida claims structures all marks or signs. Iterability does not imply a repetition of the same, for the "same," the "original," is never strictly identical with itself. A linguistic version of the repetition compulsion, iterability names a "dehiscence" or a "cleft" within the sign that, according to Derrida, both enables it to have an "original" meaning in a certain context, and to be "cited," "grafted," or translated into a potentially infinite number of other contexts and therefore to acquire different meanings. Iterability is not only an internal function of language, however; for while it could be said to operate as a kind of otherness within language, it also suggests a "linguistic" otherness operating within such tokens of indivisible "purity" as consciousness or intention.

The argument becomes perhaps easier to understand if we transfer it from the subatomic plane of marks and signs to the relation between a primary text and a secondary text. The primary text is composed of repeatable signs. These signs are in fact repeated by the secondary text in a procedure that both establishes the primary as primary and, by weaning or dislodging it from its original context, erects a version of the primary that is different. As the original signs were already iterable, the secondary text could be said to accomplish the potential for citational grafting of which the original had always been necessarily capable, and towards which in a sense it had yearned. In a strange but real sense, the secondary ensures its fidelity to the original precisely by differing from it, realizing in some particular way the difference-from-itself that had structured the very originality of the original. The secondary, then, repeats the repeatability of the primary, but does not repeat it as the same.

Iterability suggests, in other words, a kind of primary-secondary vacillation within the primary itself, with the consequence that the primary, the original sign, could be seen as having already taken an initial step towards difference. This initial step, in turn, would sanction and even compel further such steps in the secondary analysis. And these steps would then take on the character of a necessary advance that does not violate the integrity of the primary text, a fully warranted movement out of sameness and into otherness: a movement, one could say, enabled by ethicity and realized by morality.

Derrida describes these steps explicitly in the 1988 "Afterword: Toward an Ethic of Discussion," which is appended to his two earlier essays about iterability, the 1971 "Signature Event Context," which Derrida refers to dryly as *Sec*, and the 1977 "Limited Inc a b c . . . ," both republished in a 1988 volume called *Limited Inc*. In these essays, Derrida discusses, first in relatively charitable, and then in increasingly pointed and aggressive terms, the premises of speech-act theory, as established by J. L. Austin and John R. Searle. It was Searle, whose scornful 1977 reply to "Signature Event Context" called "Reiterating the Differences: A Reply to Derrida," began with the provocative charge that the encounter between Austin and Derrida "never quite takes place" because Derrida had misread Austin. The debate itself has been much discussed, by Christopher Norris, Samuel Weber, Barbara Johnson, Mary Louise Pratt, Gayatri Spivak, Jonathan Culler, and Stanley Fish, and does not need to be rehearsed here (see also Harpham, "Derrida and the Ethics of Criticism"). What is chiefly interesting in the present context is Derrida's generalization of his outrage at what he considers to be Searle's misreadings, of both his own texts and Austin's, into a general statement of scholarly ethics based on the classical model of the subordination of desire to necessity.

In the course of his writings, Derrida indicates several forms of necessity. First, within the primary text, the various textual elements and forces have been constructed and arranged in a particular way, and this construction represents a form of necessity—history is necessity. Second, any determination of the meaning of a text will entail a certain necessary stabilization of its elements that Derrida calls "repression." And third, the primary text exerts a power over the secondary text, determining what must be said about it (see *Altérités* 93; *LI* 149–50). The first two forms of necessity determine the third. That is, the ethics of analysis begins with the secondary text's obligation to represent the necessities that had determined the form and the meaning of the primary text.

Hence what Derrida calls the first "layer or moment" of analysis, that of "doubling commentary." Practical analysis ought, Derrida argues, to be governed—and in fact has traditionally been governed—by a "theoretical" duty which is also an "ethical-political duty," first of all to a lucid, exact, and minute description of its object, a scrupulous repetition that necessarily takes the form both of a faithful representation of the object, even of those elements that are marginalized, excluded, or repressed—and a defiant refusal to collaborate in those acts of repression, a strict indifference to the repressive interests of the text (*LI* 135). The principle that seeks to insure against the prejudices of the analyst determining the analysis—insofar as such insurance can be obtained, whatever the price—is that *can* implies *ought:* if the evidence makes it possible to say something, then it ought to be said, regardless of whether it accords with the inclinations or interests of the analyst (see *LI* 133). Doubling commentary aspires to a neutral account of a "minimal consensus" on the "relatively stable" meaning of a text, without which no research would be possible within a community, for one could "just say anything at all" (144). Thus, prior to interpretation proper, the first duty of the analyst is to establish a dominant interpretation (that is, an interpretation whose dominance has been established in history), using all the traditional resources of the scholar, including knowledge of the "literary, philosophical, rhetorical traditions, the history of [the] language, society, history" (144), and to employ these resources in the service of "rules of competence, criteria of discussion and of consensus, good faith, lucidity, rigor, criticism, and pedagogy" (146).

While the pretensions of such terms as "disinterestedness," "impersonality," and "neutrality" have been vigorously attacked in recent years, the practices that in Derrida's account work to secure them have never been brought seriously into question. The scholarly community maintains a systematic and principled preference for the communal over the merely personal, the authorized over the arbitrary, necessity over desire. So entrenched is this preference, in fact, that it seems impervious to questioning; and this raises the question of whether it can be considered a "preference" at all. Are not the practices Derrida describes simply the elements of a general definition of analysis? One may carry out these practices well or poorly, but if one does not carry them out at all, one has simply not performed an act of analysis. Can we, then, describe as an "ethical-political duty" a practice of repetition that is in fact compulsory? Since Kant, the principle that *ought* implies *can*—that the obligation to do something implies the freedom to do it or not to do it—has been considered crucial to the distinction between ethical choice and coercive compulsion. If a secondary text simply must repeat the primary text in order to be a secondary text at all, then repetition ought not to be considered a praiseworthy duty, but rather a value-neutral fact, an attribute of the secondary, which simply cannot fail to repeat.

While repetition grounds the ethics of analysis, however, its effects are unprogrammable, for they cannot be determined as either fully, or even primarily, primary or secondary, regressive or progressive. The primary process of the secondary text, repetition operates both within and beyond the conscious willing of the analyst, making it impossible to tell who's in charge, or whether the analysis is proceeding "instinctually" according to the primary process or binding and mastering according to the secondary process.

So it can be no surprise when repetition figures in utopian political projects, since utopian thought, too, is ambivalently progressive and regressive. One of the most impressive recent examples of this utopianism, Judith Butler's *Gender Trouble*, argues that gender is a fiction, a performance, a "*stylized repetition of acts*" rather than a biological essence or transcendental identity (140). The constructed nature of gender, Butler argues, subjects it to parody and to a proliferation of forms with the power to destabilize current political-sexual configurations, and thus to create an emancipatory "gender trouble." Since people are always imitating some practices or acts, the task, she concludes, "is not whether to repeat, but how to repeat" (148). Butler recognizes that nothing in particular is to be hoped for from repetition as such, but still maintains a dubious faith in the capacity of repetition to open up politically progressive possibilities of agency and selfhood, and, in the absence of a previously-established identity that would select, plan, and manage repetition's effects, to do so all by itself. More dubious still is the assumption that those effects could be so managed that repetition could wholly transcend its own reactionary primariness, sublimating it without reserve.

Contrary to the view, promoted by Butler as well as by Derrida, of repetition as an "ethical-political duty," I would argue that repetition is less like a virtuous act and more like an entry fee, or an ante in a poker game, which, of course, does not guarantee a winning hand. It is, to return to Freud, most like a compulsion and thus is, as Freud argues, compatible with desire and even with pleasure. Confusing a *must* with an *ought*, Derrida seems to lack one word, a word that would make the necessary distinction. The same undiscovered or repressed word impresses itself from below on a passage in the "Afterword" where he describes the inappropriately "ethical" stance taken by speech-act theorists, especially Searle, who make absolute distinctions (serious, literal speech as opposed to speeches made by an actor; non-ironic as opposed to ironic speech, etc.) that appear to be merely logical or functional discriminations, but make them on the implicit and illicit basis of value-judgments, with certain "marginal," "lateral," or "nonserious" uses of language depicted as suffering from "a *decline* or a *pathology*, an ethical-ontological deterioration" (92). Purporting only to analyze "a certain ethicity inscribed in language"—the constant and necessary possibility of marginalization, exclusion, or hierarchization—speech-act theorists, according to Derrida, "reproduce" instead "the given ethical conditions of a *given* ethics" (122). But instead of attempting to distinguish between ethicity and ethics, would it not be more precise to call the latter, the "*given* ethics," by a different name, such as "the moral?" With this adjustment, the distinction would fall not between ethicity and ethics, but between the necessary-ethical-*is* and the chosen-moral-*ought*. Pathologizing certain forms of language, speech-act theorists are applying an implicitly moral standard to the analysis of an ethical object. They thus fail, Derrida might say, to respect the epistemological moment that precedes any value judgment. In terms of this distinction, repetition as such stands not on the side of the moral but rather on the side of an "ethicity inscribed in language."

The manifest intention behind Derrida's description of this "ethical-political duty," the first "layer or moment" of analysis, is to define a formal category of obligation, to isolate the source of what he considers to be Searle's bad faith and professional irresponsibility. Searle, he charges, simply has not read *Sec* carefully; he has overleaped the epistemological moment of faithful repetition and proceeded straight through to the second, "productive" layer or moment, that of "interpretation," which can be principled only insofar as it is firmly based on the ground of doubling commentary. But in order to make such a case, Derrida has had to do precisely what he did not want to do, to distinguish sharply between a factor of "sameness" and a factor of "difference." The impossibility of such a rigorous distinction was, after all, the lesson of iterability. Now, claiming to have identified the category of Searle's perfidy, Derrida has had to forget or repress, if only for a moment, his own premise.

This forgetting, no matter how temporary or strategic, produces a streak of drollery in the debate. As we have just seen, Derrida puts himself in the position of having to propose as a duty what is in fact a compulsion, to hold up as a value what is merely a fact. But even more curiously, he has had to revert to Searle's strategy of insisting on precise distinctions in language. Thus a queer reversibility takes root, which becomes even queerer in light of Derrida's repeated insistence that it is Searle who has adopted Derrida's position by repeatedly, and apparently unconsciously, borrowing arguments from *Sec* in order to attack *Sec*. The most striking example is Searle's final statement, that iterability "is not as Derrida seems to think something in conflict with the intentionality of linguistic acts, spoken or written, it is the necessary presupposition of the forms which that intentionality takes"; to which Derrida responds, "Precisely the thesis of *Sec*, if there is one!" (*LI* 46). Over and over again, Derrida shows, Searle performs a fort-da, using what Derrida calls a "discourse from/to-*Sec*," in which, through a kind of *unheimlich* maneuver, Derrida's own arguments are uncannily recontextualized, claimed as Searle's, and turned back against Derrida. It is as if, writing on and against the primary text of *Sec*, Searle had been infected by *Sec*, somehow persuaded both that its arguments were false and that they were his own.

Such a misreading, as Derrida is at pains to establish both in his reply to Searle, "Limited Inc a b c . . . ," and in the "Afterword: Toward an Ethic of Discussion," constitutes an act of appropriative "violence" that must be criticized as a neglect of duty. But what makes the entire spectacle of the appropriation of the other's arguments especially unheimlich is the fact that Derrida himself had already argued for repetition as the basis of any "ethic of discussion" and had exemplified this principle by quoting piecemeal virtually all of Searle's "Reply" in the course of refuting it, dramatizing the logic that ties repetition to alterity.

Nor is Derrida immune to the oddly contaminatory effects of repetition, as he himself testifies in a startling moment in "Limited Inc," where he insists that Searle has falsified the issue: "I note here that I seem to have become infected by [Searle's] style: this is the first time, I believe, that I have ever accused anyone of deception, or of being deceived" (86). The "logic" that ties repetition to infection is repudiated by Searle (who, nevertheless, in his insistence on precise distinctions and rigorous categories is, Derrida suggests, "ultimately more continental and Parisian than I am") and courted by Derrida (38). But, at least at this point, it is Searle who appears to gain from it and Derrida who appears to suffer. From a longer point of view, the effects of the plague on Derrida seem even more dramatic, for Derrida has proceeded in his three texts from what he calls an "academic and 'micrological'" (112) discussion of the effects of signature, context, speech-act theory, the philosophical conceptualization of language, and so forth, to a passionate and "serious" denunciation of falsehood and error, and finally to an exhortation to ethical responsibility, justice, reason, and truth. From this longer point of view, Searle—or at least his "position"—seems decisively to have won. At the very least, he has gained a draw, for each combatant appears to have undergone a conversion-through-repetition. If the encounter between Searle and Derrida "never quite takes place," one reason might be that there is no real space between the two sides, that the distinction between them cannot be made rigorous.

Derrida anticipates and precipitates this weird circumstance by acknowledging at the very beginning that his own distinctions cannot be made rigorous, pointing out that the layer or moment—what *is* it?—of doubling commentary, no matter how passive or obedient, is already inscribed with the productive difference of interpretation; and that interpretation remains committed on principle to its basis in commentary. This commitment may in fact account for Derrida's uncertainty about whether the two are layers or moments: insofar as an "autonomous" repetitive commentary checks unwarranted assertions, analysis is a sequence of moments, with one acting as a gateway to the other; but insofar as the principle of fidelity must be honored at all times, analysis is best conceived in terms of simultaneous layers, with consciousness and intentionality laminated over doubling commentary.

Weirdest of all is the role of consciousness, in ever more transcendental forms, in providing Derrida with the only distinctions he can really sustain. Faced with the fact that Searle had repeated (the "from/to-*Sec*" style of argument), Derrida might have insisted that Searle had not understood and so had not produced a proper interpretation. Derrida concedes, however, that Searle understands *Sec* "quite well, even if everything is done to create the contrary impression, one which, it must be admitted, often seems very convincing" (54). He even concedes that Searle's "actively defensive attitude" suggests "a more certain and more vital relationship" to "what is in effect at stake" in deconstruction than that of some "avowed 'deconstructionists'" (140). So while Searle has repeated, and while he has understood, he has done neither *consciously;* the decisive but unenforceable difference, then, is between Derrida's conscious repetition of Searle and Searle's unconscious repetition of Derrida, with Derrida standing for the principle of purposive consciousness—the very principle on which speech-act theory is based, the very principle Derrida had criticized. Irony is not the word for a state of affairs in which the only way Derrida can claim victory is through the reassertion of Searle's notions, including the idea of intention in its crudest form possible, speculation about what the author knew when he was writing. Even Searle, who in one respect profits by this return of the unrepressed, might agree that consciousness is cloven and divided against itself if his own arguments proved to be the most, indeed the only, effective weapons Derrida had against him. But even Derrida, who profits in another respect, might be troubled by the cost of victory, by the necessary submission of ethics to primitivism, by what he had called in *Grammatology* the "nonethical opening of ethics."

Two morals emerge from this morality play (whose title is "Morality and Play"). First, no value based on principle can be determined without strict and rigorous categories. Only through such categories as "doubling commentary," for example—categories whose apparent neutrality indicates that they are a duty for everyone without discrimination—can a true obligation be conceived. Second, there are no such categories. As has been observed many times in this chapter already, the very convertability of "lower" compulsions into "higher" principles guarantees that the higher will remain implicated with, and permeable to, the lower. There is no formal, categorical, or value-neutral way of representing a practice that will reliably produce a positive moral value. The unrepresentable gap between fact and value, or between *is* and *ought*, will never disappear, but will invariably be bridged by the overlapping elements of the two, which will demand and legitimate a "decision" at once overdetermined (by values and facts) and underdetermined (made on principle alone). Any claims about the superiority of one practice to another must be based not just on categorical but also on hypothetical factors. If I judge Derrida to have won the debate, as I do, my judgment is not based solely on Derrida's having performed the ritual of doubling commentary, or even on Derrida's superior understanding; for as Derrida himself allows, Searle repeats and understands. My judgment must also be based on such factors as my preference for what Derrida says, and my admiration for Derrida's brilliance, style, wit, persistence, and a host of other qualities I find missing in Searle. These preferences and admirations are not categorical determinations either, for they are in turn tangled up with my disposition to praise certain things by calling them "brilliant," "witty," and so forth. And my very perception of "things" is confused with other, noncategorical factors. There is no shelter from commitment and principle, no strictly formal test of value, no absolute determination by the arguments—any more than there can be true principle without forms and categories. Even the categorical imperative must confront and respect its other. "Ethics," the name we might give to this entire spectacle, is not only a concept of fairness but a fair concept: it extends to one's opponents a sword just as long and sharp as that which it extends to oneself.

Derrida's emphasis on ethics in these and other texts written in the late 1980s suggests to many a backsliding from the dizzying prospects of unrestrained "freeplay" opened up by his work in the 1960s. The "Afterword" returns to this critical concept in an attempt to appropriate it for the "ethic of discussion," attaching to it three meanings, the most important of which is, for the purposes of this discussion, the third: "In accordance with what is only ostensibly a paradox, *this particular* undecidable opens the field of decision or of decidability. It calls for decision in the order of ethical-political responsibility. It is even its necessary condition." There can be, Derrida points out, "no moral or political responsibility without this trial and this passage by way of the undecidable" (116). The undecidability of freeplay communicates with Kantian freedom as the condition of ethical decision, the factor which, in the absence of coercion, compels choice and the taking of responsibility.

Derrida himself has surprised many in recent years by arguing for an "unconditional" opposition to, for example, apartheid or nuclear proliferation. He uses, he says in the "Afterword," the word "unconditional" "not by accident to recall the character of the categorical imperative in its Kantian form," to indicate that his decision in such a matter is "independent of every determinate context, even of the determination of a context in general. It announces itself as such only in the *opening* of context." What is necessary in opposing certain worldly evils "is to articulate this unconditionality with the determinate (Kant would say, hypothetical) conditions of this or that context" (152). Without compromising its autonomy, the context-transcending imperative must be situated within the particular context, so that it may act as a force that descends, as it were, from above; or so that—to return to a more familiar deconstructive rhetoric—"The outside penetrates and thus determines the inside" (152–53).

Why, Derrida concludes, "have I always hesitated to characterize [the unconditionality that prescribes deconstruction] in Kantian terms . . . when that would have been so easy and would have enabled me to avoid so much criticism, itself all too facile as well? Because such characterizations seemed to me essentially associated with philosophemes that themselves call for deconstructive questions." Through Kantian discourse, "another language and other thoughts seek to make their way. This language and these thoughts, which are also new responsi-bilities, arouse in me a respect which, whatever the cost, I neither can nor will compromise" (153). In a final moment of sincerity, Derrida repeats the repression of Kant by Freud, even while, like Freud, re-peating the Kantian imperative. To put it another way: Derrida re-presses Kant precisely in the name of the ethical necessity that he repeats, an uncompromising "respect" for a law that prescribes the deconstruction of all discourse, including Kant's. And all this, finally, proceeds from the imperative to go if not specifically beyond Kant, then at least beyond the pleasure principle (invoking Kant "would have been so easy"), by sacrificing desire to an unconditional law, an imperative to deconstruct that is represented as unconditional and worthy of respect even though it is his own. Just as Freud had re-pressed while repeating Nietzsche's law of repetition, and psycho-analysis represses while repeating philosophical ethics, so Derrida represses while repeating Kant. With his emphasis on enlightened reason, the dignity of rationality, and the free and open "parliament" of faculties, Kant stands, in a modern climate, a new context, as the philosopher of repression, the herald of a law that prescribes repres-sion—a law which must, in turn, be repressed by those who would follow it.

4

GETTING IT RIGHT
THE STORY OF CREATION

1. The Narrative Imperative

Where to begin? Where one is—or rather, where id or *es* is; or rather, where it *was: Wo es war*. Beginning there, one may look forward to the "emergence," as Lacan says, of *Ich*. But how does *Ich* emerge?

According to Richard Rorty's reading of Freud, the *Ich* emerges through the subject's diligent obedience to the "moral obligation" of self-understanding, an imperative that demands the construction of narratives about the self ("Freud and Moral Reflection" 6). Rorty does not try to account for the element of obligation in Freud's view of narrative, apparently regarding it as a quirk or eccentricity in Freud that happily turns out to be useful, since it encourages an aesthetic indifference to the pressures that the subject might feel radiating at him from the class or species (*pace* Aristotle), and an indifference as well to the "purity" of the law (*pace* Kant). The imperative to understand oneself by constructing narratives promotes and develops "the ability of each of us to tailor a coherent self-image for ourselves and then use it to tinker with our behavior" (19). In the ethical climate of Freud, as opposed to that of Aristotle or Kant, certain character types arise and flourish, prominent among them "the ironic, playful intellectual" who just wants to make sense of things without worrying about a "true self" or the moral status of one's acts (15).

Rorty finds this a benign conclusion, but in the course of his discussion the idea of the imperative appears to have suffered a kind of fading or evaporation. For Rorty seems to prize the Freudian imperative precisely because it creates an atmosphere in which such barbaric notions as "moral obligations" cannot be taken seriously. Rorty's own wish appears to be for a culture based on the imperative that there shall be no imperatives. This wish may account for the suspension in Rorty's work of the question of why narrative should be obligatory in a pragmatist culture. But this suspension opens up another question: what would constitute an obligation for these tinkers and tailors, these ironic handymen of the self, these smirking auto-repairmen? What can obligate those who feel no obligation? The general category under which this question arises, the question of the relation between ethics and aesthetics, is one of the deadest horses in Western thought, not because the issue has been decisively settled, but because it is, or at least has been thus far, unsettlable, stalemated. Enlightenment rationality, utilitarianism, phenomenology, and formalism converge in the argument that ethics and aesthetics are essentially separate, in that the receptive, nuanced, and nonjudgmental aesthetic experience of a unified, autonomous artifact cannot be reduced to or translated into the stern exclusionary abstractions of ethical choice. In this argument, aesthetic works stand at a distance from both the tangled and incompatible pressures of the world and from any laws or principles that may be invoked as a gauge of conduct. In the presence of the aesthetic, the viewer, reader, or listener experiences, as in a kind of trance, an image that makes no immediate demands, that does not call out for decision or action, that stands radiantly apart, enclosed, within itself. Narrative can be appropriated for such an argument because, while its retrospectively obvious closural form places it squarely within the category of the aesthetic, its referential specificity resists the crushing weight, the levelling force, of the categorical. Eve Kosofsky Sedgwick claims, for example, that narrative, especially narrative "of a directly personal sort," can, by itself and just by being itself, "disarm the categorical imperative that seems to do so much to promote cant and mystification about motives in the world of politically correct academia" (*Epistemology of the Closet* 60). The presumed hostility of narrative towards the categorical imperative can be used to prove the incommensurability of ethics and aesthetics.

But another, equally powerful and even more venerable tradition is centered on the insistence that, as Wittgenstein more than once puts it, "Ethics and aesthetics are one" (see *Notebooks* 77, and *Tractatus* 6.421). Advocates of unity generally argue for the moral utility of art, and, like their opponents, generally fix on prose narrative, which, with its often inconspicuous (during the time of reading) formal organization, seems especially intimate with ethically assessable "life" or "the world." The list of literature's ethical utilities is considerable. Literature, it is said, articulates goals, instructs people on how to picture and understand human situations, moralizes action by showing its ends, provides models of motivation and a set of character types and decisional models, structures an opportunity for the reader to test his or her capacity for discovering and acknowledging the moral law, holds the mirror up to the community so that it can identify and judge itself, represents negotiations between the community and the individual, engenders a relation between author and reader, promotes explanatory models that help make sense of different situations and that shelter the subject from the threat of the inchoate, fixes the past and so makes possible free action in the future, and models the "unity" that might be desirable in a human life (see Altieri, "Expressivist Aesthetics"; Murdoch, *Sovereignty of Good*; and Eldridge, *On Moral Personhood*). Within the aesthetic, then, it is prose narrative, with, in Matthew Arnold's phrase, its "vital connexions with other agencies," that has the strongest claim to being "one" with ethics: if ethics and aesthetics are one, they conjoin in narrative.

Generally, those who gravitate towards narrative also gravitate away from Kant. Martha Nussbaum, for example, argues that some literary texts, such as those of Proust or Henry James, can actually provide a superior picture of morality to that afforded by philosophy, especially by what Nussbaum calls "the Kantian account." Literature—or at least the work of James, Proust, and Murdoch, if not de Sade, Borowski, Kosinski—can picture what philosophy cannot, the "difficulty" of adult moral action, the need for "improvisation" as opposed to rigidity, and the necessity of being, as James puts it in the preface to *The Princess Casamassima,* "finely aware and richly responsible" to a shifting and mysterious play of appearances. Characteristically, Aristotle emerges as the champion of the anti-Kantian forces. Like Iris Murdoch, Nussbaum leans heavily on the "Aristotelian" basis of her view of ethics as "the search for a specification of the good life for a human being" ("Flawed Crystals" 139). Another Aristotelian, MacIntyre, claims suggestively that narrative "unity" is not a neutral formal attribute, but, when applied to human life, provides the key to self-knowledge and knowledge of the good (*AV* 202). Only by imagining oneself as the subject of a unified narrative, MacIntyre writes, can one overcome temptations to distraction and inconsistency and direct oneself purposefully towards the promise of achieved meaning for one's own life in the future. All three see in narrative a way not only of unifying ethics and aesthetics, but of rescuing ethics from its own worst tendencies, its own temptations to philosophical abstraction and austerity. They see, in short, narrative as a way of rescuing ethics from Kant.

Neither Murdoch, Nussbaum, nor MacIntyre has any more use for literary theory than for Kant. "If one turns from criticism to more general and theoretical writing about literature," Nussbaum complains, "the ethical vanishes more or less altogether"; she even declares that after reading Derrida, she feels "a certain hunger for blood," a hunger satisfied (for her) by reading Aristotle ("Perceptive Equilibrium" 170, 171). But while the somewhat archaic Aristotelian emphasis on roles, decisions, priorities, and forms of life clearly stands closer to the dark soil of narrative reference than do Kant's rigorously worked-out abstractions, it is in Kantian rather than in Aristotelian ethics, and in a literary theory informed by Kant, that narrative becomes interesting, if not exactly bloody.

In the *Nichomachean Ethics*, narrative is simply not an issue; but in Kant's second *Critique*, and in the philosophical tradition that descends from that text, narrative appears in a highly charged atmosphere as a necessary perversion, a perennial *distraction* of system and rationality, bearing the same relation to real philosophy as grotesque ornamentation bore to the texts of medieval illuminated psalters. For many then and for nearly all now, these often intrusive, swarming, and ludicrous illustrations—concessions to the wandering eye of the distractable and even pervertable reader—overrun and eclipse the texts themselves in interest; and ethical discourse runs the same risk of having its narrative margins compete with, overshadow, and compromise its philosophical argument. In the "Preface" to the first edition of the *Critique of Pure Reason*, Kant says that he had originally included examples but had removed them in revision. Aids to clarity from a "popular" point of view, their "bright colouring" illuminated only "details" while actually interfering with the conceptual "grasp of the whole" (13). Expunged from the first *Critique*, narrative aids worm their way into the second, and into the *Metaphysical Foundations of Morals*, as necessary examples of the application of pure reason to worldly circumstances. But however necessary they may be, narrative invariably disturbs and de-systematizes the principles it is enlisted to exemplify. Lyotard captures the high-tension ambivalence of philosophy towards narrative when he describes the philosopher's "awareness that one cannot signify that which tells itself as a prescription other than in narrations, which does not prevent the fact that at the same time one will never be able to extract this prescription out of narrations in the form of semantic content" (*Just Gaming* 99).

Pure reason represses its narrative "examples," acceding to them virtually as a kind of Passion, a humiliation that must be endured as a condition of realization in the "practical" world of action. The resistance is mutual, as narrative represses the maxims of philosophy, maxims that nevertheless seem to inform them, grow out of them, justify them, and survive them. To risk a pronouncement, we could say that narrative is the "aesthetic" countenance, and ethics the "philosophical" countenance of a discursive ensemble including theoretical rationality and aesthetic form. Neither one nor two, narrative and ethics imply the other without being exactly identical. The relation is rather one of mutual dependency, resistance, and repression.

Even the most accommodating or banal narrative is marked by this complex, the most uncompromising account of which is worked out in Hillis Miller's "ethics of reading." Miller identifies in the narrative text an imperative that paradoxically turns on the text itself, commanding the reader to renounce the very idea that literature can serve as a model at all. In following this inscrutable imperative, or imperative of inscrutability, Miller says, the reader must give up the "desire to draw direct ethical conclusions" from a thematic and referential reading, or to make one of the characters a "model for my own life" (*ER* 28). The ethics of reading dictate that no ethical instruction be derived from reading.

Beginning, then, with the premise that ethics and aesthetics are one, that narrative articulates the law for the reader, Miller discovers through narrative that that premise is a temptation, and that they are in fact two. The reader must not only surrender the intuition of unity but must even "give up the warm attractive project of looking at literature as the transmitter and creator, through language, of my culture's highest values" ("Is There an Ethics of Reading?" 97). Indeed, the value of the text lies in its power to disabuse the reader precisely of all those forms of edification and instruction that Murdoch, Nussbaum, and MacIntyre prize so highly. The text as represented by Miller does not teach its readers through faithful representations of the human subject in crisis, and certainly entails no appeal to a community, but rather works to dissolve such notions as the conscious, freely willing, socialized ego. Reading well, Miller claims, the subject focuses itself as a "relay station, so to speak, in a purely linguistic transaction" (100). Commanded by the law, the subject must freely choose to annihilate itself as a freely choosing subject.

Perhaps the situation is best described, or exemplified, by an account which is both descriptive and exemplary. The following passage is drawn from Levinas, whose infrequent and minimalistic reversions to narrative consistently betray a philosophical embarrassment:

> What we live from and enjoy is not the same as that life itself. I eat bread, listen to music, follow the course of my ideas. Though I live my life, the life I live and the fact of living it nonetheless remain distinct, even though it is true that this life itself continually and essentially becomes its own content. (*Totality and Infinity* 122)

Low-sodium white, Levinas's bread is hardly the staff of life, or the stuff of literature, suffering badly even by comparison with Hume's narrative particles in the *Treatise:* "I dine, I play a game of backgammon, I converse, and am merry with my friends . . ." (269). And the impressment in the second sentence of narrative in the service of a philosophical argument seems both a coercion of narrative and a concession that the argument could not stand without narrative. In a sense, this is exactly what the argument says, that while experience ("what we live from") and its idealized reflection ("that life itself") remain "distinct," the activity of reflection continually "becomes its own content," so that part of our experience is the process of the idealization of experience. The passage itself can be read in terms of a struggle between atemporal and temporal representations. Philosophy, we could say, consumes and transforms temporality, but in so doing, it temporalizes itself, the temporal instance exemplifying and appropriating the atemporal point in a process that knows no end, a process in which everything is transforming and transformed. The passage emphasizes, finally, neither of the two static and self-identical terms but rather the continual conversion of bread into life into bread, of philosophy into aesthetics into philosophy, of totality into infinity into totality. Insofar as ethics emerges here at all, it emerges through these struggles, these conversions.

The pivotal but unstable position of narrative may help explain the historical failure of certain longstanding debates to achieve resolution or even clarity. If any general theoretical statement about the relation of ethics and aesthetics can be supported with reference to some feature of narrative, then the clash of arguments collapses into a mere collection of statements that cannot be characterized as either agreement or disagreement, unity or disunity. This irresolute state of affairs renders even more perplexing the question with which we began: why should narrative ever be considered morally imperative?

It is perhaps easier to grasp why narrative should be considered, especially by Freud, to be therapeutically imperative, a method, as Joan Didion says at the beginning of The White Album, of "tell[ing] ourselves stories in order to live." "We live," she says, "entirely, especially if we are writers, by the imposition of a narrative line upon disparate images, by the 'ideas' with which we have learned to freeze the shifting phantasmagoria which is our actual experience" (11). Narrative, for Didion, is a requirement not for life, but for a life that "writers" could value. In abnormal circumstances, "disparate images" may stubbornly resist containment by the narrative "idea." Didion gives examples from the late 1960s: the murder of Robert Kennedy, reports from My Lai, and "the story of Betty Lansdown Fouquet . . . who put her five-year-old daughter out to die on the center divider of Interstate 5 some miles south of the last Bakersfield exit." "Certain of these images," Didion comments, "did not fit into any narrative I knew" (13). There are two ways of reading this passage. The first is as a meditation on what Freud would call "unbound" energy. The image whose sheer horror repels a narrative accommodation prevents the pleasurable reduction of tension that, Freud says, is the organism's goal—and which, Aristotle says, is the crowning effect of plotted form as well. The unbound image will be compulsively remembered and repeated, but will never be worked through because its meaning will never be settled. Having once encountered such images, one must either learn new narratives to contain them or suffer the psychological version of the cultural disintegration the images so powerfully suggest. Narrative, it seems, is a form of repetition that is also a form of repression: gathered into a narrative, the individual image takes a subordinate and determined place within a structure that limits its anarchic potential to mean everything or nothing. It is not hard to see how a therapeutic necessity can become a moral imperative. The rampant image threatens one's ethical as well as one's psychological status.

The more wild or disturbing the image, the more repressive must be the work of narrative containment. But the stronger the repression, the weaker the ethical credentials of the narrative. And this leads to the second possible reading of Didion's passage. The insistence that "these images did not fit into any narrative I knew" implies a certain view of narrative, that its formal coherence represents normality, benevolence, order. Images alien to these qualities must not, therefore, be "narrative," despite the fact that they are presented, as in the case of Ms. Fouquet, in the form of a "story." What is so appalling is that these images have already been narrativized, that narrative has already done the best it can with them. If narrative cannot repress the horror, then Didion must repress the narrative, holding out the hope that the disconcerting image could be neutralized by some as yet unimaginable discourse. But the images are so disconcerting precisely because they occur in narratives, especially in "factual" narratives whose significance is determinable and potentially threatening. Indeed, it is difficult to imagine why one would be threatened by an image that did not imply narrative extensions fore and aft, and even difficult to imagine such an image at all. What is, on the other hand, all too compulsively imaginable is the image that, within a narrative, strongly appears to resist narrative ordering, to refuse closural return, like Ms. Fouquet's daughter, whose fingers, Didion writes, had to be pried loose from the Cyclone fence on the freeway center divider by her rescuers twelve hours later. The narrative in which Ms. Fouquet and her daughter participate might, then, be "obligatory" in that it compels repetition, as in the newspapers, in Didion's text, and in this book. But it is not what Freud or Rorty would call "moral." A "moral" story ending with a normative term would, on the other hand, not be obligatory, but merely desirable. It would appear that narrative, like "ethics" as redefined in the first chapter, cannot provide what Didion would wish, an assurance of a positive, sustaining value and meaning. Narrative is rather "imperative," a precondition for the determination of the meaning and value of any event at all.

One sign that narrative condenses into itself the entire debate about ethics and aesthetics is that the analysis of narrative itself characteristically pivots on the same problem, whether narrative is one or two. For Didion, as for MacIntyre and indeed for Freud, narrative is preeminently a unified structure. Indeed, for Jameson, narrative figures an "aspiration to totality." Without narrative unity, meaning is indeterminable, events unassessable. This unity is variously construed. In one traditional approach, narrative unity is "organic," a form of structural integrity in which the identity of the system is maintained through transformation by restrictions on the possibilities of action. In the words of Stephen Jay Gould, narrative is figured by "time's arrow," a story line of "pasts that determine presents and presents that constrain futures" (*Time's Arrow, Time's Cycle* 44). The events of narrative occur within what D. H. Lawrence calls the "definite line of the story" and are subject to a host of generic restrictions that apply most directly at those moments of conversion where the transformations of some element are seen to be regulated by what has gone before, in a series that eventually produces a closure which, according to Tzvetan Todorov, represents a condition of same-but-different ("Narrative Transformations"). The expulsion from the Garden in Genesis succeeds by causal logic Adam's admission of transgression, his eating of the apple, Eve's offer of the apple, Eve's eating of the apple, Eve's decision to eat the apple, Eve's conversation with the serpent, Eve's "beguilement" by the serpent, Eve's creation, Adam's need for companionship, Adam's creation, the movement of the spirit of God over the face of the waters, the creation of heaven and earth. Narrative proceeds according to the conversional imperative to "Become what you are (not)," unfurling like a rose from a configuration of elements that is closed, latent, or implicit to one that is disclosed, realized, and explicit—but still a rose.

The biblical example is especially apt since, as Bakhtin and many others have noted, narrative tends to stress "critical junctures," those moments of character-revealing choice or decision in which some *Ich* declares or manifests itself, renouncing, and at the same time fulfilling, some inchoate or unformed *es* (*Dialogic Imagination* 115 ff.; see also Brooks, *Reading for the Plot* 40 ff.; and Harpham, *Ascetic Imperative* 67–88). What Foucault described as "the event"—the reversal of a relationship of forces, the entry of a masked other—is better conceived as the characteristic structure of the narrative event. The model is, as I argued in the previous chapter, strengthened by the codicil that the masked other is in fact a maverick fragment of sameness (hence the ease of entry) masked precisely *as* an other. With this qualification, the "event" provides us with a general picture of how a narrative system undergoes continual transformation and yet remains the same.

So powerful is the force of sameness in determining the unity of narrative that some have seen narrative as a discursive form of totalitarianism, violence, or coercion in which all difference, all "disparateness," is made to toe the "definite line" in what Derrida calls the privileged "genre of the law" ("The Law of Genre"). Kristeva has argued in this spirit that narrative—"narrow, penal, penalizing, and reductive"—is the instrument by which society produces the self-oppressing and compliant "subject" out of the originarily autonomous "individual" ("Novel as Polylogue" 203; see also "Giotto's Joy" 214 ff.). Both MacIntyre and Lyotard, in a rare moment of agreement, cite the social function of narrative as a means of justifying and "legitimating" knowledge and ethical authority. But perhaps the most rigorous and rigid case for unity is argued by Leo Bersani and Ulysse Dutoit, who claim that narrative is accurately symbolized by the military march, in which every element repeats, as it passes by, all those that went before and anticipates all those to follow (*Forms of Violence* 81–90). In the violent binding of its parts, narrative tends naturally, they suggest, to scenes like those in the seventh-century B.C. Assyrian reliefs in the British Museum in which are depicted the wars and hunts of a culture unsentimental about the death agonies of others. The argument is highly ingenious in that it goes on to discover within the ranks of similar horses, soldiers, and spears depicted in the reliefs—in other words within repetition—a principle of representation suggestive of a nonnarrative "primary process" that subverts the very violence it is enlisted to represent. Like Derrida's iterability, repetition is shown to be the essence of narrative linear violence as well as the key to an "indolent" and even "gentle" counterforce. And like Didion's "disparate images," these figures appear to stand subversively outside of narrative itself.

But Bersani-Dutoit's argument may be too ingenious in that it suppresses what may be its own most interesting implication for the sake of pursuing a polemic against what had seemed unattackable, the universal and primary form of human cognition and explanation, narrative itself. If the principle of narrative violence is unity, and if the

165

principle of unity is repetition, then repetition can hardly be said to constitute a counterforce to narrative violence. The forms of repetition within the Assyrian reliefs become most richly suggestive when they are seen not as nonnarratable and "unbound" energies but as the object or target of narrative configuration. The "primary process" is primary to narrative itself; repetition constitutes both the binding force of the narrative line and *what* is bound within that line. By what Derrida describes as the "logic that ties repetition to alterity"—and by the logic of Freudian therapy—repetition binds repetition (*Sec* 7). The claim about the unity of narrative in repetition displaces itself, then, through the disclosure of a radical otherness within repetition, an otherness that splinters the presumed unity of narrative into alterity.

Thus it is no surprise that the argument from unity has been contested from the outside, as it were, by those who have suspected narrative of structural duplicity. First indicated in Aristotle's depiction of plot as the skeleton or "soul" of narrative, the postulate of narrative doubleness has been most insistently argued by formalist criticism. Roman Jakobson's distinction between the "paradigmatic" "axis of selection" and the "syntagmatic" "axis of combination," the Russian Formalist distinction between the order of events referred to (*fabula*) and the order in which they are represented (*sjuzet*), Roland Barthes's suggestion of a dual coding of narratives by the "proairetic" (the code of actions) and the "hermeneutic" (the code of enigmas and answers), the distinctions drawn by narratology between *histoire* and *récit* or "story" and "discourse," all reflect the formalist inclination to a binary analysis (Jakobson, "Closing Statement"; Barthes, "Introduction to the Structural Analysis of Narrative"). Peter Brooks summarizes his own findings, and those of many others, when he concludes that narrative "not only uses but *is* a double logic" (29).

Indeed, the approach through disunity has proven itself to be just as productive and illuminating as the approach through unity. Only an analysis of what might be thought of as internal externalities could explain certain moments in narrative when the rules in force up to a certain point are abruptly transgressed. Take for example the scene near the end of Alfred Hitchcock's *The Shadow of a Doubt,* when a garage door abruptly shuts, trapping a girl inside with a car whose engine is running. Unable to turn off the engine because the key is not in the ignition, she is also prevented from escaping by a block of wood that had suddenly become wedged under the door from the outside, although there was nobody near the garage when she entered. Inexplicable in terms of the normal behavior of garage doors, blocks of wood, and ignition switches, the incident is also inexplicable in terms of a narrative system seen as a function of a probabilistic unity. It can, however, be accounted for by Jonathan Culler's suggestion that narrative always operates according to two different logics, a logic of events and a logic of meaning. Especially at crucial or problematic moments, the events of a narrative, Culler argues, seem to be produced not by the story "itself," but rather by the demands of narrative for a certain effect. Overriding the logic of events, the logic of meaning can take a superior and hostile position within the narrative ("Story and Discourse" 178). In this case, the entrapment of the girl—and nearly every other incident in this strange film—is determined by the requirement of the "suspense" plot that she be threatened with murder, a requirement that is met even at the cost of plausibility. On occasion, it is not only possible but necessary to regard plot as an agent of alterity within the narrative.

Even within the plot, a necessary disunity prevails in such crucial relationships as that between the narrator and the characters whose stories are narrated. As Arthur Danto points out, in a third-person or omniscient narration—which Gérard Genette regards as the only true forms of narrative—the narrator or narrative consciousness must know things the characters do not, for if the characters knew how the narrative turned out, the logic of narration would be destroyed. Narrative of this kind represents two kinds of consciousness, the kind that knows the ends and understands the causality operating in present events, and the kind that does not. The narrator's knowledge, Danto concludes, stands "*logically outside*" the order of events he describes (*Narration and Knowledge* 356).

Perhaps the most relentless form of the disunity argument has been inspired by the work of Lacan. According to Lacanians, narrative is the necessary mode of representation of a subject, as Lacan says, "born divided." The inaugural and structural division of the subject between unconsciousness and consciousness creates a gap between pleasure demanded and pleasure achieved, and this gap compels a restless psychic questing that inevitably takes narrative form, but actually obeys the imperatives of the unconscious. As the unconscious is "structured like a language," narrative, like all language, is determined by a "discourse of the Other" that cannot be made logically coherent. Narrative in particular draws on certain "capacities of the signifier," especially substitution and recombination, in structuring its "manifest content." For the most part, the surface tension of this manifest content holds, and the Other is effectively hidden. But at moments of "ellipsis," "turning," or "lapses" in logic, the narrative fissures, betraying the disfiguring power of the unconscious language from which it derives. At these moments, the repressed scene of writing is discovered like a guilty thing surprised, and the imperatives that drive the narrative reveal themselves, but never more than briefly and imperfectly. According to the Lacanian argument I have been loosely tracking, wherever one is in narrative, one is not where it's at; for, in the words of Robert Con Davis, "the subject of narration, what gives it form and meaning, will always be other than what is signified *in* narration" ("Introduction" 854).

The power of such an analysis lies in its insistence that the "manifest content" itself does not tell the whole story of narrative, an insistence essential to understanding narrative form. But the power of the La-canian approach diminishes sharply at the point, or points, of closure, when narrative form is determinable. Might there be some other way of getting at "the subject of narration" that enables us to maintain a vital connection both to the imperative but unconscious Other and to all the cultural utilities listed at the beginning of this discussion, all those features—the picturing of human circumstances, the modelling of decision-making, the production of coherence—that might make of narrative a "moral obligation?"

This other way would have to include some account of the unity as well as of the disunity of narrative. This is precisely the strength of the theory developed over the last ten years by Hayden White. Con-centrating particularly on the kind of knowledge produced in and by narrative, White says that narrative form not only endows events with meaning but virtually interprets them through what he calls "the con-tent of the form." Even in the case of "real events," the form, and hence the meaning, is never given to the narrator or author, but is always chosen; and the unity of narrative is constantly maintained against pressure from a rival account. "Unless at least two versions of the same set of events can be imagined," White says, "there is no rea-son for the historian to take upon himself the authority of giving the true account of what really happened" ("Value of Narrativity" 20). Such uncontested circumstances typically produce the "chronicle" form in which the years unfold consecutively without analysis or plot. Nar-rative "proper" is engendered by the desire to produce an accurate account over and against an inaccurate one. Thus, every historical narrative works by a "recoding" in which, as White says elsewhere, "experience is imagined to exist under at least two modes, one of which is encoded as 'real,' the other of which is 'revealed' to have been illusory in the course of the narrative" ("Historical Text as Literary Artifact" 60). The historicity of an account—like the explanatory power of an "analysis"—is established in just this way, through the convincing dismantling or repression of other possibilities. And the same applies to fictive narratives, for, as White says, "every narrative, however seemingly 'full,' is constructed on the basis of a set of events which might have been included but were left out" ("Value" 10). Narrative unity, then, is accomplished through decisions that exclude, and thereby mark, factors of disunity; and narrative as a whole originates in a choice of representational modes that is underdetermined by the facts.

White's work usefully grasps together unity and discord, but more importantly it indicates the critical relation between narrative and a particular kind of imperative. Noting Hegel's identification of the "reality which lends itself to narrative representation" as "the conflict between desire, on the one side, and the law, on the other," White suggests that the subject of narration should be seen as "the legal subject which can serve as the agent, agency, and subject of historical narrative in all of its manifestations . . ." ("Value" 12, 13). This identification, he continues, "raises the suspicion that narrative in general, from the folktale to the novel, from the annals to the fully realized 'history,' has to do with the topics of law, legality, legitimacy, or, more generally, authority" ("Value" 13). White's linkage of legitimacy and narrative is confirmed by the moment in Shakespeare's *Henry V* in which the young king anticipates the outcome of his effort to seize the throne of France, which he claims is rightfully his by the terms of an ancient law. "Either our history shall with full mouth / Speak freely of our acts," he proclaims, "or else our grave, / Like Turkish mute, shall have a tongueless mouth, / Not worshipp'd with a waxen epitaph" (I.i.230–33). If he succeeds, narrative will celebrate his victory as the reestablishment of the law. If he fails, no narrative—at least no English narrative—will be necessary or even perhaps possible.

But the truism that histories are written by the victors does not address the specific kind of authority that narrative accounts represent. Narrative does not serve all forms of law faithfully, as White demonstrates through the failure of a "chronicle" account—Richerus of Reims's *Histoire de France*—to achieve full narrative closure. What is lacking in the events described in Richerus's chronicle is, White argues, a "moral principle in light of which Richerus might have judged the resolution as either just or unjust" ("Value" 19). In the resolution of the actual conflict there was "no justice, only force" (20). Constrained by the nature of the actual events, Richerus simply could not bring his narrative to closure, and this inability suggests that, however brutally effective the social authority that authorizes a narrative may be, some forms of law resist the idealization of formal narrative closure; that is, they resist being represented under the aspect of what White calls the "moral." "If every fully realized story," White comments, "points to a moral, or endows events, whether real or imaginary, with a significance that they do not possess as a mere sequence, then it seems possible to conclude that every historical narrative has as its latent or manifest purpose the desire to moralize the events of which it treats" (14). He concludes with a question, one that refers solely to the author or narrator: "Could we ever narrativize *without* moralizing?" (25).

The answer would appear to be "No," but since 1980, when this essay first appeared, White has left this question hanging, so that in light of his recent work it appears more and more rhetorical. White has, in fact, confined himself to rhetoric, refining the theory of "tropology," which holds that the rhetorical form of any text provides a kind of content determined largely by "the structure of its dominant trope, the trope that serves as the paradigm in language for the representation of things as parts of identifiable wholes." For narrative, White claims, the content is determined by synecdoche, "the dominant trope for 'grasping together' . . . the *parts* of a totality apprehended as being dispersed across a temporal series into a *whole* in the mode of *identification*," as opposed to those modes "in which parts are related to a whole by resemblance (metaphor), contiguity (metonymy), or opposition (irony or catachresis)" ("'Figuring the nature of the times deceased'" 38).

Tropology is White's answer to the failure of structuralism to construct a logic or grammar of narrative, its inability to formalize the rules governing narrative's various "turns from one level of generalization to another, from one phase of a sequence to another, from a description to an analysis or the reverse, from a figure to a ground or from an event to its context, from the conventions of one genre to another within a single discourse, and so on" ("Figuring" 28). But what of the question left orphaned by the rhetorical emphasis of White's recent work? Why has White refused to answer his own question—why, especially when the tropological approach seems, in its autonomy from the human or historical, to cry out for some complement that credits the massive and multifarious cultural investment in narrative? What, we may ask White, actually grasps the narrative totality? Do tropes simply gather themselves into synecdoche? Or must we, in order to answer such questions, return, driven by the sheer logic of formalism itself, from the level of an abstract and enclosed narration to the figure of the subject—the hero or protagonist, but also the reader—resistant to, but ultimately bound by the law? If structuralism was unable to formalize narrative's logic or grammar, perhaps this is because the rules governing narrative turnings, like those by which the hero's turnings are assessed, are not strictly logical or grammatical, but also entail elements of ethicity. For the formal turnings White describes, while unarguably "real," can only be recognized and negotiated by a reader making underdetermined choices in the service of some principle that appears to transcend narrowly-defined interest—in the service, in fact, of the real.

Ethicity manifests itself most richly in the most dramatic of narrative turnings, the climactic point just between the knitting and unravelling of the action, the fort and the da, the moment when the rising line of complication peaks, pauses, and begins its descent into the dénouement. A kind of macro-turn, this point is the one absolutely necessary moment in narrative, the one that marks a sequence as a narrative. Gathering up and often reversing the turns that had gone before, the climax testifies more convincingly than anything else to the power of the logic of meaning, in which the sheer mechanical force of "plot" overwhelms "story," breaking the definite line, bending it, and converting it from itself to a truer, righter version of itself—the emergent *Ich*—according to an imperative that transcends the mere episodic or "proairetic" sequence of events.

Like the Kantian ethical subject, narration at its crux is seen to be commanded by a law that emerges from within, from its "deepest" interests, and yet compels its actions as if from the outside. The fact stressed by formalist criticism that the dénouement that follows is "inevitable" or "fitting after all" suggests that the principle of the turning is drawn from within forces already present within the elements of the narrative; while the fact that the ending is unpredictable suggests that some quasi-external agency is required to bring it about, if only to emphasize some factor that was there all along, to ensure its predominance over others. The emergence of the final configuration of elements produces the aesthetic closure, the "wholeness," the "completed process of change," that formalism has always ascribed to plot (see Crane, "The Concept of Plot" 306).

To see this process of change as unfolding according to the dictates of an imperative is suddenly to grasp how narrative might be said to produce a specifically "moral" authority regardless of specific, and possibly amoral, content. And to see such authority as the proper and inevitable end of narrative is finally to understand White's somewhat obscure comment that narratives conclude with a "*passage* from one moral order to another" ("Value" 23). The rather more explicitly "moral order" of action passes over, at the moment of conclusion when synecdoche declares itself as the law of the text, into the less explicitly moral order of the aesthetic, with the dark sphere of closural form eclipsing the represented human figures whose power of motion and conversion has now ceased. Tropology does not, however, eclipse ethics, either in a given narrative or in narrative theory. Rather, it marks a necessarily formal, or categorical, dimension of ethics, without which ethics would be unintelligible and incomplete.

Thus ethicity returns in the moment of its apparent erasure by formalism. Nowhere is this return more richly or productively figured than in the work of de Man, whose narrative theory is nested in other theoretical problems, including those of textuality, reading, metaphor, allegory, and ethics itself. De Man's views cannot be fully elaborated here, or perhaps anywhere, but Hillis Miller has made a noble attempt in an essay modestly titled "'Reading' Part of a Paragraph in *Allegories of Reading.*" Miller begins by noting that for de Man, ethicity is not conceptually placed at a beginning, as a basis for language, nor at an end, as "a final triumphant return to reality that validates language," but rather "in the midst of an intricate sequence" (155). It is, as it happens, sequence that de Man tries to question, asserting that narrative consists of a stringing-out along a literally fictional referential time-line of elements that exist "in fact," as Miller puts it, in a moment of synchrony (155). "Ethicity" depends upon maintaining this "fact" by resisting the temptation to referential reading in the name of a strictly textual imperative. De Man describes the form of this imperative in a famous sentence: "The paradigm for all texts consists of a figure (or a system of figures) and its deconstruction" (*AR* 205). Unpacking this paradigm leads, Miller promises, not only to the heart of de Man's thinking on narrative and ethics, but also to a richer understanding of the ethics of the narrative turn.

For de Man, all denomination illegitimately posits a necessary connection between name and essence, and thus is already what de Man calls an "aberrant" metaphor. Since such "metaphors" are inherently unstable, simply to posit one is to bring out its aberrance: the "figure" and "its deconstruction" are one and the same. "Narrative" indicates the gradual, sequential revelation of this primordial condition. Or, as Miller, breathing hard, puts it, "All texts, in de Man's somewhat idiosyncratic nomenclature, are narratives, in the sense that they are the serial presentation, as if it were a story, complete with implied protagonist, narrator, and reader, of what is in fact the synchronic positing and deconstruction of a figure or system of figures" (158). De Man takes narrative, with its inaugural instability, its dynamic groping, its pressure towards conversion, as a heavily coded representation of denomination itself, the very name of language's aboriginal error.

So now we know: naming deconstructs itself in the same way that narrative converts itself. But de Man further insists that any knowledge obtained through this process constitutes a new act of "assertion" which commits the original error once again. This new error is subject to a "second degree" deconstruction that produces what de Man calls an "allegory" whose referent is the impossibility of "reading." And since the model of a figure and its deconstruction cannot, as de Man puts it, "be closed off in a final reading, it engenders, in its turn, a supplementary figural superposition which narrates the unreadability of the prior narration" (*AR* 205). Any assertion contains the entire sequence—and more, on and on—in a state of high concentration, like the moment just before the Big Bang. Spinning out the necessary consequences of figurality, narrative, as de Man says in another essay, "endlessly tells the story of its own denominational aberration and . . . can only repeat this aberration on various levels of rhetorical complexity" (*AR* 162).

Rorty has criticized de Man for treating such terms as "language," "literature," and "reading" as "intentional objects" operating by their own peculiar laws that are incompatible with those of "natural objects" ("Two Meanings of 'Logocentrism'" 209). Chapter 2 of this book elaborates something like this criticism in different terms; but the difference is, I believe, crucial. Rorty's terms seem critically mistaken in that, in de Man, intentionality is invariably cast as a temptation to be resisted, and resisted precisely through subjection to the inhuman machinery of language, literature, and reading. Narrative performs the "ethical" negation of desire, never more decisively than at the climactic narrative turn, which can, in de Man's system, be located theoretically at the moment when an assertion—a narrative in waiting—is effectively deconstructed, its aberrance fully disclosed. At this moment, the reader, who is always, in de Man, both necessary and necessarily cancelled, confronts the choice of either ratcheting up in response to the properly linguistic imperative to the next, painful level of the textual system or sliding down towards the easeful, and somewhat contemptible, death of achieved meaning. So the internal gearing of narrative structures the moment of ethical choice for the reader.

The "ethics of narrative" seems, so far, to be a traditional exercise of discipline, of choosing the linguistic over the subjective. But in the continuation of the passage Miller is reading, de Man makes the assertion, discussed earlier, that "allegories are always ethical, the term ethical designating the structural interference of two value systems." And this might suggest that ethical imperatives simply cannot be followed, for they encode two distinct kinds of directives. This suggestion appears to be confirmed by a subsequent sentence: "The passage to an ethical tonality does not result from a transcendental imperative but is the referential (and therefore unreliable) version of a linguistic confusion" (*AR* 206). Even "ethics" seems to be crossed by two distinct value systems, one that regards it as real, prizes it, and urges obedience to its clear imperatives, and another that denigrates it as the pretentious form of a linguistic glitch. It is difficult enough for uncertain and vacillating readers to follow an imperative, but more difficult still if the imperative itself vacillates.

So "rigorous" is de Man's formulation that not even the imperative that reading ought to refuse closure and assertion itself can be closed or asserted. But what de Man has in common with the least rigorous common reader are the concepts of repetition and return. The unrigorous or worldly reading takes the narrative as a mimetic repetition of some actual or possible extratextual reality, and sees the closure of plot as an appropriate and satisfying return to quietude after disturbance in the realm of reference; the "textual" reading takes the narrative as an allegorical repetition of an aberration or disturbance that is properly located in language, an aberration to which the rigorous reading returns endlessly.

So while the reader can choose between two kinds of repetition and return, she cannot choose between repetition and return as opposed to something else. When Stephen Jay Gould contrasts the "narrative" structure of a text that tracks "time's arrow" with a structure that mimes "time's cycle"—which, he says, is "more than pure narrative"— he mistakes a constrained sequence for narrative. For narrative does not simply document a "mere aimless wandering through time's multifarious corridors," but also represents the order of "an immanent timelessness of invariant, or cyclically repeating, pattern" (*Time's Arrow* 46). De Man's is a minority view of repetition as irrational necessity; for Gould as for the referential reader, a sense of repetition operating at various levels is the signature of rationality, order, and good sense as well as the only way narrative has of escaping the boredom of interminable episodic sequence. Heidegger describes a progress that seems indelibly narrative in structure when he says that "we reach those things with which we are originarily familiar precisely if we do not shun passing through things strange to us," adding that "originarily familiar" means "what before all else has been entrusted to our nature, and becomes known only at the last" (*On the Way to Language* 33). Heidegger does not say that the "knowledge" of the origin was always known or even always available, simply that the knowledge earned by the passage through strangeness will have the character of a repetition of an original knowledge. Through the logic that decisively ties repetition to alterity, the knowledge of the end will not have the pristine quality of an origin, for the passage itself will remain within the "regained" knowledge, its strangeness preserved like a fossil as a permanent resistance to what Peter Brooks calls narrative's "temptation to oversameness" (109). This temptation is constantly risked by what Brooks calls "repetition toward recognition," the essential narrative drive, the "truth of the narrative text" (108).

Brooks dedicates his book posthumously to de Man as an "extraordinary colleague, teacher, and friend," but it is far from certain that de Man would have approved. De Man did not see narrative as a movement "toward" a decisive recognition of "truth," but rather as a series of reenactments of an original error, replicating itself like a cancer cell or a computer virus, at increasingly stratospheric levels of abstraction. For Brooks, on the other hand, the life of eroticized desire is all. Taking *Beyond the Pleasure Principle* as "Freud's Masterplot," a meditation on the "narratability" of human life, Brooks proposes that narrative plot be understood as a formalization of the "internal logic of the discourse of mortality" (22). According to this logic, the unchallenged pleasure principle drives onward, seeking the shortest possible route to death through the necessary detours and digressions that ensure "the right death, the correct end" (103). This analysis of plot contributes, Brooks suggests, to "an erotics of art," an account of the "specifically erotic nature" of writing and reading narratives—an account, finally, not of a de Manian "necessity" but of a return to worldly origins, a process of worldly renewal, with "desire as narrative thematic, desire as narrative motor, and desire as the very intention of narrative language and the act of telling" (103, 54). Especially coming from a colleague, student, and friend, such talk, with its confusion of linguistic and subjective referents, its invocation of an almighty Eros, its promises of "truth" and "correctness," might have been de Man's worst, or almost his worst, nightmare.

By the pedagogic logic of Freud's *Moses and Monotheism*—which is to say, by the logic that ties repetition to alterity, the logic of narrative itself—de Man's hard lesson seems to have become precisely inverted in the very process of faithful transmission. Brooks's "repetition" is hardly the same word as de Man's; it is more like an uncanny homonymic antonym. In *Reading for the Plot*, repetition is the constant effect of desire, both the origin of narrative as a telling of past events, and the end of narrative figured as a return. Repetition is also the very principle and essence of the middle, where, through the myriad devices of symmetry, recollection, reminder, returns *to* and returns *of*, the reader is encouraged and enabled to fit the narrative text together, to "bind one textual moment to another in terms of similarity or substitution rather than mere contiguity" (101). Finally, repetition hedges the grimmer implications of a plot that mimes the desire for death. Death is the end of life, but narrative art has its consolations, foremost among which is the promise of rebirth. The "role" of the plot, Brooks says, is to "impose an end which yet suggests a return, a new beginning: a rereading" (109).

Thus plot reassures the reader that the successful death drive inscribed in the closed plot has as yet been unsuccessful in his or her life. In order to make this point theoretically, Brooks actually turns away from the pleasure principle and towards the very different version of desire exhibited in repression, in which the repressed instinct perpetually demands a satisfaction it cannot attain. Glossing this poignant image with Lacan's dictum that desire itself is, as Brooks says, "inherently unsatisfied and unsatisfiable," Brooks derives a message exactly opposite to that carried by the mortal logic of plot (55). Whereas a "desire" modelled on the pleasure principle had produced both a comforting closure and a threatening death drive in the text, "desire" as repression retains the comfort but rejects the threat by giving the reader intimations of immortality—further proof, if any were needed, of Freud's point that repression is not incompatible with the pleasure principle. What might be hard in the text goes easy with the reader, for while the text presses on undaunted towards the edge of the world, the right kind of death, the "master trope" of narrative from the reader's point of view is not death at all but the delicious "*anticipation of retrospection*" (23). The most comprehensive and decisive example of the evasion of the implications of closure in *Reading for the Plot* is the discussion of Freud's analysis of "The Wolf Man," which becomes not merely remarkable but "heroic" and "daring" when Freud sacrifices the very coherence he had labored so mightily to establish by adding a qualifying postscript in which he questions his conclusions (277). Despite its uncompromising death drive, then, narrative does not figure the death of the individual, but actually sublimates it, as readers made "transindividual" by reading struggle heroically to remember, to repeat, to work through, and to try to recapture "that transcendent home, knowing, of course, that we cannot" (111).

At the root of this dreamy account of the reader's experience of narrative lies a doggedly sunny view of repetition based on a heavily censored reading of Freud. For Freud, as we have seen, repetition was the most powerful and unassimilable threat to the pleasure principle, the one mental imperative that preceded and exceeded the drive for mastery and a reduction in tension. For Brooks, however, instinctual repetition is restricted to what was, for Freud, just one of its potential functions: preparing the way like John the Baptist for a pleasure principle that succeeds and transcends it, "carrying out," as Brooks puts it, "a task that must be accomplished *before* the dominance of the pleasure principle can begin" (100). Repressing any dimension of repetition that does not carry out such a task, Brooks, even more forcefully than Freud, also represses the possibility of a repetition-based ethical "instinct." But such an instinct might be built into narrative in the repressed form of the anticipation of retrospection. Many narratives, Brooks points out, inscribe some expectation of their own transmission, some assessment of their own worth, through moments of "evaluation" that imply a judgmental function within the narrative itself (34). Derrida's encapsulation of Levinas in the phrase "il aura obligé" applies equally to the narrative anticipation of a judgment issuing from the future and falling on the present. Insofar as narrative could be said to contain a judgment of itself, it betrays a kind of ethical "instinct"; and Brooks, to that extent, could be charged with having mistaken the form and force of his own master trope.

At this point a marvelous symmetry emerges. De Man posits a closed system based on textual repetition, Brooks an open system based on readerly repetition. De Man argues that the reader must accede to the text and resist the temptation to interpretation; Brooks, that the reader must resist the temptation to regard the text as closed or uninterpretable by dredging it repeatedly for new, determinate meanings. De Man imagines a cleanly "cognitive" apprehension of what he calls in his later work a nontranscendent and "inhuman" language that stands implacably between the subject and anything like "home"; Brooks, a painfully "human" quest for a "home" which, however unreachable, is comfortingly transcendent and nonlinguistic. De Man's is a sentimentalism of the law in which the subject is sheltered from the threat of death by connection to a system in which there is no "life" whatsoever; Brooks's is a sentimentalism of freedom in which the subject is sheltered from the threat of death by the infinitude of desire. De Man's narrative is a repetition of error; Brooks's, a repetition leading to truth.

But however radical their differences, de Man and Brooks agree in two important respects. The first is that narrative runs against the grain of ethics. A curious inversion of the first, the second point of agreement is that the reading subject lies under an imperative arising from the nature of narrative to read in a particular way.

The apparent incoherence of theories that postulate an imperative-bound reader materializing through engagement with an anti-ethical narrative actually begins to disclose the true locus of the ethics of narrative. We may begin this process of disclosure by considering the ambivalence of Brooks's central concept, which oscillates, sometimes even within a sentence, between the formalist stasis of a text-centered "plot" and the dynamic reader-centered "plotting." Indecisively favoring the latter, Brooks explains that "the participle best suggests the dynamic aspect of narrative that most interests me: that which moves us forward as readers of the narrative text, that which makes us—like the heroes of the text often, and certainly like their authors—want and need plotting, seeking through the narrative text as it unfurls before us a precipitation of shape and meaning, some simulacrum of understanding of how meaning can be construed over and through time" (35). Brooks appears here to be following the tendency that developed through the 1960s and 1970s in narrative theory and in literary theory generally to displace attention from the text to the reader. This tendency can be tracked in the work on narrative of Barthes, Louis O. Mink, Hayden White, Paul Ricoeur, and others. Ricoeur, for example, moves from a rigorously formalist position in a 1980 article on "Narrative Time" to a more readerly position in *Time and Narrative,* published several years later. "To make up a plot," he says in the later text, "is already to make the intelligible spring from the accidental, the universal from the singular, the necessary or probable from the episodic" (1:41). But in Ricoeur as in Brooks, the move is never more than a tendency. Through a sustained rhetorical indecision, Ricoeur leaves open the question of whose "making," the text's, the author's, or the reader's, is involved. Similarly, Brooks leaves uncertain the exact origin of the factor—the "that which"—that "moves us forward," or "makes us want and need plotting." Extending a cloudy deference to the reader, such formulations permit the radical inference that the plot, that traditional sign of formal wholeness, actually signifies the disintegration of form through dependence on an unpredictable readerly creativity. They also make a mess of narrative theory, which can no longer count on even the most minimal understanding of its central component. Even more insistently than traditional formalism, recent work begs the central question: What *is* plot?

Any answer to this question must begin by conceding the strength of both the formalist and the reader-centered positions. Unlike "argument," plot is more likely to be understood by the reader as a retrospective and speculative construction. Plot is, however, a construction of a particular text that uses only materials in the text. In one sense external to the narrative, plot is also deeply internal. In a word, plot is the law of the text, arising from within and yet not precisely as its own. Orienting everything to its overall figure, plot commands the respect of its parts as the synecdochic unity inferable from each of them, the whole within which alone they might become meaningful.

Intriguingly, this account of the plot can also serve as an account of the reader who "makes" the plot. The principle of this transfer is sketched out by Nozick in the analysis of "value" in *Philosophical Explanations*. Nozick suggests that value should be considered a "choice," a "reflexive imputation" of a certain quality to things (563). Choosing value, we seek, Nozick says, a quality discoverable *in* things, and yet one that does not compromise our freedom or integrity by compelling our response. Insisting on our autonomy, we display the "full extent of the basic moral characteristic," a self-structuring *as* a "value-seeking self" (564). The imputation is "reflexive" because the quality sought is also the quality displayed by the search. Nozick calls this quality "organic unity," the fact of being contained, complete, independent. A measure of the degree of organic unity, value is thus "something whose existence is dependent upon us, but whose character is independent" (556). At the moment we ascribe value to something, we testify to our own unity and to the unity of the thing; and we become, moreover, organically unified with the object of our choosing. The very quality we discover in the object is now discoverable in our relation to the object. In this way, Nozick says, the fact-value split is overcome: in the choice of value, the subject chooses "to be identical with value, not merely to have or realize it" (569).

Nozick might well be describing the construction of plot, in which free and autonomous reading subjects impute unity to a text with which they become, by that very gesture, organically unified themselves. Responsible for their own constructions, readers can nevertheless construct only by submitting to the text as to an autonomous otherness: form is the unity of the "me" and the "not-me" in understanding. Readers are, therefore, bound in time and through the contingent details of the text to construct the law of the text. This law must be the effect of the text as it operates over time, but by determining what the reader constructs, it causes the cause of which it is the effect. Where, then, is the law? Neither strictly in the text nor in the reader, the law emerges in the binding of the reader by the text and the binding of the text by the reader. The "il" who "aura obligé" cannot be determined as either reader or text, but necessarily as a union—a mutual binding rather than a mere confusion—of the two.

Insofar as narrative demands the construction of a plot, it "allegorizes," to appropriate de Man's term, the value-event and the value-relationship. In this respect, narrative does, as de Man says, string out an event that is in fact synchronous; the event strung out, however, is most profitably construed not as the positing-and-deconstruction of self-contained "figures" but as the relation of the creative reader to the narrative, which is precisely what de Man had tried to eliminate. And this relation, rather than language "itself," is what constitutes the law of narrative. As no meaning can be established without some determination of the plot, the reader must constantly be engaged in the perception and construction of the plot, and hence, just as constantly, must grapple with the law.

The point is clinched for me by my own experience. For many years, I read Dickens's revised conclusion to *Great Expectations* as darkly threatening. The passage that most troubled me described Pip's last meeting with Estella: "I saw no shadow of another parting from her." This suggested to me the possibility that another did part from her, but cast no shadow, or perhaps that Pip failed to see the shadow. And this corresponded to the sense I had of Bentley Drummle, Pip's rival, who seemed at home in shadows. The entire text fell under the shadow of this dark ambiguity, which implied that Pip's relation to Estella remained uncertain. Later, it was explained that "another" did not refer to a person, but modified the noun "parting"; and that the ending implied Pip's marriage to Estella. Maybe so. Maybe Dickens, who revised an earlier ending in which Pip and Estella did part in response to the demand for a satisfactorily sentimental conclusion, found a way to accommodate both his audience and his own increasingly bleak sense of the world through the grammatical ambiguity of "another parting." But the point is that the "form" of the plot depends upon determinations made by a reader who must remain partly in the shadows, responsible for the creation of the law he perceives.

It is especially useful to recall this in light of certain canonical descriptions by Sterne, Fielding, Thackeray, Gide, Stendahl, and Henry James, and reinforced by numerous modern critics, of narrative literature as the site of a sprawling lawlessness, a shapeless heap of sentences, even a "disintellective" impediment to "critical" or "theoretical" thinking (Cohen, *Historical Culture* 81). It is, rather, in narrative plot that we see the law in productive resistance to the freedom of the reader and to the freedom of its own subordinate, and potentially insubordinate, elements. Indeed, the effect of narrative is to produce the clear idea of freedom only within and through the clear idea of obligation. The image of plot as the law is useful, too, as a response to those who see the "ethics of literature" as being based on the priority of the "special or unique features" of the particular instance over and against the reductive indifference to the particular of what Nussbaum calls "the Kantian account" ("Reply" 206). That account, admittedly, is not rich in illustrative narrative because of Kant's wish to separate analytically what he conceded could not be separated experientially. Nevertheless, it is the relation of reader to narrative text in the determination of plot—the marriage of Aristotle and Kant after all—that provides at once the most general and the most compelling instance of the law at work.

The union of freedom and the law in the Kantian account and in narrative compels a small but crucial revision of the plot of Jameson's "single great collective story," the master narrative into whose spacious parameters a Marxist criticism is to gather all the events and all the narratives of the past (*PU* 19). The bloody, dusty, mysterious events of the past must, Jameson argues, be retold as episodes in a "single vast unfinished plot," an "uninterrupted narrative" whose "single fundamental theme" is "the collective struggle to wrest a realm of Freedom from a realm of Necessity[3]" (20, 19). The note refers to a passage in Marx's *Capital* which indicates even more clearly what is intended. "The realm of freedom," Marx says there, "actually begins only where labor which is in fact determined by necessity and mundane considerations ceases. . . . Freedom in this field can only consist in socialized men, the associated producers, rationally regulating their interchange with Nature, bringing it under their common control, instead of being ruled by it as by the blind forces of nature" (3:820). For Marx, as for Jameson, the lamentable reign of Necessity constitutes a primitive and unredeemed condition of enslavement to be worked through and abandoned. This view of freedom as the crown of all succession leads Jameson to repudiate labor itself as "the ultimate form of the 'nightmare of history,'" and to declare in the controversial conclusion to his book that "*all* class consciousness—or in other words, all ideology in the strongest sense . . . is in its very nature Utopian" ("Marxism and Historicism" 162; *PU* 289).

Despite his insistence on the nonrandomness of all mental events, Freud, too, was utopian in this respect, as a note in *The Ego and the Id* confirms. The task of therapy, Freud says, is not "to make pathological reactions impossible, but to give the patient's ego *freedom* to decide one way or the other" (40 n.1). Resisting, often violently and explicitly, and often in the name of "realism," the bare possibility of ethics, Marx and

Freud imagine an ideal narrative leading to an unconditioned freedom in which the very determinism on which they had insisted all along simply vanishes.

From one point of view, narrative itself seems to conspire in such wishfulness. The progress of many narratives can be seen as a purposive draining of various forms of necessity or compulsion in the gradual approach to a free futurity, to a point where the protagonist dies, marries, or lights out for the territories. But narrative, as I have been arguing, also invokes and even enforces necessity. In fact, the most efficient way for contemporary readers to restrain such utopian fantasies of unrestrained liberation, in Marx, Freud, or in other discourses, would be to contemplate not just the element of mourning necessarily bound up with closure, but also the molecular implications of "narrative sentences," whose "most general characteristic," Danto says, is "that they refer to at least two time-separated events"—the event of the story and the event of the telling—"though they only *describe* (are only *about*) the earliest event to which they refer" (*Narration and Knowledge* 143). The most immediate and inescapable facts about these events are that the first is fixed, while the second is free. The sequence of narrative sentences thus produces a continual and nonsequential relation between necessity and freedom that models and anticipates the production, actually a reproduction, of such a relationship in the construction of plot.

The "passage to another moral order" that White says is effected by the closure of plot is not, then, a one-way ticket to freedom, but rather a perpetual reinscription of the relation of freedom and obligation, the reader and the other. In its very otherness, narrative also provides a way of negotiating another antinomy crucial to the history of ethics, Hume's *is* and *ought*. Narrative moves from an unstable inaugural condition, a condition that *is* but *ought not*—a severance, in other words, of *is* and *ought*—through a process of sifting and exploration in search of an unknown but retrospectively inevitable condition that *is* and truly *ought-to-be*. Narrative cannot posit a static *is;* this function is allocated, as Genette argues, to "description," which inhabits narrative like a cyst. Nor can narrative prescribe an unresisted *ought*; this is the prescriptive province of sermons. Like an Althusserian mode of production, any moment in a narrative contains and implies all others, and even the final synthesis, if there is one, recalls and preserves its *ought-nots*, the false leads, seemingly pointless complications, and digressive wanderings that went before. But if narrative is powerless to render either *is* or *ought*, it can, and ceaselessly does, figure a process of turning from a disjunction of the two, through resistance, towards their union. Plot is, in this highly qualified respect, utopian after all; for it provides what practical reason cannot, a principle of formal necessity that governs the movement towards the union of *is* and *ought*.

2. Abroad Only by a Fiction: Creation, Irony, and Necessity in Conrad's *The Secret Agent*

Tragedy is . . . an imitation of agents.
  Aristotle, *Poetics*

Socratic irony is the only completely involuntary form of disguise—and for that very reason, the only completely deliberate one. It is equally impossible for anyone to conceal or to reveal it. . . . It comprises and evokes a sense of insoluble opposition between the absolute and the relative, between the impossibility and the simultaneous necessity of total communication. It is the freest kind of poetic license, for by this means one becomes superior to oneself; and yet it is also the strictest, since it is an unconditional necessity.
  Friedrich Schlegel, *Lyceum of the Fine Arts*

On April 9, 1906, a few weeks after the first appearance of the anarchist publication *Mother Jones*, Joseph Conrad, in the midst of creating *The Secret Agent: A Simple Tale*, wrote to John Galsworthy:

I have always that feeling of loafing at my work, as if powerless in an exhaustion of thought and will. Not enough, not enough! And yet perhaps those days without a line, nay, without a word, the hard, atrocious, agonising days are simply part of my *method* of work, a decreed necessity of my production. . . . I doubt not only my talent (I was never so sure of that) but of my character. Is it indolence,—which in my case would be nothing short of baseness,—or what? No man has a right to go on as I am doing without producing manifest masterpieces. (Jean-Aubry, 2:33)

Together with those of Flaubert, Rilke, Gide, and Kafka, Conrad's letters, many of which strike this note of futility, impotence, and doubt, provide eloquent testimony to the Modernist sense of the agony of art, an agony structured in Conrad's case by the friction between what may, for simplicity's sake, be called "secrecy" and "simplicity." Conrad's letters in particular reflect the *acedia* of an extravagantly painful and, for all he knew, sterile and pointless self-punishment, a daily subjection to the spectacle of his own nonproductivity. If he had been producing masterpieces, that would have been one thing; but of that he had little assurance: despite his earnest efforts to write marketable fiction, Conrad realized in 1908, at the age of 51, less than five pounds in royalties from his thirteen published works, which included *Heart of Darkness, The Secret Sharer, Lord Jim*—which had sold fairly well eight years earlier—*Nostromo, The Nigger of the "Narcissus,"* and *The Secret Agent.* In the face of this implacable evidence of public indifference to his labors, Conrad had every reason to consider the act of creation in the light of a Levinasian other that ungratefully returned nothing to its loyal slave.

Compounding this recurrent condition of self-loathing and despair were other circumstances that, as Conrad's wife Jessie put it in her memoir, an affectionate account of Conrad's astonishing oddity, "might well have appalled the stoutest heart." *The Secret Agent* had, she wrote, "more difficulties in the way of its birth than any of the others" (*Conrad as I Knew Him* 125). Begun in Ford Madox Heuffer's house in Kent at the beginning of the year, the composition was continued in Galsworthy's London house, where the Conrads had gone to await the birth of their second son. Born in August, the infant soon became desperately ill with whooping cough and was expected to die. Shortly after, the older son contracted pleurisy and was also feared likely to die. Mrs. Conrad, who had just undergone a serious operation herself, tended the infant after the doctors had abandoned hope, while Conrad saw to the needs of the older boy. By September, he had produced just 45,000 words. But from this point on, he worked rapidly, finishing the first, serialized version in time for it to begin appearing in *Ridgway's: A Militant Weekly for God and Country* in October 1906. The family relocated, first to Montpellier, then to a hotel in Geneva, where, despite the strains of travel and dislocation, constant anxiety and sick-care, personal illness, as well as chronic, pressing, and humiliating money worries, Conrad swiftly wrote the last 15,000 words for the book version that appeared in February 1907, featuring a greatly expanded and more leisurely account of the murder of Verloc by his wife. For this efficiency under duress, Conrad earned his own wife's "additional respect" (*Conrad as I Knew Him* 55).

Still, *The Secret Agent* was in many respects an unusual production for Conrad. The first of his novels to be based on "secondary" rather than "primary" sources (reading rather than experience), it is, as Albert Guerard says, Conrad's most "professional" novel, a work of "virtuosity" (*Conrad the Novelist* 228, 231). It is, accordingly, his most elaborately and consciously "created" work, the one in which the process of composition was most accessible to him. Most strikingly, the book was actually one of Conrad's easiest creative experiences, accounting for relatively few of the agonies of art. In terms of its composition at least, *The Secret Agent* seems really to have been the "simple tale" its subtitle calls it. "I began this book impulsively," Conrad recalled in the 1920 "Author's Note," "and wrote continuously" (37). Perhaps the clue to this relative ease of production is indicated in the "Author's Note," where Conrad recounts the scraps of news, gossip, and chance reading that provided the occasion, prod, and many of the details of the narrative he eventually composed. This story of the story, the narrative of the discovery of the project, constitutes Conrad's fullest account of the process of creation. My initial hypothesis here will be that Conrad found *The Secret Agent* easy to write because he discovered in the raw materials of the story precisely the kind of agony or intrinsic difficulty that he identifies as his "*method* of work, a decreed necessity of my production." In other words, these materials appeared to possess an internal drive that disclosed to Conrad something like the germ of creation itself.

As Conrad's friends and especially his wife were constantly discovering, Conrad's memory was reliably fallible. His narrative in this case has many gaps, which have been filled in by Eloise Knapp Hay, Ian Watt's *Casebook*, Graham McMaster, and Norman Sherry. But the very imperfection of Conrad's recollection makes of the "Author's Note" a source of information on another subject: Conrad's ideas about what is likely to occur in the creative process. These ideas were themselves, of course, largely determined by ideas generally current. One of the best known early theories of creativity, Joseph Wallas's 1926 *The Art of Thinking*, proposed that creation occurs in four stages: preparation (a semiconscious gathering of material); incubation (the internal elaboration of that material, the growing sense of a "problem"); illumination (the intuited sense of a solution to the problem); and verification (the realization of that solution). Like many subsequent theories of creation, Conrad's account proceeds by clearly defined stages. Rehearsing the "very old story" of the novel's composition in the "Author's Note," Conrad says that, finding himself in a period of "mental and emotional reaction" following the completion of *Nostromo* and *The Mirror of the Sea*, he "gave myself up to a not unhappy pause" (37, 38, 39). And then . . .

> Then, while I was yet standing still, as it were, and certainly not thinking of going out of my way to look for anything ugly, the subject of *The Secret Agent*—I mean the tale—came to me in the shape of a few words uttered by a friend in a casual conversation about anarchists or rather anarchist activities; how brought about I don't remember now. (39)

The preface to *Nostromo* documents a similar sequence. After finishing *Typhoon*, "it seemed," he wrote, "that there was nothing more in the world to write about. This so strangely negative but disturbing mood lasted some little time; and then . . . as with so many of my longer stories, the first hint for *Nostromo* came to me in the shape of a vagrant anecdote completely destitute of valuable details" ("Preface to *Nostromo*" 169). The very destitution of the material invited the internal elaboration that moved the production from "preparation" to "incubation" and through to "illumination." It is a circumstance repeated in Henry James's "Preface" to *The Spoils of Poynton*, where James speaks of the "stray suggestion, the wandering word" which, despite its "air as of a mere disjoined and lacerated lump of life," contains in its vagrancy a "sacred hardness, the very stuff for a clear affirmation" (119). The sheer formal nullity of the "germ" provokes the search for its true, optimal, and necessary destiny. So, too, with *The Secret Agent.*

> I remember, however, remarking on the criminal futility of the whole thing, doctrine, action, mentality; and on the contemptible aspect of the half-crazy pose as of a brazen cheat exploiting the poignant miseries and passionate credulities of a mankind always so tragically eager for self-destruction. . . . Presently, passing to particular instances, we recalled the already old story of the attempt to blow up the Greenwich Observatory; a blood-stained inanity of so fatuous a kind that it was impossible to fathom its origin by any reasonable or even unreasonable process of thought. For perverse unreason has its own logical processes. But that outrage could not be laid hold of mentally in any sort of way, so that one remained faced by the fact of a man blown to bits for nothing even most remotely resembling an idea, anarchistic or other. ("Author's Note" 39)

The "friend"—Heuffer—commented that the man blown to bits in the attempt on the Observatory was "'half an idiot. His sister committed suicide afterwards'" (39). From this bit of information, Conrad derived a sense of "illumination" that "remained satisfactory but in a passive way." Subsequently, he came upon a book containing the "rather summary recollections of an Assistant Commissioner of Police" who had held his post "at the time of the dynamite outrages in London, away back in the eighties." The author had recounted a conversation in the Lobby of the House of Commons with the Home Secretary, Sir William Harcourt, following an anarchist incident. Harcourt had said, "'All that's very well. But your idea of secrecy over there seems to consist of keeping the Home Secretary in the dark'." "Not much in itself," this remark nevertheless "stimulated" Conrad immediately. "And then ensued in my mind what a student of chemistry would best understand from the analogy of the addition of the tiniest little drop of the right kind, precipitating the process of crystallization in a test tube containing some colourless solution" (40).

At once, "strange forms, sharp in outline but imperfectly apprehended," claimed his attention, followed by a rapid tumbling of images—of South America, the sea, a "monstrous town . . . in its man-made might"—that eventually distilled into a particular tale, "the story of Winnie Verloc," which at last "stood out complete from the days of her childhood to the end, unproportioned as yet, with everything still on the first plan, as it were; but ready now to be dealt with. It was a matter of about three days" (40, 41).

"*This* book," Conrad declares, "is *that* story . . . its whole course suggested and centred round the absurd cruelty of the Greenwich Park explosion. I had there a task I will not say arduous but of the most absorbing difficulty. But it had to be done. It was a necessity" (42). Working it out, "I was simply attending to my business" with "complete self-surrender. . . . I could not have done otherwise" (42).

But was this particular task so imperative? Where was the "necessity?" What burden did these recollected incidents, this half-conscious collection of narrative scraps, these swirling images—all concerning "meaningless," "perverse," "contemptible," or "half-crazy" acts—impose on him? One answer is that the world of violence and waste that they suggested, a world Conrad might call "unthinkable," constituted a rebuke to his beliefs, his powers, but particularly to the right and capacity of narrative art to render the world. Additionally, however, this "material" might have seemed uniquely fertile, a sociohistorical version of a certain "anarchy" intrinsic to creation. The image of the exploding human being might, in other words, have been taken by Conrad both as a challenge and as a nearly explicit invitation to creation. To such a provocation narrative *must* respond; and indeed all narrative necessarily affirms its own rights and capacities to narrativize, to crystallize from an anarchic swarm of images a story. To do so is, as Henry James comments, to discover the necessity latent in the original germ, or, as he puts it, "the *secret* of the particular case" in "drawing the positive right truth out of the so easy muddle of wrong truths," the blunders and deviations that make actual life seem so contingent ("Preface" 123).

"There is a class of human beings," Freud said in a famous essay written within months of the appearance of *The Secret Agent*, "upon whom, not a god, indeed, but a stern goddess—Necessity—has allotted the task of telling what they suffer and what things give them happiness." These are "victims of nervous illnesses, who are obliged to tell their phantasies, among other things, to the doctor" ("Creative Writers and Day-Dreaming" 146). Insofar as "anarchy" is commen-

187

surate with what Freud calls "nervous illness" and "phantasy," the possibility arises that not only neurotics—and Conrad was surely that—but all creators serve the goddess of Necessity. Generalizing from the "Author's Note," we could speculate that creation begins with anarchy.

Necessity issues, in Conrad's account, not from the particular details of his materials, but rather from what James called the "thing" of a story, the matter or issue that the story is, as Conrad says, "centred round." In the case of *The Secret Agent,* the "thing" would comprehend the style as well as the plot, the "purely artistic purpose" of the composition, which, as the "Author's Note" says, was to apply and explore "an ironic method," formulated "in the earnest belief that ironic treatment alone would enable me to say all I felt I would have to say in scorn as well as in pity" (41). At once the stimulus and instructions for work, "*this* book," this subject-in-a-certain-style, completed, ideally unflawed, fully itself and yet perfectly expressive of "all I would have to say," beckons to the creator from the future, guiding the choices necessary to produce it. The shimmering futurity of the as-yet nonexistent work *aura obligé* the creator from the very start.

In its broad outlines, this is indeed a very old story, the oldest fiction about fiction. The claim that the creator could not have done otherwise than he did is as old as the Yahwist who implores the deity to breathe the articulate spirit into him, who represents his text as a mere transcription of what has been spoken by God. It is as old as the bard who invokes the Muse for inspiration and direction, as old as the mystic who implores the Lord to "speak through me," as old as the poet who calls on Love: I' mi son un che, quando / Amor mi spira, noto, e a quel modo / ch'e' ditta dentro vo significando (*La Vita Nuova* 24.52–54. [I am one who, when Love inspires me, takes note, and goes setting it forth after the fashion which he dictates within me]). It had to be done, Dante might have said of the *Vita Nuova*; I was the poem's transcriber, not its author, an amanuensis or scrivener rather than an original creator. The finished product has taken its form not from me, but from the thing—Love—itself. An "old story" in that it precedes all stories, the narrative of creation tells the tale of the domination of the creator. Nietzsche said that creators had to be hard; but in this oldest of stories, they must also be soft, that is, responsive to the will of the other who is summoned and who summons them to the work (see *Ecce Homo* 309). It is Nietzsche, not Dante, who aligns creation with ethics, bringing both under the sign of obedience. "Every morality," Nietzsche says in *Beyond Good and Evil,* "is a piece of tyranny against 'nature,' likewise against 'reason' "; and then immediately notes "the strange fact" that "all there is or has been on earth of freedom, subtlety, boldness, dance and masterly certainty . . . in the arts as in morals, has evolved only by virtue of the 'tyranny of such arbitrary laws.'" "Every artist knows," he writes, "how far from the feeling of letting himself go his 'natural' condition is, the free ordering, placing, disposing, forming in the moment of 'inspiration'—and how strictly and subtly he then obeys thousandfold laws which precisely on account of their severity and definiteness mock all formulation in concepts. . . . The essential thing 'in heaven and upon earth' seems, to say it again, to be a protracted *obedience* in *one* direction" (§188).

Artistic obedience is a tale told again and again. E. L. Doctorow has pointed out that among the very oldest conventions of the novel—used, for example, by Cervantes and Defoe, modified, through "Marlow," by Conrad, and reinvented by Nabokov—is the fiction that the text has been "found" or "discovered" by the author, who represents himself only as its "editor" ("False Documents" 219–21). Displayed in a weaker form in any first-person fictional narrative, this pretense is typically intended, Doctorow argues, to secure a certain readerly credulity and deference towards the text as, if not a document of fact, at least a factual document, one that really existed, that was not made up or produced by an "artist" whose motives might be suspect. But as we have begun to see, the belief that the work already exists is a useful, even essential belief for the creator, who otherwise might be overwhelmed by the spectacle of an infinite number of possible paths leading to a destination that itself might be reconceived at any moment. The fact, however fictional, that a work predates any authorial agency works in a manner whose effectiveness is not in any sense undermined by its dubiety to guide the creator who would bring it into being. As "editor," the creator can labor in the "neutral" mode of repetition, a humble craftsman or functionary, avoiding—while taking—the daunting risks of creation. Thus, in the narrative of creation, the artist "receives a glimpse" of a perfected form, "remembers" some sublime harmony, "preserves" the fading ember of inspiration, "discovers" the key to the code. "I had only my ear to help me," Stravinsky says. "I heard and I wrote what I heard. I am the vessel through which the *Sacre* passed" (*Retrospectives* 32). Arnold Schoenberg reported "a sense of merely transcribing what already existed" (see Reich 242). One becomes a creator by persuading oneself that one is not a creator in the pure sense, but only a superior listener, observer, servant. The narrative of the imperative is the necessary fiction of fiction. If one believes that the perfect figure of George Bernard Shaw lies waiting within the mass of marble, then one acquires a certain kind of confidence in one's gestures: one is not chipping away as an act of ex nihilo creation, one cannot do just anything; one is simply cleaning up, liberating, or "correcting" a work already essentially completed.

Creation requires, then, a certain relation between the not-yet-created and the already-there; or, more generally, between the present yearning towards the future and the future stretching back to the past. In this, what has so far been called "creation" is entirely compatible with what Derrida calls "invention," which, he says, "*begins* by being susceptible to repetition, exploitation, reinscription" ("Psyche: Inventions of the Other" 28). "How," Derrida asks, "can an invention *come back* to being the same, how can the *invenire*, the advent of time-to-come, come to come back, to fold back toward the past a movement always said to be innovative?" It does so, he claims, by taking on the character of a repetition, representing itself only as the unfolding of the dynamics of "what was already *found* there," or as the assembly of "a stock of existing and available elements" (59, 43). The Cartesianism of invention in that it suggests a belief that the object exists in itself, independent of all desire, this notion of "finding" can apply to the "elements" of the work and even to the completed work itself, discovered by the creator already "existing in a virtual or invisible state" (47). "Thus it is," Derrida concludes, "that invention would be in conformity with its concept . . . only insofar as, paradoxically, invention invents nothing" (60).

And thus it is that, in the narrative of creation, the fiction that one is a passive non-agent, a recorder or at most an impresario, enables and even empowers the fact of decisive authorship. Creation coordinates with what Hegel calls "wit," which, as de Man puts it, "projects into the future what belongs to the past of its own invention and repeats as if it were a finding what it knew all along" ("Hegel on the Sublime" 151). This projection, de Man insists, is not duplicity but a necessity: "The poet, like the philosopher, must *forget* what he knows about his undertaking in order to accede to the discourse to which he is committed" (152). One hesitates to call invention self-determined or other-determined, constrained or free; for invention requires a prior invention of that which will make invention not merely possible, but necessary: one must produce a principle of necessity by which one will henceforth be bound.

In representing what they do as possibly uncreative, creators express what Derrida calls "a certain reserve with respect to a creationist theology," a reluctance to claim for themselves powers more properly belonging to God (47). But this reserve or "hesitation" also permits the momentary speculation that the creator does indeed possess, if only as it were on loan, a superhuman power. This power can issue from various sources, as long as it is not from the self. Necessity can, for example, issue from "within" the work, as a mass of anecdotal evidence attests. "I can tell if [things] are going well," Anne Tyler reports, "when the words start running ahead of themselves. If I set aside my work for a cup of coffee, the characters continue talking in my mind. Or I keep hearing my own rather sexless, neutral, narrator's voice spinning away at the story." There are, moreover, times "when your characters simply won't obey you. . . . Where did those little paper people get so much power? I'll have in mind an event for them—a departure, a wedding, a happy ending. I write steadily toward that event, but when I reach it, everything stops. I can't go on. The characters just won't allow this. I'll have to let the plot go their way. And when I do, everything falls into place" ("Personal View").

The work "goes well" when it goes autonomously, when the creator respects it, regarding the "little paper people" of her narrative not as means only, but as ends also, respecting their independence and capacity to determine their own fates. Sometimes this capacity is figured as the nearly daemonic possession of the creator by the creation. Noting that "poetic states" generally arise—as Conrad's account also suggests—"from no apparent cause," from "some accident or other," Paul Valéry describes the sensation as one of being "suddenly *gripped* by a rhythm which took possession of me and soon gave me the impression of some force outside myself" ("Poetry and Abstract Thought" 57). The words he murmurs in this condition are, it seems, "being murmured *through me*" (61). It is a "strange discourse" (63), a "language within a language" that appears to be "made by someone other than the speaker" (64), someone "miraculously superior to Myself" (81). The creation announces itself as the possession of an other; the sense of an imperative that overrides inclination guarantees its integrity. Creation thus reflects a reserve not just about a creationist theology, but about the self, an embarrassment about subjectivity and about the works that one might, as oneself, produce.

The dictatorial other need not be figured as the completed work; it can even be something so neutral and modest as style. Clement Greenberg describes how Jackson Pollock "lost himself" in style: "There is something of the same encasement in a style that, so to speak, feels for the painter and relieves him of the anguish and awkwardness of invention, leaving his gift free to function almost automatically" (*Arrogant Purpose* 202). Virginia Woolf describes a comparable sense of "encasement" but attributes it neither to "style" nor to the artist's "gift," but simply to immersion in what Valéry, too, had called the "rhythm" of the process of creation itself. The artist is Lily Briscoe in *To the Lighthouse*:

The brush descended. It flickered brown over the white canvas; it left a running mark. A second time she did it—a third time. And so pausing and so flickering, she attained a dancing rhythmical movement, as if the pauses were one part of the rhythm and the strokes another, and all were related. . . .

Then, as if some juice necessary for the lubrication of her faculties were spontaneously squirted, she began precariously dipping among the blues and umbers, moving her brush hither and thither, but it was now heavier and went slower, as if it had fallen in with some rhythm which was dictated to her . . . by what she saw, so that while her hand quivered with life, this rhythm was strong enough to bear her along with it on its current. (235–36, 237–38)

Begun with the very first strokes—indeed begun long before in a history of such strokes by herself and others—the "rhythm" of creation simply lifts "her," the artist, with her will, intentions, desires, and pains, and bears her along. As Nietzsche said, constraints—provided in this case by those first strokes, which are understood to indicate some task, to participate in some preexisting thing—have an effect both emancipatory and protective. Generic conventions, rhyme, meter, audience habits, and everything in any sense pre-created in the creation, all represent questions answered, possibilities realized, options foreclosed, problems solved. Anton Webern noted that the twelve-tone system, just because it was so rigidly defined, made "free fantasy" possible: "To put it quite paradoxically," Webern wrote, "only through these unprecedented fetters has complete freedom become possible!" (*The Path to the New Music* 55–56). It is in this sense that the system Chomsky described, a system in which transformational rules govern with increasing restrictiveness each successive word in a sentence—rules that language users must feel that they did not make, cannot justify, and even do not, except perhaps for Chomsky himself, understand—can be characterized as infinitely "creative." Language users can be "creative" only insofar as they submit to the laws of language. As Northrop Frye comments, "The word 'creation' involves us in a state of mind that is closely parallel with certain types of paranoia" (*Creation and Recreation* 6).

Like the behavior of the paranoiac, the gestures of the creator may seem at once compelled and coerced, and transgressive, disruptive, and unpredictable. In either event, creation is unprogrammable because the necessity that drives the work is determined as beyond human consciousness and agency. George Steiner has recently argued in *Real Presences* that creation inexorably implies an ultimate source, which he identifies as God. We must, Steiner says, live our lives, especially our creative lives, as if God existed and authorized our actions and beliefs. But, as has already been suggested, the story of creation need not refer itself to a deity. All that is required is that the authorizing other enlist what Elaine Scarry calls "belief." In Scarry's narrative of creation, the act of material making, or "making-real," is preceded by a phase of "making-up" in which "belief" is the prime mover: "Belief," Scarry says, "is what the act of imagining is called when the object created is credited with more reality . . . than oneself. It is when the object created is in fact described as though it instead created you" (*Body in Pain* 205). In the Bible, whose Old and New Testaments constitute for Scarry a massive record of making-up and making-real, the sacrifice of Abraham stands as a radiant instance of the kind of imperative exerted by an "object" or "thing" whose "believability" is demonstrated by its utter inhumanity.

Although doctrinally hostile to material culture, the Jews of the Old Testament were, on Scarry's reading, engaged in a massive production of the basic premise of material making, the most expansive single work in the history of creation: God, the Artifact. This extraordinary and idiosyncratic interpretation of both historical Judaism and of God powerfully implies what the present account has asserted in different terms: that creation characteristically occurs when the authorizing other not only liberates one's "gift" or inaugurates the creative "rhythm," but effectively destroys any sense of one's capacity even to have a gift or to initiate a rhythm. If the Jews of the Old Testament, whose perception of themselves as creators was effectively inhibited by the disembodied majesty of God, are the model of "making-up," then we must conclude that the imagination only becomes imaginative when it believes itself to be imaginary, i.e., nonexistent. Scarry's use of very similar words—Artifact and artifact—to designate the enabling other and the enabled object might seem indiscriminate; but once again the idiosyncrasy is suggestive. For the similarity between the terms richly suggests that the other is itself created, that human agency is always ultimately responsible; while the small difference of a capital letter implies that the other is not acknowledged to be created, and thus that creation occurs within the fiction of the submission of the creator to the superior force of the superhuman or nonhuman.

The unleavened theoretical solemnity of Scarry's account can perhaps be made real by comparing it with the gestation of the dancer Martha Clarke's 1987 *Miracolo d'Amore*. The chronicle of Clarke's creative process during the months before its performance suggests the delicate interplay in the creative process of belief with irreverence, the submission to an other and conscious control. What Clarke habitually referred to as "the piece" began with "a vague notion that she'd like to fool around for a couple of months with Calvino's fairy tales and Tiepolo's paintings of Pulcinello," and this notion sustained Clarke and her company through an extended period of "goofing off five hours a day." During this period, a creative process that appeared to all those participating in it as virtually random ("I'll say things like, oh, I don't know, 'Transform yourself from a virgin into a flying pig'—things like that, anything") was structured covertly by an idea, a belief in the reality and autonomy of "the piece." "The piece," Clarke says during this time, "has to find its own logic. If I don't push it, it finds its own way" (Wetzsteon 30). In the process of self-discovery, "the piece" finds that Calvino is expendable, and then Tiepolo; but this still leaves "the text," for which Clarke has already arranged for a writer. Eventually, "the piece" fired the writer when, after coming across Charles Darwin's *Expression in Men and Animals*, Clarke "realized that the piece is more about primal instincts than about intellect" (32). Shortly before the opening, Clarke reported that "the piece is becoming more like a fairy tale again"; then, at last, that "the piece is starting to breathe" (34, 35).

Only belief in the Artifact—the enabling, empowering, humbling vision of the inevitable and necessary form of "the piece"—sustained the apparently random flailing of the creative process, like that of blind and unconscious spermatozoa making their way towards the egg: miracolo d'amore! One may argue that "the piece" was entirely of Clarke's creation, but that is precisely the point: that Clarke created by first creating the believable fiction that the creation already existed that would guide those who would bring it into material being to make the "right" choices.

Perhaps the strongest, or most paranoiac, form of belief is the representation of oneself as not a self at all, but rather as a "negative capability," a faculty or power to be not just an editor, a scrivener, a lucky discoverer, but to be nothing human at all. In the most extreme form of the narrative of creation, the Artifact does not simply have more reality than oneself, but has virtually all the reality there is; and the creator, the literal agent of creation, is "depersonalized," altogether lacking in her "own" thoughts, her "own" purposes. Such a self-representation generally accompanies a fantasy of pure power. Only if the author is "nothing" can he saturate the work, existing, as Flaubert said, "in his book . . . like God in the universe, present everywhere and visible nowhere" (*Letters* 173). This fiction of one's own inconsequentiality is strongest in the strongest, most "masterly" spirits. Hence Stravinsky is a "vessel," Yeats a "medium," Pollock a "gift," and Mallarmé a "capacity." "I am now impersonal," Mallarmé writes in a letter to Cazalis, "and no longer the Stéphane that you knew—but a capacity possessed by the spiritual Universe to see itself and develop itself, through what was once me" (*Selected Letters* 74). The freedom of the creator is the freedom of the nonhuman.

One of the most recurrent fictions of creation situates it within a special, "technological" zone of being that is clean, free, exempt from the mediocrity of the resistant "ordinary" self. The act of creation is often, even characteristically, held to occur below the threshold of consciousness, in what Henri Poincaré described memorably in a 1913 essay on "Mathematical Creation" as the "subliminal self." "The poet is two people," writes Andrei Voznesensky in this vein. "One is an insignificant person, leading an insignificant life, but behind him, like an echo, is the other who writes the poetry." Conrad himself echoes this account. "There had been moments during the writing of the book," he writes in the "Author's Note," "when I was an extreme revolutionist, I won't say more convinced than they but certainly cherishing a more concentrated purpose than any of them had ever done in the whole course of his life" (42). This sentence precedes the bland declaration that in writing the book he was "simply attending to my business." The "business" of creation may well require that one, or part of one, become an extreme revolutionist.

The implication is that the creator must either become mechanical, a recording device, a sensor, or a mimic; or must permit some mechanistic faculty within himself to take charge of the work. While the ordinary self pursues the worthless freedoms of the unresisted pleasure principle, the subliminal self attends to its business at once wholly committed and detached. The subliminal self responds unhesitatingly to the task's "necessity" over the protests or indifference of the ordinary self—which are also registered in the "Author's Note": "It's obvious that I need not have written that book. I was under no necessity to deal with that subject" (38).

The work resists the world as necessity resists contingency. "I am conscious of having broken through every restriction of a bygone aesthetic," Schoenberg writes in the notes to his 1909 *George-Leider:*

> and though the goal toward which I am striving appears to me
> a certain one, I am, nonetheless, already feeling the resistance I
> shall have to overcome; I feel now how hotly even the least of
> temperaments will rise in revolt, and suspect that even those
> who have so far believed in me will not want to acknowledge
> the necessary nature of this development. . . . I am being forced
> in this direction. . . . I am obeying an inner compulsion which is
> stronger than any upbringing. (Cited in Reich 49)

If "upbringing" would encourage a reproduction of the same, a confirmation of the already-known, "inner compulsion" fosters a kind of activity that can be described in both the rhetoric of necessity or automatism and the rhetoric of deviance, as "lateral thinking," "transgressing the limits," "innovation," "chance," "luck," "amorphous thinking," "divergent thinking," or "regression." Each of these two convergent emphases sponsors its characteristic form of "invention." Within modern European thought, Derrida notes, "there are only two major types of authorized examples for invention. On the one hand, people invent stories (fictional or fabulous), and on the other hand they invent machines, technical devices or mechanisms, in the broadest sense of the word" ("Psyche" 32).

Each of these "examples" substantiates the other. It is well known that technical, scientific, or mathematical theories are often judged partly by their "beauty" or "elegance" (see Chandrasekhar). In the stories of "aesthetic" creation such as Conrad's, Mallarmé's, and Schoenberg's, the fictive or fabulous legitimates itself by claiming a warrant from the mechanical. Interestingly, if parenthetically, a comparable reversion to the strictly automatic became intensely desirable for the young Thomas Edison and especially for his potential customers, who regarded as nothing less than fabulous his capacity to devise machines that eliminated human invention, indeed human thinking, from the workplace. Edison's first major successful invention was a system of automatic telegraphy that enabled the replacement of men skilled in decoding and printing by poorly-paid, unskilled "girls" who would obediently conform themselves to the operations of a machine that required, as Edison put it, "No Intelligence" (*Papers;* quoted in Joravsky 11).

In his most intensely creative moments—but only in those moments—Conrad would have been an excellent Edisonian employee. For in his account, the creator is a functionary, governed strictly by an authority whose force and justification lay entirely within the task itself. In the humbling presence of this task, one's "inclinations," "personality," and above all intentions become supremely irrelevant. The only intention appropriate to the creator, at least in the emergent fiction we have been tracking, is obedience to the strictly formal and self-justifying imperative imposed by the task of creation itself. The power of "form," conceived as a principled indifference to intentions or even to meaning as such, is absolute over the creator. An "artist's artist" is distinguished by her reverence for technical facility or formal competence, her respect for and curiosity about materials. The primary task of such an artist is likely to be the full exploitation of the medium—especially the solution of "problems" or the overcoming of "difficulties"—rather than the urgent communication of a meaning. Such meanings as may be extracted from the work are likely to be seen by the artist as ancillary or nonessential, a precipitate of the work not to be confused with the work itself. Piero della Francesca, to take one example, is described as "a painter's painter, whose powers were concentrated exclusively upon pictorial ends, and who had no interest in the subject matter of his pictures" (Murray 6). "Pictorial"—or "musical," or "linguistic" or "dramatic"—ends assume for the creator the imperative quality of the categorical as opposed to the "softer" and corrupted quality of the hypothetical that is associated with questions of meaning.

Centered round ideas of submission, unconsciousness, automatism, and internal division, this story of creation seems to conflict starkly with Conrad's professions of single-minded moralism. These professions punctuate even his most complex and sinister works, but dominate especially his prefaces and essays. "Those who read me," Conrad says in "A Familiar Preface" to A Personal Record, "know my conviction that the world . . . rests on a very few simple ideas; so simple that they must be as old as the hills. It rests . . . on the idea of Fidelity" (19). In a well known passage from an essay on "Tradition," Conrad defends his other simple idea: "Work," he says there, "is the law. It has a simplicity and a truth which no amount of subtle commentary can destroy" (140). Such comments suggest that Conrad placed an extraordinarily high ethical premium on precisely the qualities of automatism that might appear to work against ethics itself. It is, to be sure, a "slave morality" that Conrad espouses; but it is also an artist's morality. The glorification of fidelity and work aligns Conrad with those artist's artists for whom the highest imperative is fidelity to the truth of the (aesthetic) work. In fact, by situating "work" before and against "subtle commentary," Conrad virtually models work as such on the creation of the fictive text, a creation that requires for its perfect completion a perfect submission.

The perfection of the work, and thus of the submission, may, however, be compromised rather than simply affirmed by the addition to the text of a preface, which, no matter how simple its message, constitutes "commentary," a species of "subtlety," and suggests willy-nilly that the work itself has failed to represent its author's intentions with undiluted fidelity. The "Author's Note" confirms this point explicitly in its insistence that the public scandal occasioned by the book would not have occurred if the author's intentions had been known. The "Note" also confirms the reason for misunderstanding: it is that the novel, a representation of a "bloodstained inanity," was itself sufficiently bloody and inane to appear as an anarchist text. Hence Conrad feels compelled to "justify my action," to assure his readers that he had "no perverse intention, no secret scorn for the natural sensibilities of mankind at the bottom of my impulses" (37). Responding to the challenge of social anarchy, the novel was permeable to its origins, to its others; it had, the defensive preface testifies, become itself anarchized by the materials it had appropriated, mimetically retaining some part of them, the "anarchic" part, in its formal organization. Anarchy of whatever kind constitutes an imperative—perhaps *the* imperative—to create, and it is thus this anarchistic residue in the fictive text that brings the preface into being.

The question, then, is not whether Conrad realized his intentions, but whether those intentions, or indeed any intentions to create, can be altogether un-anarchic. For the very virtues of fidelity and work, pressed into the service of creation, compel the artist to become implicated in his materials, the "thing" of his story, an implicatedness that, if this account of creation is true, requires the creator to labor faithfully in the service of anarchy. Conrad's very commitment to moral clarity through fidelity and work would, then, be largely responsible for his failure to produce moral clarity in the text. Conrad even seems aware, if not of the reasons for his failure, at least of the failure itself, offering in the preface only negative formulations of his intentions, such as that he had "no perverse intention, no secret scorn"; or that he had "not intended to commit a gratuitous outrage on the feelings of mankind" (43). There is, one could argue, an integrity to these evasions that is born of principle, for Work and Fidelity are themselves rigorously inarticulate precisely on the subject of intentions, speaking eloquently only of the intention to have no intentions. The only intentions Conrad will admit thus include within themselves a kind of cyanide capsule to be swallowed at the moment when one is captured and is about to be forced to disclose one's secrets, a factor of self-obliteration that, however grotesquely it summons up the image of a man blown to bits by his own explosives, is represented by Conrad as at once the duty of the creative artist and the highest aspiration of ethical consciousness. In fact, the very detachment of intention from effect that had, in the form of the novel's "ironic method," provoked misreading is advanced in the preface as a guarantee of proper understanding. "I expect to be believed," Conrad says of his disclaimers of anarchistic sympathies, "for the reason, which anybody can see, that the whole treatment of the tale, its inspiring indignation and underlying pity and contempt, prove my detachment from the squalor and sordidness which lie simply in the outward circumstances of the setting" (38). Accommodating both simplicity and secrecy, positivities and negativities, intentionality and unintentionality, understanding and misunderstanding, irony must have appeared to Conrad as the discovery that enabled him to create—and to create "impulsively" and "continuously"—this story of creation.

If the "Author's Note," or Conrad's statements about artistic morality in general, were to be cast in terms appropriate to the late rather than to the early twentieth century, they might take the form of the theory of creation as "morally resonant" articulated in Scarry's *The Body in Pain*. Noting that while "unmaking" or "decreation" is "widely recognized as close to being an absolute of immorality," Scarry says that creation, or material making, is "usually described as an ethically neutral or amoral phenomenon" owing to a "faulty and fragmentary" understanding (22). Material making, she argues, must be understood as a rebellion against pain. Like all cultural processes, it originates in an act of "self-extension" or "self-transcendence" that mirrors, but counters, the retreat into bodily isolation that occurs in pain. Pain, whose most extreme form is achieved during torture, robs the sufferer of speech, contracts him in upon himself, and deprives him of "consent," a faculty necessary to belief, and hence to creation. Material making begins in a dissociation of "body" from "voice," the latter being the primary form of self-extension, powerfully allegorized in the Bible by the bodiless voice of God, which is responsible for the triumphant generation of the earth, and especially of generations of the Jewish people. Singularly dedicated to acts of "rescue" (276), material making displays a tendency to largesse, excess, even surfeit that reflects the imagination's "original inseparability from compassion" (323). The chair, for example, takes the shape not of the human skeleton, not of body weight, "nor even the shape of pain-perceived, but the shape of perceived-pain-wished-gone"; it enacts "a dance entitled 'body weight begone'" (290). The maker of the chair projects "aliveness" out into the world in the form of the chair, which reciprocates by relieving sentience of its hurtability (286). Everywhere, Scarry says, the imagination is "simply, centrally, and indefatigably at work on behalf of sentience, eliminating its aversiveness and extending its acuity in forms as abundant, extravagantly variable, and startlingly unexpected as her ethical strictness is monotonous and narrowly consistent" (306). This narrowness enables Scarry to identify the intention of creation: "it is the benign, almost certainly heroic, and in any case absolute intention of all human making to distribute the facts of sentience outward onto the created realm of artifice" (288).

In one sense, the author of *The Secret Agent* had every right to claim such an intention for his creation. Thematically concerned with anarchy, the book actually depicts almost exclusively the force of compulsion, beginning with the order of Mr. Vladimir to Verloc to furnish an "anarchist outrage" that would stir up public feeling in England against anarchism, so that England would enact more repressive legislation and, ultimately, cease providing refuge for Continental terrorists, such as those active in Mr. Vladimir's country. The plot is "centred round" a radical deprivation of consent: Verloc sends his trusting, retarded brother-in-law to plant the bomb, with its delayed-action detonator, at the Greenwich Observatory, only to have him trip and set off the bomb prematurely. The tragedy of Stevie might be cast in Scarry's terms as a violation of one of the primary characteristics of material making, its link to compassion for the sentient human body. Stevie presents the same kind of affront to true creation as does capital in the work of Marx. According to Scarry, Marx undertakes a fantastically elaborate labor of reconstruction, seeking to analyze "the steps and states by which the obligatory referentiality of fictions ceases to be obligatory"; he sought to penetrate the deep "interior of capital" (260) in order to retrace "the path along which the reciprocity of artifice has lost its way back to its human source" (258); he sought to rescue and restore "the original referent" (272), the human laborer who is dissimulated by capital's "autonomy." This is the sense in which Conrad's work could be described in Scarry's terms as "morally resonant" and "inseparable from compassion": the text rescues Stevie from the spectacular anonymity of his destruction, and even represents such a rescue in its portrayal of the detection work that leads from the scene of explosion back to Stevie's home. Like Scarry's "imagination," the police are shown hard at work on behalf of sentience, reconstructing the event and promoting justice by discovering, amid the heaps of scattered and nameless fragments of bone, flesh, and clothing, a scrap of cloth from his coat inscribed by Winnie with his address. This scrap, whose inscription was intended to protect against Stevie's getting lost, seems an exemplary instance of material making in Scarry's terms. The investment of care by the coat-maker, who made it in the shape of coldness-wished-gone, and marked by Winnie in the shape of Stevie-come-home, literalizes Scarry's account of the way in which the artifact returns us ideally to origins, "like luminous breadcrumbs leading home" (37). The entire novel could be seen as constructed on the same principle, gathering into a declaration: Anarchy begone!

"Anarchy" here means not just the self-proclaimed anarchists, but every force that opposes compassion and intelligibility. As a made object, the text would, if we go along with Scarry's analysis, find it "necessary" to resist the challenge to its powers posed by anarchy, the affront to coherence, reference, and rescue. Unlike the God of the Old Testament, or capital, and unlike the anarchist bomb, the novel—Conrad might have said, but did not—would heal; it would, as Scarry puts it, "perform the counterpart of projection, reciprocation" (276). It would not represent a gratuitous outrage on the feelings of mankind.

If Conrad does not discover and lay claim to a positive argument on something like Scarry's terms, the reason must lie in an uncertainty, whose formal expression is the "ironic method," about the effect and even the intention behind the book. That is, what inhibits Conrad from expressing Scarry's confidence about the moral resonance of creation, what confines him to negative assertions about his intentions, might be the fact that the entire novel, written in the ironic mode, has an ironizing effect on morality itself. Where Scarry insists that "the distance separating the model of creation from the model of decreation is vast" (145), and insists, consequently, on a virtually absolute ethical difference between the two, Conrad's text, like irony generally, abruptly collapses these distances by making the two in a certain sense compatible, if not identical.

This ironic compatibility between creation and decreation can be brought out by redescribing the two deaths in Conrad's text—Stevie's detonation and the stabbing murder of Verloc by Winnie—in the language Scarry uses to describe material making, especially her phrases about the "reversal" of "bodily linings" that makes "what is originally interior and private into something exterior and sharable"; or about the "reabsorption of what is now exterior and sharable into the intimate recesses of individual consciousness" (285). The atrocious "fit" between act and description can be most efficiently indicated by simply providing Conradian referents to Scarry's discourse: "Thus"—one such passage might be rewritten—"the reversal of inside and outside surfaces ultimately suggests that by transporting the external object world [Winnie's knife] into the sentient interior [of Verloc], that interior gains some small share of the blissful immunity of inert inanimate objecthood; and conversely, by transporting [Stevie's] pain out into the external world, that external environment is deprived of its immunity to, unmindfulness of, and indifference toward the problems of sentience" (285). Whatever Scarry's intentions in such passages were, they assuredly did not include an account of violent death.

What really divides Conrad's practice from Scarry's theory is not, however, that he literalizes expressions she intends figuratively. It is that he has created an imaginative work that, in Scarry's terms, perverts by its very nature the act of making, whose proper medium is, for Scarry, "material." Scarry maintains the ethical "consistency" of making by exiling beyond the gates of the city of culture works that not only originate in the imagination but remain there, works, that is, in which the imagination fails to transform its operations into nonsentient material. Written fiction can only represent for Scarry a sidetrack, a spur of imaginative work, complicit with rather than opposed to pain. Torture, for example, is for Scarry a "display of the fiction of power" (57); disputes that lead to war entail a representation of the beliefs and self-conceptions of the enemy as "cultural fiction" (128); and "fictiveness" is a "major attribute of language" that both precedes and justifies physical injury, or that follows, reports, and often falsifies that injury (134). Unlike material making, language can lie.

Even when it represents the strictly imaginative suffering of strictly imaginary characters, fiction is helpless to offer any healing reciprocation. In order for the work to reciprocate, in Scarry's sense, it must be nonsentient, and since a novel is not nonsentient in the sense that a chair is, it cannot ground the circuit of pain. Perhaps the greatest perversion of the novel is that it convincingly appears to be the free creation of the writer, so that the work could actually be said to proceed exclusively from the pleasure principle. This is in fact Freud's case in "Creative Writers and Day-Dreaming," where he describes how the writer merely "transposes the things of his world into a new order that pleases him" (143–44), effecting a "liberation of tensions in our minds" that enables readers to indulge their fantasies "without any self-reproach or shame" (153). Despite Conrad's best intentions, then—despite his principled horror both at anarchist bombers and at loafers—the novel is actually vulnerable to the charge that it owes whatever pleasure it produces as a work of art to a principle of non-reciprocation whose paradigmatic form is the infliction of pain.

What might particularly pain the creator of the "Author's Note" can be most efficiently expressed in a phrase Scarry uses to describe the imagination: "nonimmunity from its own action" (324). The entire novel could be said to be tightly organized around this notion, with virtually all characters suffering unforeseen consequences of their acts. Nonimmunity may well also be the ruling idea of the Conradian protagonist who, as readers since André Gide have noted, characteristically commits some irresponsible act and spends the rest of his life trying to redeem himself. Michael Fried speaks of "Conrad's attraction to the theme of self-betrayal," a theme that takes on added depth in *The Secret Agent* in light of that novel's meditation on agency and creation ("Almayer's Face" 222). In this respect, Stevie, an "artist" whose thinking is both absolutely nonprogressive, expressing itself in endless circles, and absolutely utopian, triggered by primitive moral judgments, represents a certain "secret" dimension of agency, an "idiotic" dimension (or dementian) in which agency is diluted and determined by such factors as delusion, imperfect mechanisms, the intentions and acts of others, and accident—in short, an anarchic ungroundedness that produces a hesitation about whether to place the emphasis on the agent or on the act. The agency of representation especially displays this "nonimmunity": "irony" is the token of anarchy in the fictional text, but the preface is also permeable to the fiction it represents. Indeed, both the power and the strangeness of *The Secret Agent* derive from the fact that in the process of waging defensive warfare on behalf of the bracing ethical oppositions between creation and decreation, anarchy and Fidelity, indolence and Work, Good and Evil, Conrad has had to employ a weapon, irony, that is also an agent of anarchy and the enemy of oppositions.

Perhaps the weirdest instance of nonimmunity occurs in Conrad's account of the creative process, when he says he was "arrested by a little passage," a dialogue in a book of memoirs involving the Home Secretary. Reading this passage, Conrad reports that he experienced intense "stimulation" comparable to "the addition of the tiniest little drop of the right kind, precipitating the process of crystallization in a test tube"; followed by a succession of "strange forms" in Conrad's mind, which resolve themselves into a vision of an enormous town; and finally the emergence into high relief of the "story of Winnie Verloc" that provided the "necessity" of creation (40–41). I repeat this sequence to draw attention to the peculiarity of Conrad's account, in which, having already raised the issue of "perversion," he represents himself being "arrested," and then experiencing something like the effects of a chemical reaction. All this recalls the Professor, who would be arrested if he did not always carry with him enough explosives, to be set off by a detonator—"partly mechanical, partly chemical"—activated by the squeezing of an india-rubber ball inside his pocket, to destroy both himself and whoever tried to arrest him (91).

An extravagant figure of nonimmunity, the Professor epitomizes the mindless destructiveness of anarchism. Nevertheless, Conrad, writing what he titles the "Author's Note" but refers to within the "Note" as the "Preface," must have responded with a measure of sympathy to certain features of the Professor's description because he appropriated these features in his self-representation. The way in which the Professor raises the issue of "character," for example, might have been directly transported into the "Author's Note" as a shameless expression of what Conrad indicates in far more circumspect terms when he speaks of his "general character" and of his hopes that his readers will credit him with "decency, tact, *savoir-faire*, what you will" (37). "'In the last instance it is character alone that makes for one's safety,'" the Professor comments in phrases Conrad palpably wishes he could apply to himself; "'There are very few people in the world whose character is as well established as mine'" (92).

Of course, the Professor's "character" is an ironic inversion of the "character" Conrad aspired to, but such irony is a code easily cracked. A "moral agent" bent on making a "clean sweep," the Professor is astonished and horrified by "the mass of mankind" one encounters in the large town (102, 97, 103). Similarly, the Prefacer (who, in the first writing task undertaken after *The Secret Agent*, a preface to Jessie's *A Handbook of Cookery for a Small House*, wrote that "good cooking is a moral agent" ["Cookery" 370]) insists that his actions can be justified, and contemplates the "man-made might" of the "monstrous town" (41, 40). The Professor's mission is "to destroy public faith in legality"—the very crime of which the Prefacer had felt himself accused (102). In their own ways, the narrator says, "the most ardent revolutionists" merely seek for "peace in common with the rest of mankind . . . the peace of soothed vanity, of satisfied appetites, or perhaps of appeased conscience" (102). The Prefacer, too, is a creature of vanity ("I am not at all certain that I am modest" [37]), of satisfied appetites ("I really think that *The Secret Agent* is a perfectly genuine piece of work" [41]), and especially of appeased conscience ("I have not intended to commit a gratuitous outrage on the feelings of mankind" [43]). Most arresting of all, the Professor voices the very principle of such relationships between antipodes such as destroyer and creator, or fiction and fact, even novel and preface. Comparing anarchists to the police who oppose them, the Professor notes that they are "Like to like. The terrorist and the policeman both come from the same basket. Revolution, legality—counter moves in the same game; forms of idleness at bottom identical" (94).

Applied to the Professor and the Prefacer, the principle of "like to like" invites the reader to consider a further "anarchic" element of a certain conception of creation. This conception is the subject of a recent article by Paul Feyerabend, who attacks the idea of "creativity" exemplified in writings by and about Einstein as a "dangerous myth." In "Physics and Reality," Einstein had described as a prerequisite for the kind of insight that leads to discovery the quality of "intuition, resting on sympathetic understanding." The first stage of invention, Einstein argued, was the correlation of sense experiences with a concept in order to produce "the concept of bodily objects"; the second stage was the attribution of "significance" to this concept, a significance which, although a "free mental creation," has "justification" only insofar as it retains a connection with sense impressions (294). Up to this point, Einstein seems virtually to be describing Conrad as the latter presents himself in the "Author's Note," a man proud of what had been called his "excellent intuition of things," a creator of a work that, although wholly invented, was justified by its faithful connection to the real world of anarchism (42). But Feyerabend charges that the entire account, pivoting on the idea of the "free mental creation" of a subject in the "fictitious surroundings" of "the labyrinth of [his] sensations," posits an impossible and radically undesirable idea of creators as "self-contained entities separated from the rest of nature" ("Creativity" 708–9). Wherever the myth, or perhaps ideology, of "the fictitious process, creativity" does take hold, it provides "motives for strange and destructive actions." Thus we need to insist all the more strongly on the fact that all humans are "inseparable parts of nature and society" (710). Even creators are "citizens" who should "be prepared to accept the guidance and supervision of their fellow citizens" (711).

Feyerabend makes two of Scarry's points: that anarchy is unethical, and that fiction is implicated in anarchy. Writing from the depths of his social conservatism, Conrad nevertheless suggests a perspective that both contains and exceeds such moral assurance. Within such a perspective, it is impossible to affirm both the anarchy of ethics and the ethics of anarchy. The first affirmation has in fact been made by Levinas, for whom "anarchy" signifies "responsiveness" or "responsibility." A world that has "lost its principle, an-archical, a world of phenomena," he writes, "does not answer to the quest for the true," but rather to the quest for the ethical (*Totality and Infinity* 65). From Levinas's point of view, anarchy is the source of the ironies that reappear in the defenses against it.

The second affirmation, about the ethics of anarchy, is scattered but implicit throughout Conrad. Writing in 1907 to his friend R. Cunninghame Graham, Conrad remarks that in having the Professor say, "'madness and despair—give me that for a lever and I will move the world' I wanted to give him a note of perfect sincerity" (Conrad, *Letters to Graham* 170). Conrad often repeated key words and phrases (The horror! the horror!) even in altogether different contexts, and this one turns up several years later in the manifestly "sincere" text, "A Familiar Preface" to *A Personal Record*, where Conrad speaks of "the force of a word": "Give me the right word and the right accent," he says in the preface, "and I will move the world" (6). The implied redundancy of "madness and despair" and "the right word" suggests a rapprochement between anarchy and ethics that is explicitly invoked in an anarchist essay Conrad may have known, Auberon Herbert's "The Ethics of Dynamite." Written in 1894, the same year as the Greenwich Bomb Outrage, Herbert's essay warns that "we, too, have power. It is not like your power, disguised under innumerable forms and ceremonies. . . . Mine is the power that can be carried in the pocket of any ragged coat, if the owner of the ragged coat is sufficiently endowed with courage and ideas" (see Sherry 281). The ethics of anarchism is determined partly by those unspecified ideas, but also by the immediacy of the discharge from ideas into force, and perhaps most of all by the public, non-secret nature of the force itself. It is in this respect that the madness and despair of anarchistic self-destruction approach the force and meaning of the right word and the right accent, of what Conrad calls in "A Familiar Preface" "perfectly open talk" (17). In perfectly open talk, the public may repose its full confidence, for intention is unmediated by agency, meaning is exhausted by use, and utterance is wholly suited to context. It is the dream of logocentrism, the dream—as Herbert's essay affirms—of dynamite.

The representative in *The Secret Agent* both of Herbert and of the metropolitan police is the Professor, who cherishes his own dream, of a "perfect detonator," a "really intelligent detonator" that would "adjust itself." Like the perfect word, the perfect detonator would strike everyone immediately and without prejudice. Perfection is, however, as elusive as justice; even the Professor's own detonator has a twenty-second "delay" between intention and effect, the squeezing of the bulb and the explosion. "'The manner of exploding,'" the Professor explains, "is always the weak point with us'" (92). "Delay" is also an inhibiting factor in the perfection of language. In his discussion of Husserl, Derrida shows why, by describing delay as a necessary structural deferment of what Husserl too-hastily called "the natural origin." "Here delay is the philosophical absolute," Derrida says, in terms a "Professor" would appreciate, "because the beginning of methodic reflection can only consist in the consciousness of the amplification of *another* previous, possible, and absolute origin in general. . . . The Absolute is *present* only in being *deferred-delayed* without respite" (*Edmund Husserl* 152–53). Anarchism has history on its side, for its power, however immediate it may appear, is conditioned by the factor of delay that converts presence into history and makes of all knowledge a knowledge of the past. Anarchism thus aligns with writing, the dimension of language which, as Derrida argues, most insistently confirms the anarchic non-presence of the origin.

All knowledge may be knowledge of the past, but anarchism is not, it must be pointed out, interested in knowing about the historical past anything other than that it does not embody the putatively just dispensations of an origin. Anarchism is, as Hayden White comments, "inclined to idealize a *remote* past of natural-human innocence from which men have fallen into the corrupt 'social' state in which they currently find themselves" (*Metahistory* 25). Conrad registers this inclination in his adherence to values "old as the hills," and in his attraction for "very old" or "already old" stories, stories that required a reworking that, however temporarily, transported the creator back to the beginning. As a creator, Conrad necessarily shared the anarchist idealization of a magnetic but literally repellent origin, an origin that cannot be fully known. Also as a creator, Conrad entertained, especially in his prefaces and essays, the anarchist dream of the annulment of time through an explosive act of realization. As White continues: "they [anarchists], in turn, project this utopia onto what is effectively a non-temporal plane, viewing it as a possibility of human achievement *at any time*, if men will only seize control of their essential humanity, either by an act of will or by an act of consciousness which destroys the socially provided belief in the legitimacy of the current social establishment" (25). Or, Conrad might have added, if they find, speak, and heed "the right word."

Drawing particular attention to the Professor as a "Nietzschean" figure, Edward Said argues that Conrad and Nietzsche shared an "attitude to language" based on a sense of "utterance as inevitably and endlessly leading to another without recourse to a single originating or unequivocally privileged first fact" ("Conrad and Nietzsche" 65). At first glance, Said seems to have gotten it dead wrong, describing a regrettable fact—"delay"—about detonators and writing as definitive of Conrad's "attitude," ignoring the many expressions in the prefaces of a fervent belief in first facts such as Work and Fidelity. But considering that Conrad represented the Professor's power as merely fictive or imaginary, a power that must not be used, then perhaps Said is unexpectedly right—perhaps Conrad inscribed in his fictions, if not his sincere statements of belief, not only the dismal inevitability but also the positive humanistic virtue of deferral. But if so, then the conclusion seems perverse: that the factual moralistic preface dreams irresponsibly of the perfect word whose effects are literalized in the fictive novel as an anarchist bomb.

Conrad was not the only creator to justify such dreams. In fact, the discourse of creation has been impressively resourceful in finding ways to reinvent anarchy. In the *Salon de 1859*, Baudelaire described his own creativity as being "à tout casser, comme une explosion de gaz" (quoted in Burton 170). This explosion is repeated in Jacob Burckhardt's point in *The Civilization of the Renaissance* (1860) that "creativity" became the human activity on which most reliance was placed when the state, politics, and religion lost their power to center and organize the culture. In the Renaissance, Burckhardt said, individual creation acquired fantastic new opportunities, mixed with nihilistic potentialities; and the greatest art coexisted with political terrorism and villainy. For recent theoreticians, nothing seems more natural than to describe creativity as, in the words of Silvano Arieti, "barrier-breaking," a loosening of the imprisoning effects of individuality (*pace* Stevie). The most anarchic of all theories of creation is actually that of Scarry, who says that imaginative "making-up" "may entail a revolution of the entire order of things, the eclipse of the given by *a total reinvention of the world*" (171).

So it is to be expected that the discourse of anarchism lays particular emphasis on the idea of the world as the vast product of countless acts of individual creation. In one of the most famous of all anarchist writings, "Anarchism: What It Really Stands For" (1911), Emma Goldman represents a world wholly man-made as both a profound shame and an unparalleled opportunity. In Goldman's view, the enemies of anarchism are the loafers, "the lazy class" (67), or "the lazy men" who think that "government rests on natural laws" (64) when in fact it rests on "violence" and is therefore "wrong and harmful, as well as unnecessary" (56). Anarchism attacks at this point of non-necessity, promoting the liberation of the "sovereign individual" (73), to be positioned at the center of "a new social order" based "on liberty unrestricted by man-made law" (56). Indeed, Goldman claims, the force of liberty was already busy "reconstructing the world," "usher[ing] in the Dawn" (73).

Anarchism could be described in Scarry's terms as a social movement based on the power of the imagination to reinvent the world. The imaginative writer, impressed as Conrad was by the "monstrous town . . . in its man-made might," a human creation whose "darkness" devours the world's light and defers the Dawn, actually stands in close proximity to a certain concentration of "anarchic" forces, a primary configuration not just for this particular novel but for creation in general. For what anarchism does, in attacking, for example, the Greenwich Observatory, is to try to unmask the most fundamental and natural-seeming of laws—the global grid by which the precise hour of the Dawn is calculated—as man-made (Universal Standard Time had in fact been established only in 1888) and therefore fictive and therefore unnatural and therefore revisable through the human capacity for making-up and making-real.

Anarchism is a marginal social movement, but its founding premise structures many of the diplomatic protocols of the nation-state. These protocols are the subject of a discussion between Mr. Vladimir and the Assistant Commissioner. The latter, who suspects the former's involvement in the bomb outrage, tells him that the crime seems to have been planned abroad. "You admit it was planned abroad?" Mr. Vladimir asks.

> "Theoretically. Theoretically only, on foreign territory; abroad only by a fiction," said the Assistant Commissioner, alluding to the character of Embassies which are supposed to be part and parcel of the country to which they belong. (209)

Both real and theoretical, established and revisable, national boundaries not only enable but virtually necessitate secret agents, which are employed freely by embassies, by anarchists, by fictionalists of all kinds. They are even employed by the police. Later that same evening, the Assistant Commissioner tells the Secretary of State, Sir Ethelred, that he has discovered, in the wake of the bomb incident, not just a suspect but a "psychological state." To get to the bottom of the affair, he intimates, he may have to employ a secret agent. "'In principle,'" he tells Sir Ethelred,

> 'I should lay it down that the existence of secret agents should not be tolerated, as tending to augment the positive dangers of the evil against which they are used. That the spy will fabricate his information is a mere commonplace. But in the sphere of political and revolutionary action, relying partly on violence, the professional spy has every facility to fabricate the very facts themselves, and will spread the double evil of emulation in one direction, and of panic, hasty legislation, unreflecting hate, in the other. However, this is an imperfect world—' (144)

And—the sentence might be finished—in such a world the secret agent is perhaps the most effective way of realizing one's intentions. Mere fabrications, these agents possess a monstrous power to create a reality they purport to mime; they serve as primary agents—direct causes of action—in the guise of secondary agency—the representation of an other.

The irreducible duplicity of agency itself, a duplicity emerging with special clarity in the case of "fabrication," suggests once again the peculiar affinity Conrad may have intuited between his "materials" and the creative process; and suggests, too, why he nominated the "ironic method" as the "purely artistic purpose" of the entire novel. For irony represents a species of anarchic nonimmunity-from-its-own-action in the domain of language. Detaching speaker from utterance, intention from meaning, irony unlinks the entire communicative chain of narrator, character, author, and reader. For this reason, irony is manifestly unsuited to serve most worldly purposes. Hence the anxiety of moralistic criticism when it confronts irony. Such criticism characteristically responds to ironic detachment by urging that irony ought, in normal or ideal circumstances, to be neutralized or stabilized through the principled conversion of doubt into certainty. This is notoriously the case with Wayne Booth's 1974 *The Rhetoric of Irony*, and also with Gary Handwerk's 1985 study of *Irony and Ethics in Narrative*, where irony is conceived as "a form of discourse that insists upon the provisional and fragmentary nature of the individual subject and thus forces us to recognize our dependence upon some mode of intersubjectivity that exceeds the furthest extension of any individual subject" (viii). Irony, itself, however, resists moralization. Whatever it is that insists and forces is more like "ethics" than like "irony," which disappears from Handwerk's sentence at about the same time that the fragmented subject assembles itself into "us." Indeed, perhaps the only "purpose" that irony *can* serve is that of a "purely artistic" or Kantian art in which sensation is unhinged from idea, desire from judgment, purposiveness from purpose, an art based on an idea of "beauty" that stands autonomously midway between the pleasure of incarnation and the good of rational law, an art conceived as "something within the subject as well as without him, something which is neither nature or freedom" (*Critique of Judgment* 199). What Conrad discovers in *The Secret Agent* is that art conceived on the Kantian model, pure art, is "at bottom identical" with perversion, terrorism, and anarchy.

The largest formal setting of irony in *The Secret Agent* is what critics have called the "mood" of the narrative, which Jocelyn Baines contrasts with the "theme" or plot. The latter has been a disappointment to many who, like Baines, find it "very hard to decide what the central interest is; for, although the ironical treatment provides a unity of mood, the book lacks . . . a unifying theme, and when it is carefully examined falls apart into a succession of only superficially related scenes; in fact the 'crystallization' of which Conrad speaks in the Author's Note never occurs" (*Conrad* 340). Often treated as a principle of fragmentation, irony is for Baines the source of a unity that the theme or plot—putative agents of unity—only dissimulate.

The smallest scale on which the irony-effect is generated is the pluralized individual word, especially such oft-repeated key words as "reaction," "effect," "wise," "agent," "necessity," "thoughtless," "indolent," and, preeminently, "simple"—words used to such violently differing effects that the simplest of them falls under suspicion. The term "moral," for example, attaches to the Professor, the "moral agent"; to Heat, who, though "not insensible to the gravity of moral differences," still recognized the "morality" of anarchists as being "of

the same kind" as that of the police (110); and to the Assistant Commissioner, who feels "pangs of moral discontent" (118); to Stevie,
whose "morality" was "very complete" (169); once again to Heat,
whose attempt to incriminate the innocent Michaelis is "not without
its moral value" (191); and to Verloc, who senses "subtle moral affinities" between himself and Mr. Vladimir (82). The basis of principled
distinctions, morality ironically becomes a linguistic placeholder for a
general commonality or kinship. Even the Professor's meditation on
the underlying likeness between antagonists is repeated, and ironized,
by his enemy Heat, who reflects that "the mind and the instincts of a
burglar are of the same kind as the mind and the instincts of a police
officer" (110). The same simple words, the same preoccupations with
morality, necessity, kindness, likeness, and so forth, are constantly re-
worked, explored for internal differentiations, so that to read the book
is to reread it, to encounter once again the same, but different.

Perhaps the word "kind" is subjected to the most grotesque rework-
ings. The term of Stevie's compassion for "poor people" and abused
horses, kindness also informs Conrad's solicitude for the "feelings of
mankind." A suggestion of both kindness and kinship determines
Winnie's heartfelt fantasy that Verloc and Stevie "might have been
father and son"; and indeed the issues of kindness, the unity of mankind, kinship, the feelings of mankind, the relation of like to like, and
affinities between different kinds, thoroughly saturate the text. It may
seem merely incidental, or horribly ironic, that Conrad describes in
the preface the crucial moment of inspiration through the "analogy"
of crystallization, the addition to a "solution" of "the tiniest little drop
of the right kind," for the image disconcertingly recalls the Professor's
detonator. But of all characters in the novel it is the Professor who
sustains the most persistent sense of the global oneness of "mankind."
The Professor himself is an ironic figure, "calling madness and despair to the regeneration of the world" (269); and the juxtaposition of
his detonator and the creative act suggests the vast and unexpected
reach of irony, deep into, and well beyond, the boundaries of language as such. Linguistic irony and acts of creation are of the same
kind as the combination of unlike elements in the Professor's flask.

More improbable still, perhaps, is the notion that irony's exploration of the kinship between unlikenesses provides not only a ruling
principle for this particular text (which serially couples Verloc and
Winnie, Verloc and Stevie, Heat and the Professor, Verloc and Mr.
Vladimir, Verloc and anarchists, Winnie and Ossipon) but for creation
itself. Nevertheless, this hypothesis is supported by classical accounts
of wit, discovery, invention, metaphor, inspiration, and creativity,
which repeatedly stress the "yoking" or "bringing-together" of dispa-

rate elements (see Hadamard), the "union of dissimilars" familiar from Romantic aesthetics, or what Arthur Koestler calls creative "bissociation," a mental occurrence simultaneously associated with two habitually incompatible contexts. Scarry's allegorical narrative of material making continues this tradition, pivoting on the operation of a two-sided tool/weapon that temporarily conflates wounding and creating in the process of producing a freestanding artifact.

At the center of Scarry's account of creation is the notion of a power-generating "distance from the body" of "voice" that precedes and enables any creative act. Assuming that freestanding artifacts must display in coded or displaced form some trace of their own origins, the residue of some generative "distance," two figures in *The Secret Agent* emerge as candidates, both ironic. The first is Stevie, who becomes "creatively" distanced from his body in the very moment of becoming mortally "wounded." The second is the toneless, unfathomably detached narrator, or narrative voice, which records even the knifing murder of Verloc by Winnie with an undisturbed and protracted leisureliness, as though it had no woundable body. Scarry nearly describes this famous scene when she says that "there are certain instruments (such as those in medicine and dentistry) that we call 'tools' even though they enter human tissue." But so vast is the "gulf of meaning" that separates the tool-function from the weapon-function that "a conscious mental act" is required to sustain the "perception of the flesh-cutting knife as a tool" (173). Even adults "tend to watch the approach of the knife toward an arm with complete equanimity only if they know that the tissue of the arm has been anesthetized and thus made almost nonsentient" (174). Indeed, Verloc watches Winnie's approach with a fascinated but very incomplete equanimity, all too aware of his own hurtability. The narrator, on the other hand, is so composed as to appear anesthetized.

Once again, *The Secret Agent* resists an easy assimilation to the theory that seems to express its highest aspirations. For Stevie as the detonator of creation represents a collapse of the distance between creation and decreation that Scarry insists is "vast," while the narrator stands at a distance from bodiliness that is not strategic, temporary, or metaphorical, but absolute. Moreover, neither figure contributes to a narrative of compassion; they collaborate not in "rescue," but in rejection: Stevie begone! Verloc begone! By closing some distances and opening others, *The Secret Agent* actually indicates a larger, if less edifying vision than that disclosed in *The Body in Pain*. The narrator is critical to this vision. Not merely the voice of indifference to human suffering, the narrator also fulfills several traditional functions of narrative that would otherwise be left disturbingly vacant. The first is indicated by Freud, who says that every story features "a hero who is the centre of interest, for whom the writer tries to win our sympathy by every possible means and whom he seems to place under the protection of a special Providence. If, at the end of one chapter of my story, I leave the hero unconscious and bleeding from severe wounds, I am sure to find him at the beginning of the next being carefully nursed and on the way to recovery. . . . It is the true heroic feeling, which one of our best writers has expressed in an inimitable phrase: 'Nothing can happen to me!'" In this fantasy of invulnerability we can, Freud adds, "immediately recognize His Majesty the Ego, the hero alike of every day-dream and of every story" ("Creative Writers and Day-Dreaming" 149–50). But who qualifies? Not Verloc, although the working title of the text was simply his name; for Verloc does not recover. Nor can it be Stevie; nor Winnie, although it is as "the story of Winnie Verloc" that the work finally crystallized. None of these is under the special care of Providence, or even of the metropolitan police. The narrative voice, however, proceeds unmolested through scenes of anarchy, murder, and perversion, measuring the possibility that Winnie will be hanged without fear for its own neck. (Hanging would, indeed, be redundant: ironic meaning is, as commentators since Schlegel have pointed out, "suspended.") That voice alone meets the inviolability criterion, and meets it because it *is* alone, and not only alone but without an identifiable body, and not only without a body but without a voice either: it is just text, the most radical reduction possible of the human imperative to communicate. *The Secret Agent* is the first Conradian text to be drawn from reading rather than from experience; it is also the first, and really the only, *written* text in Conrad's entire oeuvre.

The second contribution of the narrator to narrative's humanism is suggested by Said, who writes that "the Conradian encounter is not simply between a man and his destiny," but between "speaker and hearer. Marlow is Conrad's chief invention for this encounter, Marlow with his haunting knowledge that a man such as Kurtz or Jim 'existed for me, and after all it is only through me that he exists for you.' The chain of humanity—'we exist only in so far as we hang together'—is the transmission of actual speech" ("The Text, the World, the Critic" 176). This would seem to make *The Secret Agent*, the first major Conradian text without such an "invention," radically un-Conradian. But in fact the novel is hyper-Conradian; for the indifference of the narrative to readers and characters alike effaces distinctions, rendering everything within its representational orbit indeed "alike." A story

without an identifiable teller, a particular implied audience, a protagonist, a unified plot, or a turning point, *The Secret Agent* still has a hero
and invokes, and even helps to create, a community.

Through the agency of the preface, this community includes Conrad himself, who draws the terms of his self-description as a creator,
and of humanity at large, from the figures of his fiction. It is Verloc
who "originally" utters "a few ominous generalities on the theme of
necessity" (185), the ancestors of those Conrad utters in the preface.
And it is Chief Inspector Heat who, "though what is called a man,
was not a smiling animal" (133), inspires by inversion this odd echo
from *Hamlet* in the preface: "Man may smile and smile but he is not
an investigating animal" (38). And it is Winnie, with her belief that
"things do not stand looking into" (172)—Winnie, "guiltless of all
irony" (169)—who is the original for what follows that sentence in the
preface: "He [man] loves the obvious. He shrinks from explanations"
(38). Winnie shares with her mother, her husband, Michaelis, and Vladimir a corpulence that suggests "constitutional indolence" (167), a
charge, as we have seen, to which Conrad was especially sensitive and
to which the assurances of "difficulty" and "attending to business"
were meant as responses. And Winnie, once again, who first exemplifies "detachment" (192). Impressed with this quality, Heat nevertheless warns her that "you won't be believed as much as you fancy you
will" (196). To this—it must be—Conrad replies in the preface that he
"expect[s] to be believed" on the subject of the nonperversity of his
intentions precisely because of his "detachment" from the subject (38).

The creation of the intricate kinship system within the novel was
what Conrad referred to in the preface as an "absorbing" difficulty.
This difficulty was redoubled as the novel itself was absorbed into the
preface, whose earnest account of motives, intentions, and character
was determined by agents of the novel operating in certain embassy-
sentences of the preface. Lacan uses the term *aphanisis* to describe the
"fading of the subject in the field of the other," a curious and vague-
sounding formulation until we see it happening to author, narrator,
characters, and reader in *The Secret Agent* (see *FFC* 207–8, 215, 221).

The ensemble of preface and narrative presents the spectacle of a
general fading in the field of the other, a demystification of difference
on the principle that the other is "abroad only by a fiction." Fiction
itself maintains a tenuous distinction from its other, as its other, the
moralizing preface, immediately asserts. "I must conclude," the preface begins, "that I had still preserved some of my pristine innocence
in the year 1907. It seems to me now that even an artless person might
have foreseen" the scandal created by the novel (37). Allied with art-
lessness, innocence reveals itself in the capacity to commit an uninten-

tional crime. In 1920, the author of the preface, no longer innocent or artless—he was an older and more worldly man, and the anarchy of the Great War had intervened—is in a position to assure the public that he had not intended to commit a crime because the artistic text had been produced by an artless person. Crimes are committed by innocent people, while proclamations of innocence, proclamations that their proclaimers "expect to be believed," are made by artful persons no longer innocent. One cannot be innocent and declare it at the same time, but one can declare that one was once innocent, and point to a crime as proof. The "Author's Note" and the text hang together as evidence and plea of innocence—but also as evidence and plea of guilt in an aphanisis of even the most elementary distinctions.

So far, the argument has centered round Conrad's contention that all this was a necessity and has sought to define that necessity in two ways. The first, which might be called the "special theory of necessity," referred to the particular circumstances of Conrad and his materials, such as the social situation of anarchy, the attempt on the Greenwich Observatory, the image of the exploding body, and also the "ironic method." These local materials inexorably suggest the phenomenon of creation itself, or what might be thought of as the "general theory of necessity." According to this theory, creation occurs under the direction of an imperative exerted paradoxically by some conception of the eventual form of the created work that dictates the very decisions and choices required to bring it into being. The special materials of *The Secret Agent* resonate with peculiar force on this second level, corresponding almost allegorically to the broadest and most ambitious conception of imaginative creation—that it can revolutionize and recreate the world. Indeed, these very terms—resonance, allegory, correspondence—all suggest the principle of unity, kinship, or likeness that relates everything within the system of creation, a principle that makes both theories into theories of relativity after all.

A bit more must, however, be said about the kinship between the moralistic author and his amoral materials, a bit more about the imperative that determined this particular novel. To get at this bit, let's replay the exact moment of crystallization in slow motion. Conrad had the facts about the bomb outrage, he had a few comments from Heuffer about the bombing, and a good deal of variously-acquired information about anarchists. He had the sibling relation between the dead man and the woman whose husband was responsible, and, as stated earlier, a great deal of other heterogeneous material with which he had come into contact. The preface is, in a word, incomplete in its account of sources. But concerning the moment when sources were converted to necessity, the preface is precise. It is the moment when

Conrad comes upon Sir William Harcourt's "angry sally": "All that's very well. But your idea of secrecy over there seems to consist of keeping the Home Secretary in the dark." Reduce this sally to its kernel: Home Secretary in the dark, or home in the dark, darkness in the home. This kernel unfolds into the opening scene of the novel, *chez* Verloc, with Winnie and Stevie and Verloc living above the poorly illuminated pornography shop with its "shady wares" (47), a detail that illuminates, as if from below, the kind of home it is. In *The Secret Agent*, the dark home underlit by antifamilial perversions represents something like a primal scene of creative bissociation, the juxtaposition of conventionally incompatible elements.

The simple, stolid Winnie stands within, but against, this domestic darkness. Or does she? Her intuition that things don't bear too much looking into suggests a subtle moral affinity with dark interiors. Of course, this is not how she appears. Indeed, she murders Verloc for making Stevie's dark interior as public and visible as a pyrotechnics display. This antipathy to interiority apparently commands Conrad's respect, for in the preface he elevates it into a veritable definition of "mankind," which, he asserts, "shrinks from explanations. Yet," he immediately adds, renouncing any claim he might have on the sympathies of mankind, "I will go on with mine" (38). Going on with it, Conrad assures his readers of the nonperversity of his intentions, of the principled superficiality of his novel. Conrad of the preface stands close, then, to Winnie in his rejection of the perversity of depth. But Conrad of the novel, the author of a perversely complex untruth, finds a model in Winnie as well. What does Winnie create? This local interpretive question can be answered by moving up to the general theory of necessity. According to J. Chasseguet-Smirgel, creation includes within its routine powerful elements of perversion, which she describes as a "universal human temptation" not just to transgress limits but to "make a new universe where anything becomes possible" (13). Historically, she argues, times of rich creative energy, including social upheavals, have been marked by "the confusions between sexes and generations, peculiar to perversion, as if the hope for a new social and political reality went hand in hand with an attempt at destroying sexuality and truth" (2). It is Winnie who is brought into high relief by this account of creation, for it is she who imagines that her brother might be her son—"Might be father and son," she muses to herself as Verloc walks out with Stevie, contemplating their relation as "her work" (179).

Thus, despite having had a working title of *Verloc*, *The Secret Agent* is, as Conrad insists in the preface, "the story of Winnie Verloc." For the representation of the simple Winnie involves a remarkable number of figures, functions, and images integral to the act of creation as Conrad understood it and described it in the preface. The "perversion" of her "work" constitutes a fictive form of the relation with which Conrad struggled, between a socially conservative purpose and an anarchic, world-transforming means. And, describing the murder of Verloc, she registers the force of "necessity." "'You guessed what I had to do,'" she tells Michaelis; "'Had to!'" (244). She is, moreover, the image of Conrad's doggedly unreflective but suspicious readership ("it was borne upon her with some force that a simple sentence may hold several diverse meanings—mostly disagreeable" [173]). Intriguingly, she also helps to define a crucial Conradian idea—the idea of the idea, as invoked in the preface, which speaks of "the fact of a man blown to bits for nothing even most remotely resembling an idea" (39). "Idea" reemerges in the text when, soon after the Greenwich incident, Verloc tells Winnie that they may have to emigrate. "Mrs Verloc, as placidly as if her husband had been threatening her with the end of the world, said: 'The idea!'" (184). To consider "emigration" not just as *an* idea but as *the* idea is to see the entire creation—both the narrative and the preface—as a nesting of others within, a system of traversals from one context to another, a system some of whose components are ironic meanings, foreigners in England, darkness in the home, narrative in the preface, others in the self, nonsimplicity within simplicity.

Finally, Winnie provides a key transition from accident to premeditation. *The Secret Agent* pursues the track of death from unintended explosion, through Winnie's act of "preternaturally perfect control" (233), and finally, in Winnie's frenzied imaginings, to the prospect of hanging, an act that would have no trace of passion or affect. The murder of Verloc represents the decisive move and models the creator's transformation of anarchy into justice by "simply attending to my business."

We may speculate about one last traversal of context into which Conrad himself might not have chosen to probe. At one point, the Assistant Commissioner finds himself in an Italian restaurant which gives off "an atmosphere of fraudulent cookery mocking an abject mankind in the most pressing of its miserable necessities" (151). The phrase "fraudulent cookery" reappears, having emigrated to Conrad's preface to his wife's cookbook, where he claims not only that cooking is a "moral agent" but that "simple" cooking must be distinguished from the productions of the "quack without a conscience" (372) who creates "idle feasts and rare dishes" (370). Conrad's admiration not just for simple cooking but specifically for cookbooks (which, however, "I own that I find it impossible to read through" [370]) leads him to proclaim that "of all the books produced since the most remote ages by human talents and industry those only that treat of cooking are, from a moral point of view, above suspicion" (370). Only cookbooks can be read without the possibility of irony, without doubt as to the author's intentions. Perhaps the unintellectual, corpulent Jessie served as the pattern not only for Winnie and for the incurious, easily outraged "mass of mankind," but for Conrad himself, Conrad as he wished he could be, writing the book he wished he could write, and perhaps would if only he were not so foreign, if only he were above suspicion, if only he were not an emigré.

For cookery seems to be connected for Conrad to the idea of the indigenous, the native, the homegrown, the real, even the English. The quack whom Conrad condemns subverts not just eaters anywhere; he "preys mainly upon the races of Anglo-Saxon stock"; thus, "No virtues will avail for happiness if the righteous art of cooking be neglected by the national conscience" (371). Conrad's treatment of simple cooking suggests the complex of ideas that Robert Weimann gathers into the term "appropriation": "The process of making certain things one's own," Weimann writes, "becomes inseparable from making other things (and persons) alien, so that the act of appropriation must be seen always already to involve not only self-projection and assimilation but alienation through reification and expropriation . . . " ("History, Appropriation, and the Uses of Representation" 184). In the preface to Jessie's cookbook, Conrad at once appropriates the moral stability and transparency of the cookbook, and alienates those "rare" and "idle" aspects of his own art, and his own identity.

To return to the Assistant Commissioner tucking into his pasta, the unwitting victim, as Conrad tells it, of fraudulence, of mockery, and of his own abject misery. A British restaurant in Britain, no matter how bad the food, would have at least the salutary effect of establishing indigeneity: anybody who patronized it would know that they were either British or not-British. The alienating effect of the Italian restaurant in Britain is to create a special race of anonymities, people

> as denationalized as the dishes set before them with every circumstance of unstamped respectability. Neither was their personality stamped in any way, professionally, socially or racially. They seemed created for the Italian restaurant, unless the Italian restaurant had been perchance created for them. But that last hypothesis was unthinkable, since one could not place them anywhere outside those special establishments. One never met these enigmatical persons elsewhere. It was impossible to form a precise idea what occupations they followed by day and where they went to bed at night. (152)

Perhaps the creation of fictions whose motives, unlike those of simple cookbooks, were not above suspicion had, for Conrad, the same feeling as eating spaghetti. Fictions about embassies, emigration, secret agency—fictions written in the ironic method—confirmed not just his foreignness but also the anarchic thought that he belonged nowhere, that his intentions could never be determined, that his "ideas," even the very idea of himself, would never be "precise."

Occurring under the sign of irony, creations, as written fictions so palpably and painfully demonstrate, are not moral agents in Scarry's sense, for their effect is never unambivalent. Those looking to literature for the promotion of the good seek agency in the wrong place, for everything in a creation is shadowed and compromised by its others. Creations are rather the cause or the effect of agency—the burden of which, however, falls on those who must make decisions based on evidence that is conflicting and imprecise, on those who must choose and act on principle despite the suspicion that principle is "at bottom identical" with interest. There may be, as some have argued, a textual "imperative" *not* to decide on a correct or final interpretation and *not* to permit the emigration of moral truths from the text to the world. Conceived in this way, "literature" is a figure for agency's anarchic ungroundedness. But anarchy bears its own obligations; and the horizon of indecision is reached whenever necessity imposes upon agents a fresh imperative to hazard simplicity despite its secrets: to understand, to make, to create and recreate not just the text and its meaning, but themselves and the world.

WORKS CITED

Abrams, Meyer H. *Doing Things with Texts: Essays in Criticism and Critical Theory.* New York and London: W. W. Norton, 1989.

Ainley, Alison. "Amorous Discourses: The Phenomenology of Eros and Love Stories." In Robert Bernasconi and David Wood, eds., *The Provocation of Levinas,* 70–82.

Althusser, Louis. *For Marx.* Translated by Ben Brewster. London: NLB, 1977.

———. "Ideology and Ideological State Apparatuses (Notes towards an Investigation)." In *Lenin and Philosophy,* 127–86.

———. *Lenin and Philosophy.* Translated by Ben Brewster. New York: Monthly Review Press, 1971.

Altieri, Charles. "Contemporary Philosophy and Modernist Writing: Or How to Take Seriously the Unmaking of Empiricism." *The CEA Critic* 50, nos. 2–4 (Winter 1987-Summer 1988): 2–18.

———. "From Expressivist Aesthetics to Expressivist Ethics." In Anthony Cascardi, ed., *Literature and the Question of Philosophy,* 134–66. Baltimore and London: The Johns Hopkins University Press, 1987.

Andolsen, Barbara Hilkert, Christine E. Gudorf, Mary D. Pellauer, eds. *Women's Consciousness, Women's Conscience: A Reader in Feminist Ethics.* San Francisco: Harper and Row, 1985.

Anscombe, G. E. M. "Modern Moral Philosophy." In G. Wallace and A. D. M. Walker, eds., *The Definition of Morality,* 211–34. London: Methuen, 1970.

Arieti, Silvano. *Creativity: The Magic Synthesis.* New York: Basic Books, 1976.

Aristotle. *The Nichomachean Ethics.* In J. A. K. Thomson, ed., *The Ethics of Aristotle.* Baltimore, Md.: Penguin Books, 1965.

Baier, Kurt. "The Moral Point of View." In G. Wallace and A. D. M. Walker, eds., *The Definition of Morality,* 188–210. London: Methuen, 1970.

Baines, Jocelyn. *Joseph Conrad: A Critical Biography.* London: Weidenfeld and Nicolson, 1960.

Bakhtin, Mikhail. *The Dialogic Imagination. Four Essays.* Edited by Michael Holquist; translated by Caryl Emerson and Michael Holquist. Austin: University of Texas Press, 1981.

Barthes, Roland. "Jeunes Chercheurs." *Communications* 19 (1972): 1–5.

———. "Introduction to the Structural Analysis of Narratives." In *Image, Mu-*

sic, Text, translated by Stephen Heath, 79–124. New York: Hill and Wang, 1977.

de Beauvoir, Simone. *The Second Sex*. Translated by J. Parshley. New York: Bantam Books, 1970.

Beck, Lewis. *Kant Studies Today*. LaSalle, Ill.: Open Court, 1969.

Bennington, Geoffrey. "Aberrations: de Man (and) the Machine." In Lindsay Waters and Wlad Godzich, eds., *Reading de Man Reading*: 209–22.

Bentham, Jeremy. *An Introduction to the Principles of Morals and Legislation*. London: W. Pickering, 1823.

Benveniste, Emile. "Categories of Thought and Language." In *Problems in General Linguistics*, translated by Mary E. Meek, 55–64. Coral Gables: University of Miami Press, 1971.

Berlin, Sir Isaiah, "On the Pursuit of the Ideal." *New York Review of Books* 35, no. 4 (March 17, 1988): 11–18.

Bernasconi, Robert. "Levinas and Derrida: The Question of the Closure of Metaphysics." In Richard A. Cohen, ed., *Face to Face with Levinas*, 181–204.

———, and Simon Critchley, eds. *Re-Reading Levinas*. Bloomington: Indiana University Press, forthcoming.

———, and David Wood, eds. *The Provocation of Levinas: Re-Thinking the Other*. London and New York: Routledge, 1988.

Bersani, Leo, and Ulysse Dutoit. *The Forms of Violence*. New York: Schocken Books, 1985.

Blanchot, Maurice. *The Unavowable Community*. Translated by Pierre Joris. Barrytown, N.Y.: Station Hill Press, 1988.

Booth, Wayne. *The Rhetoric of Irony*. Chicago and London: University of Chicago Press, 1974.

Borsch-Jacobsen, Mikkel. "The Law of Psychoanalysis." *Diacritics* 15, no. 1 (Spring 1985): 26–36.

Bresnan, J., ed. *The Mental Representation of Grammatical Relations*. Cambridge, Mass., and London: MIT Press, 1982.

Brooks, Peter. *Reading for the Plot: Design and Intention in Narrative*. New York: Vintage Books, 1985.

Burckhardt, Jacob. *The Civilization of the Renaissance in Italy*. 2 vols. New York: Harper & Brothers, 1958.

Burke, Kenneth. *A Grammar of Motives*. New York: Prentice-Hall, 1945.

Burton, Richard. *Baudelaire in 1859: A Study in the Sources of Poetic Creativity*. Cambridge: Cambridge University Press, 1988.

Butler, Judith. *Gender Trouble: Feminism and the Subversion of Identity*. New York: Routledge, 1990.

Calvino, Italo. *Mr. Palomar*. Translated by William Weaver. San Diego, New York, London: Harcourt Brace Jovanovich, 1985.

Cameron, Deborah. *Feminism and Linguistic Theory*. New York: St. Martin's Press, 1985.

Cascardi, Anthony J. "Genealogies of Modernism." *Philosophy and Literature* 11, no. 2 (October 1987): 207–25.

Cavell, Stanley. *The Claim of Reason: Wittgenstein, Skepticism, Morality, and*

Tragedy. Oxford: Clarendon Press; New York: Oxford University Press, 1979.

———. *Themes out of School.* Chicago and London: University of Chicago Press, 1984.

Chalier, Cathérine. "Ethics and the Feminine." In Robert Bernasconi and Simon Critchley, eds., *Re-Reading Levinas.*

———. *Figures du féminin.* Paris: La nuit surveillé, 1982.

Chandrasekhar, S. *Truth and Beauty.* Chicago and London: University of Chicago Press, 1987.

Chanter, Tina. "Feminism and the Other." In Robert Bernasconi and David Wood, eds., *The Provocation of Levinas,* 32–56.

Chase, Cynthia. "Oedipal Textuality: Reading Freud's Reading of Oedipus." In *Decomposing Figures: Rhetorical Readings in the Romantic Tradition,* 175–95. Baltimore: The Johns Hopkins University Press, 1986.

———. "The Witty Butcher's Wife: Freud, Lacan, and the Conversion of Resistance to Theory." *Modern Language Notes* 102 (December 1987): 989–1013.

Chasseguet-Smirgel, Janine. *Creativity and Perversion.* London: Free Association Books, 1985.

Chomsky, Noam. "Linguistics and Philosophy." In Sidney Hook, ed., *Language and Philosophy,* 51–94. New York: New York University Press, 1969.

Clark, Stanley G., and Evan Simpson, eds. *Anti-theory in Ethics and Moral Conservatism.* Albany: State University of New York Press, 1989.

Cohen, Richard A., ed. *Face to Face with Levinas.* Albany: State University of New York Press, 1986.

Cohen, Sande. *Historical Culture: On the Recoding of an Academic Discipline.* Berkeley and Los Angeles: University of California Press, 1986.

Conrad, Jessie. *Conrad as I Knew Him.* London: William Heinemann Ltd., 1926.

Conrad, Joseph. "Cookery." Preface to Jessie Conrad, *A Handbook of Cookery for a Small House.* In *Almayer's Folly * Last Essays,* 370–72. Edinburgh, London, and Melbourne: Nelson, [1963].

———. "A Familiar Preface." In *A Personal Record.* London and Toronto: J. M. Dent & Sons, 1919. Orig. pub., 1912.

———. *Joseph Conrad's Letters to R. B. Cunninghame Graham.* Edited by C. T. Watts. Cambridge: Cambridge University Press, 1969.

———. "Preface to *Nostromo.*" In Walter F. Wright, ed., *Joseph Conrad on Fiction,* 169–75. Lincoln: University of Nebraska Press, 1964.

———. *The Secret Agent: A Simple Tale.* Edited by Martin Seymour-Smith. Harmondsworth: Penguin, 1984.

———. "Tradition." In *Notes on Life and Letters,* 194–201. London: J. M. Dent & Sons. Ltd., 1921.

Corngold, Stanley. "On Paul de Man's Collaborationist Writings." In Werner Hamacher, Neil Hertz, and Tom Keenan, eds., *Responses: On Paul de Man's Wartime Journalism,* 80–84. Lincoln: University of Nebraska Press, 1989.

Crane, R. S. "The Concept of Plot and the Plot of *Tom Jones.*" Reprinted in

J. L. Calderwood and H. E. Toliver, eds., *Perspectives on Fiction*, 303–18. London and New York: Oxford University Press, 1968.

Critchley, Simon. "'Bois'—Derrida's final word on Levinas." In Bernasconi and Critchley, eds., *Re-Reading Levinas*.

———. "The chiasmus: Levinas, Derrida and the ethical demand for deconstruction." *Textual Practice* 3, no. 1 (April 1989): 91–106.

Culler, Jonathan. "Meaning and Convention: Derrida and Austin." *NLH* 13, no. 1 (1981): 15–30.

———. "Story and Discourse in the Analysis of Narrative." In *The Pursuit of Signs: Semiotics, Literature, Deconstruction*, 169–87. London: Routledge and Kegan Paul, 1981.

———. *Structuralist Poetics*. Ithaca: Cornell University Press, 1975.

Daly, Mary. *Beyond God the Father: Toward a Philosophy of Women's Liberation*. Boston: Beacon Press, 1973.

———. *Gyn/Ecology: The Metaethics of Radical Feminism*. Boston: Beacon Press, 1978.

Dante Alighieri. *La Vita Nuova*. Translated by Mark Musa. Bloomington: Indiana University Press, 1973.

Davis, Robert Con. "Introduction: Lacan and Narration." In Robert Con Davis, ed., *Lacan and Narration: The Psychoanalytic Difference in Narrative Theory*, 848–59. Baltimore and London: The Johns Hopkins University Press, 1983. Originally published as a special issue of *Modern Language Notes* 98, no. 5 (December 1983).

Derrida, Jacques. *Altérités*. Paris: Editions Osiris, 1986.

———. "At this very moment in this work here I am." In Robert Bernasconi and Simon Critchley, eds., *Re-Reading Levinas*. Orig. pub. as "En ce moment même dans cet ouvrage me voici." In *Textes pour Emmanuel Levinas*. Paris: Editions Jean-Michel Place, 1980.

———. *Edmund Husserl's "The Origin of Geometry": An Introduction*. Translated by John Leavey, Jr. Stony Brook, New York: Nicolas Hays Ltd., 1978.

———. "The Law of Genre." Translated by Avital Ronnell, *Critical Inquiry* 7, no. 1 (Autumn 1980): 55–81.

———. *Limited Inc*. Translated by Samuel Weber and Jeffrey Mehlman. Evanston, Ill.: Northwestern University Press, 1988.

———. "Of an Apocalyptic Tone Recently Adopted in Philosophy." Translated by John P. Leavey. *Oxford Literary Review* 6, no. 2 (1984): 3–37.

———. *Of Grammatology*. Translated by Gayatri Spivak. Baltimore and London: The Johns Hopkins University Press, 1978.

———. *Positions*. Translated by Alan Bass. Chicago: University of Chicago Press, 1981.

———. *The Post Card*. Translated by Alan Bass. Chicago: University of Chicago Press, 1987.

———. "Psyche: Inventions of the Other." In Waters and Godzich, eds., *Reading de Man Reading*, 25–65.

———. "Signature Event Context." In *Limited Inc.*, translated by Samuel Weber and Jeffrey Mehlman, 1–23. Evanston: Northwestern University Press, 1988.

————. "Structure, Sign, and Play in the Discourse of the Human Sciences." In *Writing and Difference,* translated by Alan Bass, 278–94. Chicago: University of Chicago Press, 1978.

de Saussure, Ferdinand. *The Course in General Linguistics.* Ed. Charles Bally and Albert Sechehaye, in collaboration with Albert Riedlinger; trans. Wade Baskin. New York: Philosophical Library, 1966.

Dews, Peter. *Logics of Disintegration: Post-Structuralist Thought and the Claims of Critical Theory.* London and New York: Verso, 1987.

Didion, Joan. *The White Album.* New York: Pocket Books, 1979.

Doctorow, E. L. "False Documents." *American Review* 26 (1977): 215–32. Rpt. in Richard N. Trenner, ed., *E. L. Doctorow: Essays and Conversations,* 16–27. Princeton: Princeton University Press, 1983.

Dodds, E. R. *The Greeks and the Irrational.* Berkeley: University of California Press, 1971.

Edison, Thomas A. *The Papers of Thomas A. Edison.* Vol. 1, *The Making of an Inventor, February 1847-June 1873.* Edited by Reese V. Jenkins et al. Baltimore and London: The Johns Hopkins University Press, 1989.

Edwards, James C. *Ethics Without Philosophy: Wittgenstein and the Moral Life.* Tampa, St. Petersburg, Sarasota, and Ft. Myers: University of South Florida Press, 1982.

Einstein, Albert. "Physics and Reality." In *Ideas and Opinions,* edited by Carl Seelig; translated by Sonja Bargmann, 290–323. New York: Bonanza Books, 1954.

Eldridge, Richard. *On Moral Personhood: Philosophy, Criticism, and Self-Identity.* Chicago and London: University of Chicago Press, 1989.

Eliot, T. S. "The Function of Criticism." In *Selected Essays 1917–32,* 12–22. London: Faber & Faber, 1932.

Ellison, Julie. *Delicate Subjects: Romanticism, Gender, and the Ethics of Understanding.* Ithaca: Cornell University Press, 1990.

Feyerabend, Paul. "Creativity—A Dangerous Myth." *Critical Inquiry* 13, no. 4 (Summer 1987): 700–11.

Fish, Stanley. *Doing What Comes Naturally: Change, Rhetoric, and the Practice of Theory in Literary and Legal Studies.* Oxford: Clarendon Press, 1989.

————. "With the Compliments of the Author: Reflections on Austin and Derrida." In *Doing What Comes Naturally,* 37–67.

Flaubert, Gustave. *The Letters of Gustave Flaubert 1830–1857.* Edited by Francis Steegmuller. Cambridge, Mass., and London: Harvard University Press, 1980.

Foot, Philippa. "Is Morality a System of Hypothetical Imperatives?" *Analysis* 35 (1973–74): 53ff.

Forster, E. M. *Aspects of the Novel.* London: E. Arnold, 1927.

Foucault, Michel. "The Ethic of Care for the Self as a Practice of Freedom." Interview with Raúl Fornet-Betancourt, Helmut Becker, and Alfredo Gomez-Müller (January 20, 1984). In James Bernauer and David Rasmussen, eds., *The Final Foucault,* 1–20. Cambridge, Mass., and London: The MIT Press, 1987.

————. "Nietzsche, Genealogy, History." In *Language, Counter-Memory, Prac-*

tice, edited by Donald F. Bouchard, translated by Donald F. Bouchard and Sherry Simon, 139–64. Ithaca: Cornell University Press, 1977.

———. "Power, Moral Values, and the Intellectual." Interview with Michael Bes (November 3, 1980). *History of the Present Newsletter* 4 (Spring 1988): 1–2.

———. *The Use of Pleasure.* Vol. 2 of *The History of Sexuality.* Translated by Robert Hurley. New York: Vintage, 1986.

Freud, Sigmund. *An Autobiographical Study.* Translated by James Strachey. In vol. 20 of *The Standard Edition of the Complete Psychological Works of Sigmund Freud,* edited by James Strachey, 7–74. 24 vols. London: Hogarth Press and the Institute for Psycho-Analysis, 1953–74. (Hereafter referred to as *SE.*) Orig. pub., 1924.

———. *Beyond the Pleasure Principle.* Translated by James Strachey. New York and London: W. W. Norton and Co., 1961. Reprint of translation in vol. 18 (1955) of *SE,* 3–64. Orig. pub., 1920.

———. *The Complete Letters of Sigmund Freud to Wilhelm Fliess, 1887–1904.* Edited and translated by Jeffrey Moussaieff Masson. Cambridge: Belknap Press of Harvard University Press, 1985.

———. "Creative Writers and Day-Dreaming." In *SE* 9 (1959), 141–54. Orig. pub., 1907.

———. *The Ego and the Id.* Translated by Joan Rivière, revised and edited James Strachey. New York and London: W. W. Norton and Co., 1962. Corrected reprint of text in vol. 19 (1962) of *SE,* 3–66. Orig. pub., 1923.

———. "Notes Upon a Case of Obsessional Neurosis." In *Three Case Histories,* edited by Philip Rieff, 15–102. New York: Collier Books, 1979. Orig. pub., 1909.

———. "Observations on Transference-Love." In vol. 12 (1958) of *SE,* 157–71.

———. "Recommendations to Physicians Practising Psycho-analysis." In vol. 12 (1958) of *SE,* 109–20.

———. "Some Psychical Consequences of the Anatomical Distinction Between the Sexes." In vol. 19 (1961) of *SE,* 248–60. Orig. pub., 1925.

———. "The Theme of the Three Caskets." In vol. 12 (1958) of *SE,* 291–301. Orig. pub., 1913.

Fried, Michael. "Almayer's Face: On 'Impressionism' in Conrad, Crane, and Norris." *Critical Inquiry* 17, no. 1 (Autumn 1990): 193–236.

Frye, Northrop. *Anatomy of Criticism.* New York: Atheneum, 1969.

———. *Creation and Recreation.* Toronto, Buffalo, and London: University of Toronto Press, 1980.

Gasché, Rodolphe. "In-Difference to Philosophy: de Man on Kant, Hegel, and Nietzsche." In Waters and Godzich, eds., *Reading de Man Reading,* 259–96.

Gilligan, Carol. *In A Different Voice: Psychological Theory and Women's Development.* Cambridge, Mass., and London: Harvard University Press, 1982.

———, Janie Victoria Ward, and Jill Taylor, with Betty Bardige, eds. *Mapping the Moral Domain: A Contribution of Women's Thinking to Psychological Theory and Education.* Cambridge, Mass.: Harvard University Press, 1989.

Goldman, Emma. "Anarchism: What it Really Stands For." In *Anarchism and Other Essays,* 51–73. New York: A. C. Fifield, 1911.

Gould, Stephen Jay. *Time's Arrow, Time's Cycle: Myth and Metaphor in the Discovery of Geological Time.* Harmondsworth: Penguin Books, 1988.

Greenberg, Clement. *Arrogant Purpose, 1945–1949.* Vol. 2 of *The Collected Essays and Criticism.* Edited by John O'Brian. Chicago and London: University of Chicago Press, 1986.

Griffiths, Morwena, and Margaret Whitford. *Feminist Perspectives in Philosophy.* London: Macmillan, 1988.

Guerard, Albert. *Conrad the Novelist.* Cambridge, Mass.: Harvard University Press, 1958.

Habermas, Jürgen. "Arnold Gehlen: Imitation Substantiality." In *Philosophical-Political Profiles,* translated by Frederick G. Lawrence, 111–28. Cambridge, Mass., and London: Harvard University Press, 1983.

———. "Questions and Counter-Questions." In Richard Bernstein, ed., *Habermas and Modernity,* 192–216. Cambridge, Mass.: The MIT Press, 1985.

Hadamard, Jacques Salomon. *An Essay on the Psychology of Invention in the Mathematical Field.* Princeton: Princeton University Press, 1945.

Hamacher, Werner. "LECTIO: de Man's Imperative." In Waters and Godzich, eds., *Reading de Man Reading,* 171–201.

Hampshire, Stuart. *Freedom of the Individual.* Princeton: Princeton University Press, 1975.

———. *Morality and Conflict.* Cambridge, Mass.: Harvard University Press, 1983.

Handwerk, Gary J. *Irony and Ethics in Narrative.* New Haven and London: Yale University Press, 1985.

Hare, R. M. *Freedom and Reason.* Oxford: Clarendon Press, 1963.

———. *The Language of Morals.* Oxford: Oxford University Press, 1952.

———. *Moral Thinking; Its Levels, Method, and Point.* Oxford: Clarendon Press, 1981.

Harpham, Geoffrey Galt. *The Ascetic Imperative in Culture and Criticism.* Chicago and London: University of Chicago Press, 1987.

———. "Derrida and the Ethics of Criticism." *Textual Practice* 5, no. 3 (Winter 1991): 383–99.

———. *On the Grotesque: Strategies of Contradiction in Art and Literature.* Princeton: Princeton University Press, 1982.

Hartman, Geoffrey. "Looking Back on Paul de Man." In Waters and Godzich, eds., *Reading de Man Reading,* 3–24.

Hawkes, Nigel, and Adrian Hamilton, Farzad Bazoft, and Eric Silver. "Iran Slams the Door on the West." *The Observer,* 7 May 1989, 21.

Hay, Eloise Knapp. *The Political Novels of Joseph Conrad.* Chicago: University of Chicago Press, 1963.

Heidegger, Martin. *Being and Time.* Translated by J. Macquarrie and E. Robinson. New York: Harper & Row, 1962.

————. "Letter on Humanism." In *Martin Heidegger, Basic Writings, from Being and Time (1927) to The Task of Thinking (1964)*, edited by David Farrell Krell, 193–242. New York: Harper and Row, 1977.

————. *On the Way to Language*. Translated by Peter D. Hertz. San Francisco: Harper and Row, 1971.

Heller, Agnes. *General Ethics*. Oxford and New York: Basil Blackwell, 1988.

Henley, Nancy M. "This New Species That Seeks a New Language: On Sexism in Language and Language Change." In Joyce Penfield, ed., *Women and Language in Transition*, 3–27. Albany: State University of New York Press, 1987.

Herbert, Auberon. "The Ethics of Dynamite." *Contemporary Review*, May 1984, 679. Cited in Sherry, *Conrad's Western World*, 281.

Hertz, Neil. "Lurid Figures." In Waters and Godzich, eds., *Reading de Man Reading*, 82–104.

Howe, Irving. "Notes from Jerusalem." *The New York Review of Books* 35, no. 14 (29 September 1988): 13–14.

Hudson, W. D. "Editor's Introduction: The 'is-ought' problem." In W. D. Hudson, ed., *The Is-Ought Question*, 11–31. London: Macmillan, 1969.

Hume, David. *An Enquiry Concerning the Principles of Morals*. In *Hume's Ethical Writings*, 23–156.

————, *Hume's Ethical Writings: Selections from David Hume*. Edited by Alasdair MacIntyre. Notre Dame, Ind.: University of Notre Dame Press, 1965.

————. *A Treatise of Human Nature*. In *Hume's Ethical Writings*, 177–252.

Irigaray, Luce. *Éthique de la différence sexuelle*. Paris: Editions de Minuit, 1984.

————. "The Fecundity of the Caress." Translated by Carolyn Burke. In Cohen, ed., *Face to Face with Levinas*, 231–56.

————. "Questions for Emmanuel Levinas. On the Divinity of Love." In Bernasconi and Critchley, eds., *Re-Reading Levinas*.

————. *This Sex which is Not One*. Translated by Catherine Porter with Carolyn Burke. Ithaca: Cornell University Press, 1985.

Jakobson, Roman. "Closing Statement: Linguistics and Poetics." In Thomas Sebeok, ed., *Style in Language*, 350–77. Cambridge, Mass.: MIT Press, 1960.

————. "Two Types of Language and Two Types of Aphasic Disturbances." In *Word and Language*, Vol. 2 of *The Selected Writings of Roman Jakobson* (1971), 239–59. The Hague, Paris, New York, Berlin, Amsterdam: Mouton Publishers, 1962–85.

James, Henry. "Preface" to *The Spoils of Poynton*. In *The Art of Fiction*, edited by R. P. Blackmur, 119–25. New York: Charles Scribner's Sons, 1934.

James, William. *Habit*. New York: Henry Holt & Company, 1890.

————. *Principles of Psychology*. 2 vols. New York: Henry Holt & Co., 1890.

Jameson, Fredric. "Beyond the Cave: Demystifying the Ideology of Modernism." In *The Ideologies of Theory: Essays 1971–1986*, vol. 2, *Syntax of History*, 115–32. Theory and History of Literature, vol. 49. Minneapolis: University of Minnesota Press, 1988.

————. "Criticism in History." In *The Ideologies of Theory: Essays 1971–1986*, vol. 1, *Situations of Theory*, 119–36. Theory and History of Literature, vol. 48. Minneapolis: University of Minnesota Press, 1988.

————. *Fables of Aggression*. Berkeley: University of California Press, 1979.

————. "Marxism and Historicism." In *The Ideologies of Theory: Essays 1971– 1986*, vol. 2, *Syntax of History*, 148–77.

————. "Pleasure: A Political Issue." In *The Ideologies of Theory*, vol. 2, *Syntax of History*, 61–74.

————. *The Political Unconscious: Narrative as a Socially Symbolic Act*. Ithaca: Cornell University Press, 1981.

Jay, Gregory. "The Subject of Pedagogy: Lessons in Psychoanalysis and Politics." *College English* 49, no. 7 (November 1987): 783–800.

Jay, Martin. "The Morals of Genealogy: Or, Is There a Post-Structuralist Ethics?" *The Cambridge Review* 110, no. 2305 (June 1989): 70–74.

Jean-Aubry, G. *Joseph Conrad: Life and Letters*. 2 vols. London: William Heinemann, 1927.

Jennings, Bruce. "Beyond the Rights of the Newborn." *Raritan* 7, no. 3 (Winter 1988): 79–93.

Johnson, Barbara. "Mallarmé and Austin." In *The Critical Difference: Essays in the Contemporary Rhetoric of Reading*, 52–66. Baltimore: The Johns Hopkins University Press, 1980.

Joravsky, David. "Machine Dreams." *New York Review*, 7 December 1989, 11–15.

Kain, Philip J. *Marx and Ethics*. Oxford: Clarendon Press, 1988.

Kamuf, Peggy. "Pieces of Resistance." In Waters and Godzich, eds., *Reading de Man Reading*, 136–54.

Kant, Immanuel. *Critique of Judgment*. Translated by J. H. Bernard. New York: Macmillan, 1951.

————. *Critique of Practical Reason*. In *Critique of Practical Reason and Other Writings in Moral Philosophy*, edited and translated by Lewis White Beck, 118–260. Chicago: University of Chicago Press, 1949.

————. *The Doctrine of Virtue*. Part 2 of *The Metaphysic of Morals: With the Introduction to the Metaphysic of Morals and the Preface to The Doctrine of Law*. Translated by Mary J. Gregor. New York: Harper & Row, 1964.

————. *Immanuel Kant's Critique of Pure Reason*. Translated by Norman Kemp Smith. New York: St. Martin's Press, 1965.

————. *Metaphysical Foundations of Morals*. Translated by Carl J. Friedrich. In *The Philosophy of Kant: Immanuel Kant's Moral and Political Writings*, edited by Carl J. Friedrich, 140–208. New York: Random House, 1977.

————. "On the Proverb: That May Be True in Theory, But Is of No Practical Use." In *Perpetual Peace and Other Essays on Politics, History, and Morals*, 61–92.

————. "To Perpetual Peace, A Philosophical Sketch." In *Perpetual Peace and Other Essays on Politics, History, and Morals*, 107–43.

————. *Perpetual Peace and Other Essays on Politics, History, and Morals*. Translated by Ted Humphrey. Indianapolis and Cambridge: Hackett Publishing Company, 1983.

Kaplan, Cora. "Language and Gender." In *Sea Changes: Essays on Culture and Feminism,* 69–94. London: Verso, 1986.

Kenner, Hugh. "Modernism and What Happened to It." *Essays in Criticism* 37, no 2 (April 1987): 97–109.

Koestler, Arthur. *The Act of Creation.* New York: Macmillan, 1964.

Kramarae, Cheris. *Women and Men Speaking: Frameworks for Analysis.* Rowley, Mass: Newbury House, 1981.

Kristeva, Julia. *Desire in Language: A Semiotic Approach to Literature and Art.* Edited by Leon S. Roudiez; translated by Thomas Gora, Alice Jardine, and Leon S. Roudiez. New York: Columbia University Press, 1980.

———. "The Ethics of Linguistics." In *Desire in Language,* 23–35.

———. "Giotto's Joy." In *Desire in Language,* 210–36.

———. "The Novel as Polylogue." In *Desire in Language,* 159–209.

———. *Revolution in Poetic Language.* Translated by Margaret Waller. New York: Columbia University Press, 1984.

Lacan, Jacques. "The agency of the letter in the unconscious or reason since Freud." In *Ecrits,* 146–78.

———. *Discours de clôture des Journées sur les psychoses chez l'enfant.* In *Recherches,* special issue, *Enfance aliénée,* 11 December 1968. Translated by and quoted in Derrida, *The Post Card,* 482.

———. *Ecrits: A Selection.* Translated by Alan Sheridan. New York: W. W. Norton and Co., 1977.

———. *Encore: Le Séminaire, Livre XX.* Paris, 1975. Translated by and quoted in Michel de Certeau, *Heterologies: Discourse on the Other,* 242 n. 50. Theory and History of Literature, vol. 17. Translated by Brian Massumi. Minneapolis: University of Minnesota Press, 1986.

———. *Éthique de la psychanalyse* (1959–60). Paris: Editions du Seuil, 1986.

———. *The Four Fundamental Concepts of Psycho-analysis.* Edited by Jacques-Alain Miller; translated by Alan Sheridan. New York and London: W. W. Norton and Co., 1981.

———. "The Freudian thing." In *Ecrits,* 114–45.

———. "The function and field of speech and language in psychoanalysis." In *Ecrits,* 30–113.

———. "Kant avec Sade." In *Ecrits,* 763–92. French edition, Paris: Editions du Seuil, 1966.

———. "The signification of the phallus." In *Ecrits,* 281–91.

———. *Television: A Challenge to the Psychoanalytic Establishment.* Translated by Denis Hollier, Rosalind Kraus, Annette Michelson, and Jeffrey Mehlman; edited by Joan Copjec. New York and London: W. W. Norton & Co., 1990. Orig. pub., 1974.

Lakoff, Robin. *Language and Woman's Place.* New York: Harper & Row, 1975.

Lemann, Nicholas. "The Unfinished War." *The Atlantic Monthly,* January 1989, 53ff.

Levelt, William J. *Speaking: From Intention to Articulation.* Cambridge, Mass.: MIT Press, 1989.

Levinas, Emmanuel. *En découvrant l'existence avec Husserl et Heidegger.* Paris: J. Vrin, 1974.

———. *Time and the Other, and Additional Essays.* Translated by Richard A. Cohen, Pittsburgh: Duquesne University Press, 1987.

———. *Totality and Infinity; An Essay on Exteriority.* Translated by Alphonso Lingis. Pittsburgh: Duquesne University Press, 1969.

———, and Richard Kearney. "Dialogue with Emmanuel Levinas." In Cohen, ed., *Face to Face with Levinas,* 13–34.

Lyotard, Jean-François. *The Differend: Phrases in Dispute.* Translated by Georges Van Den Abbeele. Theory and History of Literature, vol. 46. Minneapolis: University of Minnesota Press, 1988.

———. "Figure Foreclosed." In *The Lyotard Reader,* edited by Andrew Benjamin, 69–110. Oxford, England, and Cambridge, Mass.: Basil Blackwell, 1989.

———. "Levinas' Logic." In *The Lyotard Reader,* 275–313.

———, and Jean-Loup Thébaud. *Just Gaming.* Translated by Wlad Godzich. Theory and History of Literature, vol. 20. Minneapolis: University of Minnesota Press, 1987.

MacIntyre, Alasdair. *After Virtue.* Notre Dame, Ind.: University of Notre Dame Press, 1981.

———. "Hume on 'is' and 'ought.'" In Hudson, ed., *The Is-Ought Question,* 35–50.

———. *Whose Justice? Which Rationality?* Notre Dame, Ind.: University of Notre Dame Press, 1988.

MacRae, Donald G. *Weber.* London: Woburn Press, 1974.

Mallarmé, Stéphane. *Selected Letters of Stéphane Mallarmé.* Edited by Rosemary Lloyd. Chicago and London: University of Chicago Press, 1988.

de Man, Paul. *Allegories of Reading: Figural Language in Rousseau, Nietzsche, Rilke, and Proust.* New Haven and London: Yale University Press, 1979.

———. "Foreword," to Carol Jacobs, *The Dissimulating Harmony.* Baltimore and London: The Johns Hopkins University Press, 1978.

———. "Hegel on the Sublime." In Mark Krupnick, ed., *Displacements: Derrida and After,* 139–53. Bloomington: Indiana University Press, 1983.

———. "The Resistance to Theory." In *The Resistance to Theory,* foreword by Wlad Godzich, 3–20. Theory and History of Literature, vol. 33. Minneapolis: University of Minnesota Press, 1986.

———. *The Rhetoric of Romanticism.* New York: Columbia University Press, 1984.

Martin, Judith, and Gunther S. Stent. "I Think, Therefore I Thank: A Philosophy of Etiquette." *The American Scholar* 59 (Spring 1990): 237–54.

Marx, Karl. *Capital.* New York: International Publishers, 1977.

———. "The Communist Manifesto." In *The Portable Karl Marx,* edited by Eugene Kamenka, 203–41. Harmondsworth: Penguin, 1983.

———, and Fredrick Engels. *The German Ideology,* Pt. 1. In *The Marx-Engels Reader,* edited by Robert C. Tucker, 162–95. New York: W. W. Norton, 1978.

Massey, Irving. *Find You the Virtue: Ethics, Image, and Desire in Literature.* Fairfax, Va.: George Mason University Press, 1987.

McMaster, Graham. "Some other Secrets in *The Secret Agent.*" *Literature and History* 12 (Autumn 1986) 2: 229–42.

Mehlman, Jeffrey. "Trimethylamin." *Diacritics* 6, no. 1 (1976): 42–45.

Miller, J. Hillis. *The Ethics of Reading; Kant, de Man, Eliot, Trollope, James, and Benjamin.* New York: Columbia University Press, 1987.

———. "Is There an Ethics of Reading?" In James Phelan, ed., *Reading Narrative: Form, Ethics, Ideology,* 79–101. Columbus, Ohio: State University Press, 1989.

———. "Reading Part of a Paragraph in *Allegories of Reading.*" In Waters and Godzich, eds., *Reading de Man Reading,* 155–70.

Miller, Jacques-Alain. "Interview." *Newsletter of the Freudian Field* 1, no. 1 (Spring 1987): 5–10.

Mink, Louis O. "The Autonomy of Historical Understanding." *History and Theory* 5 (1965): 24–47.

———. "History and Fiction as Modes of Comprehension." *New Literary History* 1, no. 3 (Spring 1970): 541–58.

———. "Philosophical Analysis and Historical Understanding." *Review of Metaphysics* 20 (1968): 667–98.

Mitchell, Basil. *Morality, Religious and Secular: The Dilemma of the Traditional Conscience.* New York: Oxford University Press, 1980.

Moi, Toril. *Sexual/Textual Politics: Feminist Literary Theory.* London and New York: Methuen, 1985.

Murdoch, Iris. "Against Dryness: A Polemical Sketch." In Stanley Hauerwas and Alasdair MacIntyre, eds., *Revisions: Changing Perspectives in Moral Philosophy,* 43–50. Notre Dame, Ind.: University of Notre Dame Press, 1983. Murdoch essay orig. pub. 1961.

———. *The Sovereignty of Good.* New York: Schocken Books, 1971.

Murphy, Jeffrie G. "Kant's Concept of a Right Action." In Lewis W. Beck, ed., *Kant Studies Today,* 471–95. LaSalle, Ill.: Open Court Press, 1969.

Murray, Peter. "Introduction" to *The Complete Paintings of Piero della Francesca,* 5–7. Harmondsworth: Penguin, 1967.

Nagel, Thomas. *Mortal Questions.* Cambridge: Cambridge University Press, 1979.

———. *The View from Nowhere.* New York and Oxford: Oxford University Press, 1986.

Nietzsche, Friedrich. *Beyond Good and Evil: Prelude to a Philosophy of the Future.* Translated by R. J. Hollingdale. Harmondsworth: Penguin, 1973.

———. *Ecce Homo.* In *On the Genealogy of Morals and Ecce Homo.* Translated by Walter Kaufmann. New York: Random House, 1969.

———. *On the Genealogy of Morals.* In *On the Genealogy of Morals and Ecce Homo.* Translated by Walter Kaufmann. New York: Random House, 1969.

———. *Human, All too Human: A Book for Free Spirits.* Translated by R. J. Hollingdale. Cambridge and New York: Cambridge University Press, 1986.

———. *Twilight of the Idols*. In *Twilight of the Idols; and, The Anti-Christ*. Translated by R. J. Hollingdale. Harmondsworth: Penguin, 1968.

Norris, Christopher. "De Man unfair to Kierkegaard? An allegory of (non)-reading." In *Deconstruction and the Interests of Theory*, 156–86. Oklahoma Project for Discourse and Theory, vol. 4. Norman: University of Oklahoma Press, 1989.

———. *Derrida*. Cambridge, Mass.: Harvard University Press, 1987.

Nozick, Robert. *Philosophical Explanations*. Cambridge, Mass.: Belknap Press of Harvard University Press, 1981.

Nussbaum, Martha Craven. "'Finely Aware and Richly Responsible': Literature and the Moral Imagination." In *Love's Knowledge*, 148–67.

———. "Flawed Crystals: James's *The Golden Bowl* and Literature as Moral Philosophy." In *Love's Knowledge*, 125–47.

———. *The Fragility of Goodness*. Cambridge: Cambridge University Press, 1986.

———. *Love's Knowledge: Essays on Philosophy and Literature*. New York: Oxford University Press.

———. "Perceptive Equilibrium: Literary Theory and Ethical Theory." In *Love's Knowledge*, 168–94.

———. "Reply to Richard Wollheim, Patrick Gardiner, and Hilary Putnam." *New Literary History* 15, no. 1 (Autumn, 1983): 201–8.

Olsen, Tillie. *Silences*. London: Virago, 1980.

Plato. *Protagoras and Meno*. Translated by W. K. C. Guthrie. Harmondsworth: Penguin, 1985.

Platts, Mark. "Introduction." In Mark Platts, ed., *Reference, Truth and Reality: Essays on the Philosophy of Language*, 1–18. London, Boston and Henley: Routledge, 1980.

Poincaré, Henri. "Mathematical Creation." In *The Foundations of Science*, translated by George Bruce Halstead, 383–94. Lancaster: The Science Press, 1946.

Poovey, Mary. "Feminism and Deconstruction." *Feminist Studies* 14, no. 1 (Spring 1988): 51–65.

Pratt, Mary Louise. "The Ideology of Speech-Act Theory." *Centrum* n.s. 1, no. 1 (Spring 1981): 5–18.

Putnam, Hilary. "Taking Rules Seriously—A Response to Martha Nussbaum." *New Literary History* 15, no. 1 (Autumn, 1983): 193–200.

"Rafsanjani backs down on his 'kill Westerners' call," *The Observer*, 6 May 1989, 2.

Rajchman, John. "Ethics under Analysis." Photocopy of a paper given at the MLA Covention, New York City, December 1986.

———. "Lacan and the Ethics of Modernity." *Representations* 15 (Summer 1986): 42–56.

———. *Michel Foucault: The Freedom of Philosophy*. New York: Columbia University Press, 1985.

Rasmussen, David. *Universalism vs. Communitarianism: Contemporary Debates in Ethics*. Cambridge, Mass.: MIT Press, 1990.

Readings, Bill. "The Deconstruction of Politics." In Waters and Godzich, eds., *Reading de Man Reading*, 223–43.

Reich, Willi. *Schoenberg: A Critical Biography*. Translated by Leo Black. New York and Washington: Praeger Publishers, 1971.

Ricoeur, Paul. "Narrative Time." In W. J. T. Mitchell, ed., *On Narrative*, 165–86. Chicago and London: University of Chicago Press, 1981.

———. *Time and Narrative*. 2 vols. Translated by Kathleen McLaughlin and David Pellauer. Chicago and London: University of Chicago Press, 1984–85.

Rieff, Philip. *Freud: The Mind of the Moralist*. New York: Viking Press, 1959.

Rorty, Richard. *Contingency, Irony, and Solidarity*. Cambridge and New York: Cambridge University Press, 1989.

———. "Freud and Moral Reflection." In Joseph H. Smith and William Kerrigan, eds., *Pragmatism's Freud: The Moral Disposition of Psychoanalysis*, 1–27. Baltimore and London: The Johns Hopkins University Press, 1986.

———. *Philosophy and the Mirror of Nature*. Princeton: Princeton University Press, 1980.

———. "Solidarity or Objectivity?" In John Rajchman and Cornel West, eds., *Post-Analytic Philosophy*, 3–19. New York: Columbia University Press, 1985.

———. "Truth and Freedom: A Reply to Thomas McCarthy." *Critical Inquiry* 16, no. 3 (Spring 1990): 633–45.

———. "Two Meanings of 'Logocentrism': A Reply to Norris." In Reed Way Dasenbrock, ed., *Re-Drawing the Lines: Analytic Philosophy, Deconstruction, and Literary Theory*, 204–16. Minneapolis: University of Minnesota Press, 1989.

Ryle, Gilbert. "Pleasure." In *Dilemmas*, 54–67. Cambridge: Cambridge University Press, 1954.

Said, Edward. "The Text, the World, the Critic." In Josué V. Harari, ed., *Textual Strategies: Perspectives in Post-Structuralist Criticism*, 161–88. Ithaca: Cornell University Press, 1979.

———. "Conrad and Nietzsche." In Norman Sherry, ed., *Joseph Conrad: A Commemoration*, 65–76. London and Basingstoke: Macmillan, 1976.

Sapir, Edward. "The Status of Linguistics as a Science." In *Culture, Language, and Personality*, edited by David G. Mandelbaum, 65–77. Berkeley, Los Angeles, and London: University of California Press, 1949.

Sartre, Jean-Paul. "The Last Words of Jean-Paul Sartre." *Dissent* 27 (Fall 1980): 397–422. Orig. pub. as "L'Espoir, maintenant . . . ," *Le Nouvel Observateur*, 10, 17, 24 March, 1980.

———. *Un Théâtre de situations*. Paris: Gallimard, 1973.

Scarry, Elaine. *The Body in Pain: The Making and Unmaking of the World*. New York and Oxford: Oxford University Press, 1985.

———. "Introduction." In Elaine Scarry, ed., *Literature and the Body: Essays on Populations and Persons*, vii–xxvii. Baltimore and London: The Johns Hopkins University Press, 1988.

Schalow, Frank. *Imagination and Existence: Heidegger's Retrieval of the Kantian Ethic*. Lanham, Md.: University Press of America, 1986.

Schopenhauer, Arthur. *The Basis of Morality.* Translated by A. B. Bullock. London: Swan Sonnenschein, 1903.

Searle, John. "Reiterating the Differences: A Reply to Derrida." *Glyph* 2 (1977): 198–208.

———. *Speech Acts: An Essay in the Philosophy of Language.* Cambridge: Cambridge University Press, 1969.

Sedgwick, Eve Kosofsky. *The Epistemology of the Closet.* Berkeley and Los Angeles: University of California Press, 1990.

Shakespeare, William. *The Merchant of Venice.* In *William Shakespeare: The Complete Works,* edited by Peter Alexander. London and Glasgow: Collins, 1971.

Shammas, Anton. Translation and quotation of article by Yitzhak Shamir in the publication *Hehazeet* (1943) in "The Morning After," 47. *The New York Review of Books* 35, no. 14 (29 September 1988): 47–52.

Sheehan, Thomas. "Heidegger and the Nazis." *The New York Review of Books* 35, no. 10 (16 June 1988): 38–47.

Sherry, Norman. *Conrad's Western World.* Cambridge: Cambridge University Press, 1971.

Spender, Dale. *Man Made Language.* London: Routledge & Kegan Paul, 1980.

Spinoza, Benedict. *Ethics.* Translated by George Eliot; edited by Thomas Deegan. Salzburg: Institut für Anglistik und Amerikanistik, Universität Salzburg, 1981.

Spivak, Gayatri Chakravorty. "Revolutions that as Yet Have No Model." *Diacritics* 10, no. 4 (Winter 1980): 29–49.

Steiner, George. *Real Presences: Is There Anything in What We Say?* London: Faber, 1989.

Stevenson, Charles. *Ethics and Language.* New Haven: Yale University Press, 1944.

Stout, Jeffrey. *Ethics after Babel: The Languages of Morals and their Discontents.* Boston: Beacon Press, 1988.

Stravinsky, Igor, and Robert Craft. *Retrospectives and Conclusions.* New York: Knopf, 1969.

Taylor, Charles. *Human Agency and Language.* Vol. 1 of *Philosophical Papers.* Cambridge: Cambridge University Press, 1985.

Todorov, Tzvetan. "Narrative Transformations." In *The Poetics of Prose,* translated by Richard Howard, 218–33. Ithaca: Cornell University Press, 1977.

Trotsky, Leon. *Their Morals and Ours.* New York: Pathfinder Press, 1973.

Tyler, Anne. "Personal View." *The Sunday Times* (London), 8 January 1989, G4.

Valente, Joseph. "Joyce's Sexual Differend: An Example from *Dubliners.*" *James Joyce Quarterly,* forthcoming.

Valéry, Paul. "Poetry and Abstract Thought." In *The Art of Poetry,* 52–81. New York: Vintage, 1961.

Voznesensky, Andrei. *An Arrow in the Wall: Selected Poetry and Prose.* Edited by William Jay Smith and F. D. Reeve. London: Secker and Warburg, 1987.

Walesa, Lech. "A Letter to the Polish Electorate" (dated 27 April 1989). *The New York Review of Books* 36, no. 15 (28 September 1989): 72.

Wallas, Joseph. *The Art of Thought.* New York: Harcourt Brace, 1926.

Waters, Lindsay, and Wlad Godzich, eds., *Reading de Man Reading.* Theory and History of Literature, vol. 59, Minneapolis: University of Minnesota Press, 1989.

Watt, Ian, ed. *The Secret Agent: A Casebook.* London and Basingstoke: Macmillan, 1973.

Weber, Samuel. "It." *Glyph* 4 (1978): 1–31.

———. *The Legend of Freud.* Minneapolis: University of Minnesota Press, 1982.

Webern, Anton. *The Path to the New Music.* London: Theodore Presser Co., 1963.

Weimann, Robert. "History, Appropriation, and the Uses of Representation in Modern Narrative." In Murray Krieger, ed., *The Aims of Representation: Subject/Text/History,* 175–216. New York: Columbia University Press, 1987.

West, Cornel. "Ethics and Actions in Fredric Jameson's Marxist Hermeneutics." In Jonathan Arac, ed., *Postmodernism and Politics,* 123–44. Theory and History of Literature, vol. 28. Minneapolis: University of Minnesota Press, 1986.

Wetzsteon, Ross. "Miracolo d'Martha." *Village Voice,* 21 June 1988, 29–36.

White, James Boyd. *When Words Lose Their Meaning.* Chicago and London: University of Chicago Press, 1984.

White, Hayden. *The Content of the Form: Narrative Discourse and Historical Representation.* Baltimore and London: The Johns Hopkins University Press, 1988.

———. "'Figuring the Nature of the Times Deceased': Literary Theory and Historical Writing." In Ralph Cohen, ed., *The Future of Literary Theory,* 19–43. New York and London: Routledge, 1989.

———. "The Historical Text as Literary Artifact." In Robert H. Canary and Henry Kozicki, eds., *The Writing of History: Literary Form and Historical Understanding,* 41–62. Madison: University of Wisconsin Press, 1978.

———. *Metahistory: The Historical Imagination in Nineteenth-Century Europe.* Baltimore and London: Johns Hopkins University Press, 1973.

———. "The Value of Narrativity in the Representation of Reality." In *The Content of the Form: Narrative Discourse and Historical Representation,* 1–25.

Whiteside, Anna. "Conclusion: Theories of Reference." In Anna Whiteside and Michael Ischaroff, eds., *On Referring in Literature,* 175–204. Bloomington and Indianapolis: Indiana University Press, 1987.

Whorf, Benjamin Lee. "Language, Mind, and Reality." In *Language, Thought, and Reality,* 246–70.

———. *Language, Thought, and Reality: Selected Writings of Benjamin Lee Whorf.* Edited by John B. Carroll. Cambridge, Mass.: MIT Press, 1988.

———. "The Relation of Habitual Thought and Behavior to Language." In *Language, Thought, and Reality,* 134–59.

Williams, Bernard. *Ethics and the Limits of Philosophy.* Cambridge, Mass.: Harvard University Press, 1985.

———. *Moral Luck.* New York: Cambridge University Press, 1981.

Wimsatt, W. K. "Battering the Object: the Ontological Approach." In Malcolm Bradbury and David Palmer, eds., *Contemporary Criticism*, 73–98. London: Edward Arnold, 1970.

Wittgenstein, Ludwig. *On Certainty*. Edited by G. E. M. Anscombe and G. H. von Wright; translated by Denis Paul and G. E. M. Anscombe. Oxford: Basil Blackwell, 1974.

———. "A Lecture on Ethics." *The Philosophical Review* 74, no. 1 (January 1965): 3–26.

———. *Notebooks 1914–1916*. Translated by G. E. M. Anscombe. New York: Harper Torchbooks, 1969.

———. *Philosophical Investigations*. Translated by G. E. M. Anscombe. New York: Macmillan, 1953.

———. *Tractatus Logico-Philosophicus*. Translated by D. F. B. Pears and B. F. McGuiness. London: Routledge and Kegan Paul, 1974. Orig. pub. 1921.

Wittig, Monique. *The Lesbian Body*. Translated by David Le Vay. New York: William Morrow, 1975.

Wolin, Sheldon S. "On the Theory and Practice of Power." In Jonathan Arac, ed., *After Foucault: Humanistic Knowledge, Postmodern Challenges*, 179–201. New Brunswick and London: Rutgers University Press, 1988.

Wollheim, Richard. "Flawed Crystals: James's *The Golden Bowl* and the Plausibility of Literature as Moral Philosophy." *New Literary History* 15, no. 1 (Autumn 1983): 185–91.

———. *The Thread of Life*. Cambridge, Mass.: Harvard University Press, 1984.

Woolf, Virginia. *To the Lighthouse*. London: Harcourt Brace, 1927.

INDEX

A

Abrams, Meyer, 144
Adorno, T. W., 6
Aesthetics, 158–62
Ainley, Alison, 15
Althusser, Louis, 9, 12, 45. Works: *For Marx*, 9; "Ideology and Ideological State Apparatuses," 45–46; *Lenin and Philosophy*, 9
Altieri, Charles, 2, 41, 159. Works: "Contemporary Philosophy and Modernist Writing," 41; "Expressivist Aesthetics," 159
Analysis, 122–24, 129, 132, 134–36, 169; and ethics, 138–56. *See also* Secondary process
Anarchy, 200, 206–9, 213; and creation, 187, 197–200, 202, 204, 207–8; and ethics, 205–6; and irony, 203
Andolsen, Barbara Hilkert, 17
Anscombe, G. E. M., 18–20
Arieti, Silvano, 208
Aristotle, 12, 17, 19, 27, 44, 51–53, 111, 157; on action, 43; ethic of virility of, 13; and narrative, 159–60; on pleasure, 10, 112–13, 163; on plot, 163, 166, 181. Works: *Nichomachean Ethics*, 13, 43, 113, 160; *Poetics*, 183
Arnold, Matthew, 62, 159
Ascesis, 119–20, 131. *See also* Renunciation
Augustine, St., 111
Austin, J. L., 148

B

Baier, Annette, 47, 56–57
Baines, Jocelyn, 210

Bakhtin, Mikhail, 6, 164
Barthes, Roland, 1–2, 7, 86, 145, 166. Works: "Introduction to the Structural Analysis of Narratives," 166; "Jeunes Chercheurs," 1–2
Bataille, Georges, 6, 11, 13
Baudelaire, Charles, 207
Beauvoir, Simone de, 6, 15
Bennington, Geoffrey, 91
Bentham, Jeremy, 78, 111, 113–16, 121
Benveniste, Emile, 79
Berlin, Isaiah, 14
Bernasconi, Robert, 74
Bersani, Leo, 165–66
Bible, the, 193, 199
Blanchot, Maurice, 6, 13
Booth, Wayne, 2, 210
Borsch-Jakobsen, Mikkel, 131
Bresnan, J., 104
Brooks, Peter, 165–66, 175–78
Burckhardt, Jacob, 207–8
Burke, Kenneth, 60–61, 107

C

Calvino, Italo, 41, 194
Cameron, Deborah, 71
Cascardi, Anthony, 61
Categorical imperative, 12, 25, 44, 46, 56, 59, 59, 78, 155–56; and countercategorical imperative, 101; and creation, 197; and language, 97, 101, 103; and narrative, 158, 172
Cavell, Stanley, 2, 6, 39, 49, 56, 61, 75, 94; on ethical "mode of presentation," 18; on ethical knowledge, 59–60; on the ethical *ought*, 24, 32; on the distinction between persuading and con-

239